HENRY,

I hope that
you Enjoy my Book...

" TRADITION
NEVER
GRADUATES!"

1/5/2019

Go
QUAKERS!

Also by Stan Beck

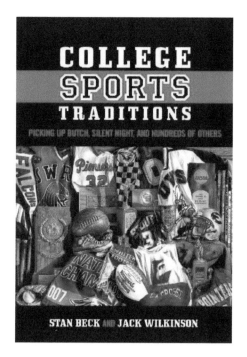

"Some books are really good, some are fun, and a
very few are both ... this is one of those."
— American Reference Books Annual

"The authors offer a fun catalog of traditions that will likely spark
nostalgia or school spirit among readers."
— Publishers Weekly

"Covering subjects that range from the eccentric and outlandish
to the touching and meaningful, the book captures the spirit and
importance of college sport rituals and campus culture. Anyone
who enjoys tidbits about college life will find it hard to put down."
— Library Journal

College Sports' Traditions

Before, During, and After a Game

Stan Beck

Published by College Sports' Traditions, LLC.
390 Gunston Hall Circle, Alpharetta, GA, USA
www.collegesportstraditions.com

Library of Congress Cataloging-in-Publication Data
Beck, Stan, 1948–
College Sports' Traditions: Before, During, and After a Game / Stan Beck.

Includes bibliographical references, photography credits, and index.
ISBN 978-1-68026-044-1 (hardback)
ISBN 978-1-68026-043-4 (softback)
ISBN 978-1-68026-045-8 (eBook)

™ The paper used in this publication meets the minimum requirements of American National Standard for Information Sciences—Permanence of Paper for Printed Library Materials, ANSI/NISO Z39.48-1992.

Printed in the United States of America.

CONTENTS

Introductions

"I've had the pleasure of working in college sports for almost twenty years, and the even greater pleasure of witnessing some of its most honored traditions. The strange thing is that I am not even really a college sports fan – at least not in the traditional sense of having grown up living, eating, breathing and sleeping for my team. I'll say that I am more of a college sports' enthusiast.

I was never really exposed to college sports growing up in what was largely a professional sports town in Washington, DC. Sure, I was there during the Georgetown Hoyas / John Thompson hey days, and one of the local teams would occasionally have a year worthy of note, but college sports was largely relegated to the last few pages of the Washington Post and whatever games were on television. I also didn't get any additional exposure by going to a school with a powerhouse athletic program. James Madison had its share of unique quirks, but it was no Alabama or Texas.

After college, a job brought me to Atlanta – what many see as the capital of college football. For those of you that may have followed a similar path from a non-college sports market, you'll understand the culture shock that comes with moving to the South, where college sports is a 24x7x365 all-consuming passion.

I recall very vividly my first memory of driving to Athens, GA for a UGA game 'between the hedges' and seeing all of the flags on cars along the drive, talking to people that had been tailgating for DAYS leading up to that opening game of the season, the roar of the crowd when the infamous mascot 'Uga' had his arrival announced, and the "oh, you HAVE to listen to that Larry Munson" guy referrals.

Fast forward several years, where I had the opportunity to work with the traveling carnival that is affectionately known as ESPN's College GameDay. For four years, I crisscrossed the country with Chris Fowler, Lee Corso and Kirk Herbstreit to the best college football match-ups each week. Who could forget students dressed in full team gear – some sober, some not so much – greeting you as you arrived for an early morning set call? Most slept at the production site all night, just so they could scream their heads off on television the next morning. This is just one of the more recent traditions in college sports lore.

I often felt bad about having a job that someone who truly LOVED college football would die for, but not being a fan of any one team allowed me to witness, and truly appreciate, all those fantastic traditions that college sports has to offer – without getting swept up in the result of the game. Over time, I touched 'Howard's Rock', witnessed 'Ralphie' the Buffalo run (and even got to pet her) and I helped toilet-

paper 'Toomer's Corner'. I was able to feed 'Reveille' a dog biscuit at 'Midnight Yell Practice' in College Station. That's also where I got scolded for wearing my hat in their library. Yeah, there were also some great games, but what swept-me-up was the pomp and circumstance surrounding the game – much more so than the game itself.

Traditions, you see, are what truly make college sports remarkable.

Even if you disregard the names on the back of the jerseys (or numbers on the helmets), and even the score of the game, these traditions will leave a lasting legacy, and bind together generations. I hope you'll take the opportunity to experience many of them for yourself. Trust me, it's well worth it … and this advice comes from a non-college sports fan."

J.W. Cannon
Sponsorships & Events

Introductions

"There is no better place, or environment, in the WORLD, than a college football stadium on a Saturday in the fall – for Tradition or Traditions. In his first book, 'College Sports' Traditions: Picking-up Butch, Silent Night, and Hundreds of Others', Stan Beck perfectly captured the essence of why multi-generations of families, friends and fans gather every Saturday, DON'T plan their weddings during the fall, and even plot their entire year's schedule around these special occasions each Saturday.

The color, the pageantry, the spirit and the unbridled enthusiasm of the student-athletes, the students, the legacies, the alumni and all fans alike are unmatched anywhere in the world – even with the Olympics, soccer and other sports, with all due respect to each of them. The college football experience bonds and stretches across age, color, gender and race, as we all gather together to cheer 'our' team on. Whether we 'went' there, or not.

For me, this all began the first time I set foot in Auburn's Jordan-Hare Stadium in 1971, with my mom, to watch the famous Sullivan-Beasley combination, as Auburn Quarterback Pat Sullivan began his quest for The Heisman Trophy.

It continued to grow, in 1973, as I set foot for the first time inside Bryant-Denny Stadium to watch Coach Paul "Bear" Bryant dismantle his former protégé Howard Schnellenberger, and his nascent Miami Hurricanes, 73-0 in a routine (for The Bear) homecoming victory.

This passion continued each time I also set foot in Tiger Stadium, aka, Death Valley to watch my Chatom, Alabama hometown heroes – the Jackson Brothers – and their legendary coach, Charles 'Cholly Mac' McClendon, wreak havoc on whichever team was brave enough to face the conditions on a Saturday Night in Baton Rouge, Louisiana.

In short. It never gets old for me. Or for millions of others.

When Stan asked me to write a 'brief' Introduction to his second book on college sports' traditions, I pondered for many, many days regarding where I would start, or where it would end. It doesn't end. It never does.

From Auburn's War Eagle 'Nova' circling proudly around Jordan-Hare; to the University of Alabama 'Million Dollar Band'; to LSU's 'Mike the Tiger'; to 'Uga' the mascot at UGA; to the Florida State Seminoles and the 'Burning Spear'; to the University of Southern Mississippi's 'Dixie Darlings'; to 'Hotty Toddy'; to the FAMU

Rattlers' 'Drum Major and Drum Corps'; to The University of Texas' 'Bevo'; to Clemson's 'Howard's Rock'; to Notre Dame's 'Play Like a Champion Today'; to Texas A&M's '12th Man'; to 'Rocky Top'; to the 'Gator Chomp'; to Keith Jackson's honey voice; and to Verne Lundquist's soothing Saturday tone. Nothing and I mean NOTHING, can, or will ever, replace how and what we've grown-up-with and how it still influences, inspires, touches us, and conjures up the best memories in each of us – now and forever. And, I hope it never does. At least not for me.

I realize I may have left-out a few of your favorites, and you all have great traditions: way too many to cover in this brief introduction of an amazing book.

Congratulations Stan for reminding us why college football and its traditions, are, and remain, a scared ritual in all of our lives. And, thank you for bringing them to life for us in this book."

Vince Thompson
Chairman / CEO

a premiere agency for activating
sports and entertainment properties
in ways that drive fans to respond

Introductions

"In all my years covering sports all over the world, there's one sport that keeps me energized — and that's college football. There's something about those crisp autumn Saturday's that separates college football from all the rest.

Traditions.

College sports, football in particular, has the most unique collection of traditions.

Where else can you see over 80,000 people going ballistic watching their Clemson Tigers gain magical powers by rubbing 'Howard's Rock' before 'running down the hill' in rowdy Death Valley?

Or how about the chill that goes up your spine watching the precision of the 'Best Damn Band in the Land' perform 'Script Ohio'? The Ohio State Marching Band makes the 'dotting-of-the-i' a bucket list item.

There are plenty of animal mascots in college sports — too many to name. But the thrill of watching 'Ralphie run' onto Folsom Field leading the Buffalos to battle is incredible. The same goes for the pre-game festivities at Auburn when you see 'Nova', the eagle, circle Jordan-Hare Stadium before making a perfect landing at midfield.

And if you want to tailgate in luxury, how about 'sailgating' in Lake Washington? You gotta love docking your boat alongside beautiful Husky Stadium before catching a Washington football game.

College football, and the traditions that take place every season, are very special. There is nothing more American than friends, food and football ... and the traditions associated with the game truly do separate it from every other sport."

Mark Packer
Host of *College Sports Today*

Introductions

"Having grown up on the West Coast, my experience with college traditions generally were limited to, "Do you want to skip class and head to the beach?" and, "What's the best chiliburger near campus?"

It wasn't until years later, when I lived in San Francisco and was covering Stanford football in 1986, that I first was fully exposed to the unique traditions that make college athletics so special. Stanford / Cal's rivalry is unique: It's 'The Big Game', 'The Axe', 'Tightwad Hill', and their legendary 'pranks' (that make almost everyone hearing about them, smile).

That year Stanford finished 8-3 in the regular season under the late coach, Jack Elway, its best year since the days of Bill Walsh, and the team was invited to play in the Gator Bowl to play Clemson. My research for that game exposed me to all of the great traditions of Clemson football, like 'Howard's Rock,' and, 'Running down the Hill.'

When I made my first trip to Clemson years later after coming to work for the Atlanta Journal-Constitution, I thought the players' entrance down the hill into 'Death Valley,' was one of the coolest things I had ever seen. (In full disclosure, part of me also hoped one of the players would stumble, starting an amusing 27-player pileup.)

*Stan Beck has done a great job researching the wonderful sports traditions at more **500 schools,** like those at Clemson. His first book on this subject is a great book for sports fans and it sits on my bookshelf, where I can reach for it at any time to learn about a college team's tradition.*

I'm sure you'll enjoy this latest edition."

Jeff Schultz
Sports Columnist

Honored by Associated Press Sports Editors (APSE), National Sportscasters and Sportswriters Association (NSSA) and many others

Introductions

"Intercollegiate sports got it right from the beginning.

The first intercollegiate event was the 1852 'Harvard-Yale regatta'. With a few exceptions it has been held every year since. It became a tradition.

Hundreds, if not thousands, of intercollegiate traditions would follow over the next 165 years. All sports and all schools have them. Some like basketball's 'cutting down the nets' after a championship win are universal to every team that ever sought to add some shiny hardware to their trophy case.

But most are uniquely school specific – each tradition having its own story.

Some origins are humorous, and many are solemn. Some traditions may be a bit contrived, while others are deeply rooted in school, state or regional history. And others are created by pure accident, or folly. Regardless of how they began, we all hope they continue …

Traditions. They are the rotes and customs that link generations of fans and alumni.

As a historian – who has not always been accepting and adaptable to change – it's comforting to know that these time-held traditions, the very best part of collegiate sports, will always be with us and will be carried-on long after the memories of scores and seasons have passed."

Kent Stephens
Historian & Curator
College Football Hall of Fame

Traditions. We all have them. It can be what a family does for a holiday meal, or it can be how you choose to celebrate your birthday, or the birthday of others. Or it can even be a ritual that you do before any event that is special to you. Traditions. The actions which bind us together. We all have them.

And then there are the traditions of college sports. I saw my first one over fifty years ago, when my Boy Scout troop volunteered at an Auburn home football game. An eagle was released, then circled around the stadium and landed at midfield. I will never forget it. As you are reading this book, I am very likely witnessing my most-recent college sports' tradition. I have seen many hundreds of them (see pages 272-281 if you are interested), and each one has touched me in a way that I can't describe. Many of them are quite famous, and even a part of pop culture, while others have been celebrated for 150+ years by one small school – which year after year does the same wonderful thing around a sporting event – and no one outside of those students, or alumni base have a clue that it goes on.

Each time you witness a college sports' tradition, you are making a memory for a lifetime. One college athletic staff recently received a package from a former player, now a Marine, donating all of his service medals. "You taught me about tradition and how to earn these", was the message enclosed. That school may have been one with a very famous tradition, or a school with a tradition that very few are aware of. It really doesn't matter. But I will wager on one thing: at that college they viewed that, "a tradition without heart is simply a habit." It wasn't a habit that inspired that Marine. It was a tradition with heart.

On the following pages, you will find hundreds of college sports' traditions from 260+ colleges and universities. I hope they make you smile, as they do me. My first book on this subject contained 1,200+ traditions from 500+ schools, and it has been very easy to add to the collection with this book. But one thing is certain, the day after I send this manuscript for publication, I will begin finding out about other traditions – of which, I had no clue they existed. It's a journey along a life-long destination path that celebrates all that's good about college sports, their players, alumni, students, and fans. Welcome to that journey.

Stan Beck
August 2017

Alabama (Football): *Bacon Strips Equals the Number of Tide Championships*

The *Rama Jama* is a Tuscaloosa eatery, with two very famous items on their menu. You can order either a *National Champ Burger*, or a *National Champ BLT*. The burger has *the number of ounces that equals the number* of **Alabama** *National Championships*, while the BLT is *topped with that same*

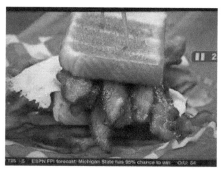

number of bacon strips. Sixteen is the number of *National Championships* that **Alabama** currently claims so when you visit *the Rama Jama*, go hungry.

Alabama (Football): *Countdown Clock to the Spring Game*

A few schools (e.g., **Ohio State** and **Michigan** before they recently stopped) have *Countdown Clocks* in their locker rooms to indicate the day / time / minutes remaining until that next big game with their rival. And rather than have only one countdown clock, **Clemson** is known to have one in *every meeting room*, for the countdown to their yearly contest with the **South Carolina** Gamecocks. But **Alabama** makes all other schools pale in comparison. The team's official website has a *Countdown Clock to each year's Spring Game*.

Alabama (Football): *Celebrating Bear Bryant's Birthday*

Bear Bryant was born on September 11, 1913 and each year on September 11th many die-hard **Alabama** fans make a pilgrimage to the museum in Tuscaloosa which honors the Bear. The museum opened in 1988 (five years after coach Bryant's death), and many fans have made the trip each year on the Bear's birthday. One fan drives from Memphis each year to pay-her-regards. That's a 460 mile round trip.

Alabama (Football): *Namesake Reunion Party*

For the past twenty-one years, the hundreds of Paul's, William's, Bear's and Bryant's whose parents revered the former **University of Alabama** coach enough *to name their kids after him* gather at the *Namesake Reunion Party* on the Saturday of **Alabama's** first home game, at the *Paul W. Bryant Museum* to celebrate coach Bryant. The coach's first namesake, his son Paul Bryant Jr., developed the idea for the tailgating event after many, many

people approached him to say they were named after the coach. And since there is a need for precision for an event like this, the first or middle name has to be Paul, Paula, William, Bear or Bryant. It cannot be a last name. The rules need to be clearly understood since many Roll-Tide-babies are still being named after coach Bryant.

Alabama Rankings

In 2016, *Fortune* magazine ranked **Alabama's** Nick Saban as 11th on its list of *the world's greatest leaders*. But not to be outdone, *Soldier of Fortune* magazine named the Tide *the world's 9th best infantry*.

Alabama (Football): Victory Cigars Smoked After a Tennessee Victory

Each year, **Alabama** football players continue a long tradition of smoking a victory cigar following a win over **Tennessee** – just one of their many rivals. And it isn't just the players that have a desire to celebrate. The owner of Cigars & *More* in Birmingham indicates that

his sales are generally up 30-40 percent the week of this game.

Alabama (Football): *Walk of Fame at Denny Chimes*

The *Walk of Fame at Denny Chimes* has been an **Alabama** tradition since the spring of 1948. Some consider the ceremony at *Denny Chimes one of the most important Alabama traditions*. The **University of Alabama** is the only school that honors its *team captains, MVP's, All-Americans*, etc. by capturing their names, achievements, handprints, and footprints in concrete. One hundred eighty **Alabama** football players have been honored to-date.

Alabama (Football): *Fan to be Buried Closest to the Stadium*

While Bryant-Denny Stadium was built in 1929, *Evergreen Cemetery –* adjacent to the stadium – was there first. It was built in the mid 1830's. And on any given Saturday when the Tide is playing a home game, a few fans, looking for something to do, inevitably wander thru the cemetery. Over the years, the

cemetery's proximity to the stadium has caused a few problems, i.e., prevented expansion of the stadium area, impacted positioning of cranes doing work, etc. You would think Bama fans would be lining-up to be buried there, but they can't. New burials are limited to existing family plots. But one super fan was able to obtain the plot closest to the stadium. And rumor has it that since the plot contained places for both him and his wife, he ensured that his resting place was closer to the stadium than his wife's. And in a nod to the fans that sometimes wander thru on game day, his headstone is already in place. It says, "Hi. Thanks for stopping by."

Alabama (Football): *Wrestling Title Belt for Turnovers*

Alabama players have a tradition that involves keeping a *wrestling belt* on the sideline. When a defensive player creates a turnover, they are awarded the *title belt*. The tradition started in 2015 as the *Ball-Out Belt*. The coaches conceived it, because many of the defensive players were not stripping-at-the-ball the prior season, and as a result turnovers were down year-to-year. The belt often changes hands during a game, if the Tide defense causes more than one turnover.

Alabama (Football): *NFL First Round Draftees*

Alabama has a currently active tradition: *football players being drafted in the first round of the NFL Draft*. The year 2017 was their 9th consecutive year with a player selected in the first round of the NFL Draft. It's the current record for all NCAA schools. And, in 2017, **Alabama** had four players selected in the First Round – that ties a record set previously by **Auburn**, **LSU**, and the Tide on two earlier occasions. When might this streak end? If ever?

Alabama: *Roll Tide*

ESPN has the most-clever commercials. And one of my very favorites was in 2010, and featured the phrase *"Roll Tide,"* and how the fans of **Alabama** *use the phrase in everyday life*. If you can't recall the commercial, some day when you need a smile, just search for it online. It will make your day. Most fans know the story of how **Alabama** became known as the *Crimson Tide*. *The nickname was given to the team by sportswriter Hugh Roberts in 1907*, when red clay covered the players' uniforms during a particularly dominating game. Roberts is said to have characterized that the players looked like a *Red Tide* rolling in. So by the time **Alabama** traveled west to play in the 1926 *Rose Bowl*, the name *"Crimson Tide"* was in common usage and that year's victory in Pasadena ensured it would, from that point forward, be associated with the football team. But was the phrase *"Roll Tide"* being used at that time as well? As true **Alabama** fans know, the phrase appears in **Alabama's** fight song, *"Yea Alabama."* That song was composed by an **Alabama** engineering student, in a campus-wide contest following the 1926 *Rose Bowl*. But if you look-up the original sheet music to the composition, the phrase *"Roll Tide"* is nowhere in it. The explanation seems to be that *"Roll Tide"* was a chant folks inserted at the end of the song which later was incorporated into it (e.g., like the way fans chant *"Roll Tide Roll"* in the middle of *Sweet Home Alabama* during games). So where did it come from? One clue might be from the song, *"Roll Alabama*

Roll" that tells the story of the *CSS Alabama*. This merchant raider ship had an illustrious career during the Civil War before being sunk by the *USS Kearsarge* in June 1864 outside the port of Cherbourg, France. There are accounts of the song being sung as early as 1870 and the first printed reference to it was in 1903. Now the phrase *"Roll Alabama Roll"* is used constantly throughout the song but there is no mention of the *tide*. So was there a confluence of this Civil War-era song and the **Alabama** football team's nickname at some point? Who knows?

Alabama / Auburn University (Baseball): *Iron Derby*

In 1997 Tim Hudson led **Auburn** to the *College World Series*. Now he hosts a *Home Run Derby* the night before **Auburn** and **Alabama's** annual *Iron Bowl* football game. Former baseball players (and very likely a few ringers) from each school compete, and all proceeds go to charity.

Alabama / Auburn (Football): *Iron Bowl Viewing*

In the state of Alabama, when **Auburn** plays **Alabama**, the state-wide tradition is to listen to the game on your radio, or watch the game on TV. For most years, the city of Birmingham (which is surveyed) indicates that *85-88 percent of the TV's that are turned-on are tuned to the game*.

Alabama / Auburn (Football): *Cremation Remains Spread at Iron Bowl*

It is more than urban legend that super fans of both **Alabama** and **Auburn** wish to have their ashes left on the field after a victory over their rival in the annual *Iron Bowl*. The **Auburn** Turfgrass Management team recently identified remains, and also indicated that they have become quite adept at spotting the remains. In 2015 a TV news reporter was on the sidelines of the *Iron Bowl* when a college-aged man made eye contact with her. "These are my grandfather's ashes, and I'm going to dump them on the field," the student said grasping a Ziploc bag. His grandfather, who passed away the previous August, requested that his ashes be spread at *Bryant-Denny Stadium* during the *Iron Bowl*. The young man's actions illustrated a curious trend: *fans spreading ashes on a field after a game*. Before social media, few people might have heard about *the ashes being spread*, and there is no way to estimate how often it is done, although all schools discourage the practice. "It's probably happened dozens of times," said a professor of crop, soil and environmental sciences at **Auburn**. "These are not the first and only incidents, and they certainly won't be the last." After the 2013 *Iron Bowl*, the **Auburn** professor received calls from across the USA about *cremated remains being spread at other athletic venues, golf courses and parks.* It was then that he realized that what happened at *Jordan-Hare Stadium* wasn't that rare. "I don't want to overstate this, but in my discussions with people – both with golf courses and athletic fields – this is extremely common," the professor said. "It's not like this is a single incident. It really speaks to our culture, I think. These people have such affection for their university or the places they golf; they want their final remains to be interred there." Suzan McClelland didn't spread ashes at an *Iron Bowl*, but did spread some at **Alabama's** *Fan Day* in 2012. With her brother along for moral support, the woman pulled out a plastic bag and spread her husband John's remains inside *Bryant-Denny Stadium*. "I was worried I'd get arrested doing this, but he loved **Alabama** football and wanted to have his *ashes spread on the field* here," McClelland told the *New York Times*. "I was worried I'd get arrested, but this was his dying wish, and I didn't want him to haunt me for the rest of my life if I didn't do it." No matter the intentions of the deceased, dumping ashes on football fields isn't well-received. There is a lot of calcium and

phosphate in human remains and that dries out the turf and causes a salt burn. The irony in *choosing your favorite football field as your final resting place* is that your remains will destroy the turf, and that area of the field will have to be replaced. In **Auburn's** case, if they realize remains are involved, they remove the piece of turf but don't simply discard it. They do something respectful with the remains.

Allstate's Goalpost Nets

In 2003, the NFL was first to toy-with the idea of placing their logo on goalpost nets. But Allstate decided to do it in a big way with colleges in 2004. We've all seen them, and it seems quite simple, but it is far from it. Allstate has to obtain a *net sponsorship* with each school and in 2013, they had 78 schools, 23 bowls, 10 neutral site games, and 4 conference championships agree to sponsorship. The exposure to Allstate is estimated at $48,739 of value per game. The deals with each school range from $50,000 to $250,000, and believe it or not, *each goalpost must be licensed separately*. The **University of New Mexico** once sold one end zone to Allstate and the other end zone to a local casino. When coach Bob Stoops first saw them, he didn't like them so demanded that they be removed. Years later, **Oklahoma** came around. Construction isn't always straightforward. Some nets are attached to the stadium while others are strung from the ground. The nets come in a variety of sizes, but the *"Good Hands"* logo is always a 22' square. Each net is hand painted with the logo. But Allstate doesn't have a monopoly. The nets in the *Rose Bowl* are sponsored by *AAA of Southern California* when **UCLA** is at home. **Army** has *Jeep*, **Oregon** and **Wisconsin** have *American Family Insurance*, and **Michigan State** has *Auto-Owners Insurance*. Allstate's nets made their regional TV debut on *Labor Day Weekend* during a game with **Temple** playing at **Arizona State**. But for the *first nationally televised game*, things did not go very smoothly – and Allstate senior executives were watching. With **Miami** playing at **FSU**, when the home team scored, the nets went up as planned. But when **Miami** scored, the nets were not raised. Seems the local workers responsible for raising the nets thought it was for home team scores only. Allstate has various sponsorships with both **Notre Dame** and **Michigan**, even though each school traditionally frowns on in-stadium sponsorships. But **Michigan** does allow the *"Good Hands Net"* to be used during their *Spring Game*.

Alumni Games

Alumni games have become the latest source for offseason fun in college football. Roddy White was on the field making insane catches at the **University of Alabama Birmingham's** *alumni game* in the 2016 offseason and also recently, **South Carolina** honored their first-ever *All-American*, 94-year old Lou Sossamon, with a *walk-in touchdown*. The Gamecocks are not the first to set their alumni up for these moments. Bryan Sperry, a member of **Kansas'** 1947 *Orange Bowl* team, scored a touchdown in the *alumni game* in 2015 and was back at it in 2016, spry as ever at the age of 90.

Amherst College: *New Mascot*

Amherst College, the prestigious liberal arts school, recently concluded that their school would no longer have any reference to *Lord Jeffery Amherst*. The debate over *Lord Jeff* erupted amid a series of other campuses' controversies over the use of historical figures, like slaveholders,  Confederate generals, stereotypes of American Indians, etc. So the *Lord Jeff* mascot needed to go. How hard could it be to select a new mascot? Here is how it went: The nominating process for mascot suggestions launched in October 2016, and closed at the end of November. *A total of 2,046 mascot suggestions were received by the deadline.* A committee spent December reviewing submitted mascot ideas and rationale, applying criteria, and winnowing the suggestions down to a list of *30 semifinalists*. In February 2017, the *Mascot Committee* sought input from a representative group of 441 alumni and student delegates, who were asked to rate the semifinalists according to the criteria and alumni feedback. The *Mascot Committee* then used the ratings to identify *the top five mascot ideas*. The five finalists were announced in March 2017 as *Fighting Poets, Mammoths, Purple and White, Valley Hawks, and Wolves*. Alumni, students, faculty, and staff all voted the last two weeks of March, and the winning mascot was announced in the spring of 2017, and *Mammoths was the winner*.

Amherst, Wesleyan, & Williams (Various Sports): *The Little Three*

Amherst and **Williams** first became league rivals in 1882, and **Wesleyan** joined them in 1899 to form the Triangular League, or *Little Three*. This partnership lasted only three years before disputes caused a breakup, but it was reformed in 1910 and has been *played continuously in every sport in which each school fields a varsity team*.

Arizona (Football): *Crazy Train*

Students and fans sing along with Ozzy Osbourne's *"Crazy Train"* each time an opponent faces a third down.

Arizona (Football): *Haka*

Many football teams (and sometimes other sports) use a pregame *Haka* as a ritual to get them into the spirit of the contest, and in some cases, as a

form of intimidation. **Arizona** football players *perform the Haka* in front of their student section four minutes before kickoff, and *the students join-in*.

Arizona (Football): *Beanie Bowl*

This annual event is held in **Arizona** *Stadium* and is the first chance for new students to support the football team and sit in the *ZonaZoo*. It's an open practice / scrimmage for the football team and is run like an actual game. The *ZonaZoo* crew (student section) is on-hand to teach new students the chants and cheers. The name *"beanie"* comes from the yellow beanies that scout team members wear over their helmets.

Arizona (Softball): *Linda Ronstadt Songs*

There is no tradition on the **Arizona** Wildcats campus more fantastically obscure, lovely and regionally perfect than the one at *Hillenbrand Stadium* that is 25+ years old. For well over 600 home games since *Hillenbrand* opened in 1993, *players and fans have heard the same two first-inning Linda Ronstadt songs*. When the Wildcats take the field, the public address system blares *Palomita de los Ojos Negros*, a track from the Tucson-born Ronstadt's 1991 album, *Mas Canciones*. The announcer follows with *"Juegen pelota"* – *play ball*. In the bottom half of the inning, *La Mariquita*, another traditional song from the same album, serenades the opposing team's pitcher as she throws warm-up tosses. There's also protocol. *Each song starts when the first player crosses the baseline, and ends when the warmed-up pitcher steps on the rubber to start the frame.* On rare occasions, in tournaments when **UA** is a visiting team, the songs are swapped so the Wildcats feel at home. In a time where every utterance at **UA** games seems to come with a sponsor's message, the first inning sails along, unencumbered, while the music plays. *Both songs are entirely in Spanish.* Most players have no idea what they mean, and opposing teams often have expressions of: "What the heck is going on right now?" And this tradition, like many others, *was never meant to be a tradition.* **UA** media relations director Tom Duddleston was given *Mas Canciones* by his mom, Betty, after it came out in late 1991. The album featured Ronstadt's brothers, Peter and Mike, on vocals. At the time, Peter was Tucson's police chief. Duddleston had seen Linda Ronstadt, a Tucson native, play with the *Stone Poneys*, and was a fan. "We were thinking of things to do to make things festive," Duddleston said. "What's more festive than that?" He stumbled upon *Palomita* first, when the team took the field, and soon added *Mariquita*. At first, they were played from a tape recorder, with a microphone propped on a plastic cup with the bottom torn out. *Maybe one day Linda will sing these two songs live, in the first inning?*

Arizona: *Race Track Industry Program*

In the early 1970's **Arizona** created a program geared for future workers / executives in the horse racing industry. The  program typically has about 45 students enrolled, and 70 percent of the program's budget comes from industry sources. *It's the only such program in America* and counts as its graduate's industry icons like Bob Baffert and Todd Pletcher. Other alumni are racing secretaries, track managers simulcast coordinators, racehorse auction company presidents, breeding farm executives, and even the race and sports book supervisor at a major Las Vegas casino. Baffert & Pletcher's association with **Arizona** turned them both into huge fans. Pletcher has hosted former coach Lute Olson at the *Kentucky Derby* and has invited current coach Sean Miller to his home. Baffert is often seen on TV wearing an **Arizona** baseball hat.

Arizona State: *Camp Tontozona*

Camp Tontozona provides the Sun Devils with a unique setting for concentration and preparation for each new season ahead. The camp began hosting **Arizona State** football's preseason practice in 1960 and continued through 2008. The camp borders the *Tonto National Forest*, which provides

the first two syllables of *Tontozona*. The state of Arizona offers the last pair. In 2012 a campaign to return the team to the camp was successful. No conversation about *Camp-T* would be complete without mentioning *Mount Kush* (coach Frank Kush began the tradition). Coach Kush had his team's *climb the nearby mountain as a group*, and when they got to the top, rookie players had to sing their high school's fight song.

Arizona State (Basketball): *The Curtain of Distraction*

Home teams – especially students – have tried for years to distract visiting teams' players during free throw attempts. There was *Speedo Guy* at **Duke**, and the giant cardboard heads, and pinwheels that popped-up everywhere. But in my view, **Arizona State** has achieved the holy grail of *free throw distraction*. It's called the *"Curtain of Distraction"* and has even gained credibility with some full-fledged quantitative-nerds arguing that it works. The notion of *"free-throw defense"* – that a home team's fans might rattle opposing players into missing shots – is being treated as something other than a quirky sideshow. **Arizona State** supporters say their method even helped them upset **Arizona**, their much higher-ranked rival in the Pac 12, in 2015. For those of you that have not witnessed this wonderful tradition, the **Arizona State** students construct a curtain on the corner of the baseline, and just before a free throw shooter releases the ball, they pull the curtain open, and you never know what will be behind it. It is hilarious, and how any free throws are made by opponents amazes me. *What's behind the curtain is always surreal, and sometimes disturbing.* But hey, they're clever college kids. You might see a pair of students making out while wearing unicorn heads and tutus, or they could start twerking in their underwear, while wearing animal masks. The *scenes are sometimes improvised, and sometimes planned ahead*; they're always strange and shocking. But are they effective? In a front page article in the *New York Times* an economist and sports-statistics guy wrote a recent story that included a graph showing how the free-throw rate of **Arizona State's** opponents dropped once its fans introduced the *Curtain of Distraction* for the 2013–14 season. During the three years prior, visiting opponents made about 70 percent of their free throws; in the one and half seasons since the curtain began, opponents have made just 61 percent. The researcher also found that **Arizona State's** opponents had not gotten any worse against other teams, so this didn't seem to be a matter of the school's facing weaker competition. Also, visitors' stats only seemed to be affected at the free-throw line; their field-goal percentage did not diminish. "Statistics can never fully prove a causal link," wrote the researcher, "but this case is pretty strong." Still, the numbers might seem a little odd. Opposing players only face the *Curtain of Distraction* during the second half, when they're shooting on the basket in front of **Arizona State's** rambunctious student fans. One of my favorite examples of this tradition happened in 2016 when Michael Phelps added to the mystique of *the Curtain*. He made his appearance after *the Curtains* were drawn to

distract a free throw shooter during the second half of a Sun Devils' game with **Oregon State**. Naturally,

Phelps sported a swimsuit and six-pack abs with gold medals around his neck and a swim cap on his head while standing between two shirtless male students wearing bow ties. **Oregon State's** player missed both of his free throws.

Arkansas: *Woo Pig Sooie Trademarked*

One of the most recognizable cheers in all of college sports is **Arkansas'** *"Woo Pig Sooie"* cheer. But did you know that **Arkansas** *was the first school to obtain a trademark for their collegiate cheer?* It was obtained in 2014 as a *"sound or sensory mark."* Sound trademarks are most often associated with a certain brand (i.e., Intel's jingle, or *ESPN's Sports Center's* catchy introduction). The *Hog Call originated in the 1920's* so it was very simple to provide the Patent Office with numerous examples where *the hogs were called.* Some examples even were of famous individuals' leading the cheer. This tradition began when a lagging Razorback football team was struggling for a win and a *group of farmers started squealing like hogs to offer encouragement.* The farmers' support seemed to work, as the Razorbacks came out victorious. The surrounding crowd took notice and put their nonsensical squeals to use at the next game when a group of men organized the *"Woo Pig Sooie"* cheer. Since then, it has become the school's best-known cheer, garnering national attention for its uniqueness.

Arkansas (Football): *Linemen Fly First Class*

When coach Bielema arrived at **Arkansas**, he began a tradition: *the offensive linemen always fly first class*. Literally. It's the coach's way of recognizing the efforts of the guys who power his smash mouth attack by giving them the best seats – and the biggest, too – right up front, on team charters. In 2014, one of the Razorback's senior tackles said, "It's huge," and he means it literally, too. "Those airplanes are tiny. Road trips can be miserable. First class is great. You get to spread out and relax." In other words, it's *Hog heaven*.

Armed Forces Classic

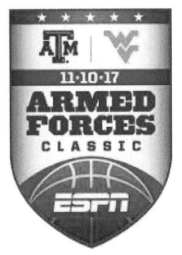

What better day to play the 5th annual *State Farm Armed Forces Classic* than to play it on *Veterans Day*, and in Hawaii, just under a month from the *75th anniversary* of the attack on *Pearl Harbor*? In 2016, **Arizona** played **Michigan State** and **Kansas** played **Indiana**. These games were originally scheduled to take place at *Joint Base Pearl Harbor-Hickam*, but were relocated to provide basketball fans of both the military and the community an opportunity to see the games up close. Previous *Armed Forces Classic* games were played in Ramstein, Germany in 2012 (**UConn** vs. **Michigan State**), Pyongtaek, South Korea in 2013 (**Georgetown** vs. **Oregon**), Aguadilla, Puerto Rico in 2014 (**Louisville** vs. **Minnesota**) and Okinawa, Japan in 2015 (**Gonzaga** vs. **Pittsburgh**). The games are televised on ESPN as part of the network's *America's Heroes: A Salute to Our Veterans* initiative honoring the men and women who are serving and who have served in the United States military, both at home and abroad. The 2017 event will return to Ramstein Air Base in Germany, this time showcasing **Texas A&M** against **West Virginia**. The 2018 game is planned for Fort Bliss, Texas, the 2019 game in Joint Base Elmendorf-Richardson, Alaska, and the 2020 game at Marine Corps Base Camp Lejeune, N.C.

Army (Football): *The Marshall Plaque*

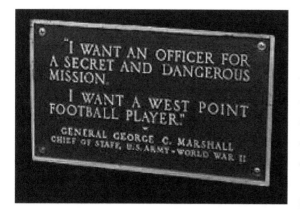

During World War II, General George C. Marshall, then chief of staff for the Army, needed an officer to train and lead a secret mission. *"I want an officer for a secret and dangerous mission. I want a **West Point** football player,"* he told the secretary of the general staff, who was tasked with selecting the officer. It was a simple, concise request but also an incredible compliment to all **West Point** football players. *That quote has become a part of a **West Point** tradition*: Before every football game – both home and away – the **Military Academy's** players *touch a plaque that has the quote inscribed on it*, known as *the Marshall Plaque*.

Army: (Football): *T-shirt Tank*

Every sports team has air cannons to fire up the crowd with the one thing people crave more than anything – a *"one-size-fits-all" branded T-shirt*. Those flying cotton beauties never fail to get people on their feet. For most teams, it's just a few people running around firing off cannons. And there are some that have stepped their game up and have giant T-shirt Gatling guns. But then there's the **US Military Academy**, which bests all competitors with its *T-shirt tank*.

Army (Football): *Coach wears a T-shirt Representing One of Army's Divisions*

When Rich Ellerson was the coach at **Army**, he wore for each game, a *T-shirt that represented one division of the 10-division army*. But which division? Coach Ellerson never revealed which division was represented on that week's T-shirt.

Army: *Pillow Fights*

In 2015, **US Military Academy** officials banned cadet *pillow fights* like the bloody one earlier that year that left 30 cadets injured. Traditionally first-year students (including all athletes), known as *"plebes,"* organized the *annual pillow fight* as a way to build camaraderie after a grueling summer of training. But the *pillow fight* in 2014 led to multiple injuries, including a broken nose and 24 diagnosed concussions. **West Point's** superintendent indicated that the unsanctioned event has *"no place in the future"* in an academy developing Army officers. He said an investigation showed *"ineffective communication"* between cadet leadership and senior military personnel before the *pillow fight*, and that he was taking unspecified administrative actions against both groups.

Army (Football): *When Army Beats Navy*

At **West Point**, due to the proximity of the game's date to Christmas leave, many *Fourth Classes* are permitted to sit *"at ease"* for all meals until Christmas leave if **Army** wins. That includes being able to eat without the strict order of motions they are normally required to perform. In 1998, when **Army** defeated **Navy**, the plebes were permitted to have their rooms in *PMI inspection condition* all day until Christmas leave. *PMI inspection condition* means that their wardrobe doors may be closed, there may be some trash in the trash cans, and a small amount of dust would be tolerated.

Army (Football): *Army Divisions Represented in a Specific Game*

For each of **Army's** eleven games, *the team wears a different helmet sticker for each of the army's eleven division* (i.e., *the 82nd Airborne*). When they play more than eleven games, they add a Regiment (i.e., *75th Ranger Regiment*). In addition to *carrying the American flag on the field, as they enter,* they also *carry the flag of that week's division.* Also, each week, *by position group, players wear an emblem of each of the different divisions.*

Army (Football): *Goats versus Engineers*

At **West Point**, the students in the *lowest 5 percent academically* must play in a *football game on Thanksgiving morning.* They are named the *"Goats"* in reference to the **Navy** mascot, and intended as an insult as they play the *"Engineers."* Traditionally the top performers in each class at **Army** chooses engineering as their field of study. The game is said to predict the outcome of the **Army** / **Navy** game with the saying: *"that as go the Goats, so goes Army against Navy."*

Army and Navy (Football): *The Greatest Game Ever Played*

*The first **Army** / **Navy** game was played in 1890* and was won by **Navy** 24-0. But after that game the yearly matchup

was suspended for the next five years after a dispute between an Army brigadier general and a Navy rear admiral almost led to a duel. After the 1946 **Army / Navy** football game, the legendary sportswriter, Grantland Rice, called the game, *"the greatest game ever played"* While many, many legendary games have been played since 1946, Grantland was certainly right about this game being special. **Army** was in the midst of their third consecutive undefeated season, while **Navy** had just one win that year. A disputed play ended the game with time running-out before **Navy** could kick a game tying field goal. The sidelines were overcrowded (hence the **Navy** player could not get out-of-bounds), because President Truman had left the game shortly before its end, and all of the local security departed with the president. More than 100,000 fans are said to have attended, and both General Dwight Eisenhower and Admiral Nimitz gave their seats to veterans that were wounded in World War II. To celebrate the 70th anniversary of this famous game, surviving players from both teams received signed footballs, and *the traditional **Army** and **Navy** bathrobes and helmets*. But the helmets left the players laughing, since these modern-day helmets had face masks, while the ones in 1946 certainly did not. **Army / Navy** week isn't just about football. Many athletic events (including intramurals) between the two schools take place that week. One year, I even attended an **Army / Navy** *boxing match* the night before the football game.

Army and Navy (Football): *Comrades for Life!*

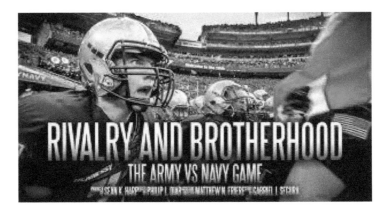

Most every year at both **Army** and **Navy**, one hundred plebes and midshipmen join the football team. Four years later, each academy will have about 30 seniors – *athletes that will be playing their last football game*, after probably ten plus years of competing. A common theme for these athletes is *"I lay me down to bleed awhile, but I will rise to fight with you again."* The hard part for these graduating seniors isn't acknowledging that they will *rise to fight again*, but in knowing that there is *no other football battle left to fight*. So this is why each year at the **Army / Navy** game, the *"reunion of all reunions"* is held. They understand what only those that have served understand: they are *comrades for life.*

Army / Navy (Football): *Spirit Spots*

What began with a few cadets or midshipmen, or maybe a public affairs officer, and a point-and-shoot camera has turned into the *cinematic event of the year* for **Army** and **Navy** fans, as both teams trade *Spirit Videos* across the web in the run-up to each annual game. And if you're one of the fortunate fans attending the game, during each timeout – on the stadium's big screen – they show these clever videos with our nation's finest making great fun of the opposite academy. They are a riot! They are wonderful parodies and always end with either the traditional *"Go **Army**, Beat **Navy**!"* or *"Go **Navy**, Beat **Army**!"* One year the Secretary of the Army was in a video, blowing the whistle on the so-called *"Gridiron Directive,"* which he said had been in place since the early 2000s and, apparently, forces **West Point** to throw the **Army / Navy** game each year so sailors don't come down with a fatal case of *service envy.* There was another that parodied the

Matthew McConaughey Lincoln commercials. And one of my favorites is an **Army** produced one that has a character playing the Secretary of the Navy playing a board game with a baby – and losing a battleship to the winning baby.

Athletes' Opportunities for Degrees after Their Playing Careers

Most sports fans realize that *scholarships are actually offered to athletes on a one-year basis*, although most coaches do not want the negative association that would come with not renewing scholarships when the time comes each year. But how about this for a tradition? In 2014, the **University of Maryland** began offering a *lifetime degree guarantee* for all student athletes. The program promises aid for student athletes who have completed their eligibility before earning degrees. The aid continues until they graduate. It also applies to athletes that leave school early to play professionally. **Maryland** was a leader with this trend, but many other schools subsequently considered and / or implemented similar commitments. **Nebraska** has post-eligibility-opportunities which offer athletes scholarships for internships, study abroad, and **Nebraska** graduate school use. Former players have up to three years from the time of their graduation or the end of their playing career to participate in the program. The objective is to give athletes experiences that other students may have: *time to find a job, time to build a resume, and time to experience a different culture*. And, rightly so, **Nebraska** uses this program as a recruiting tool. In 1989 the NCAA created a *Degree Completion Award Program* that has awarded over $20 million to almost 3,000 athletes. *The National Consortium for Academics and Sports* is over thirty years old and has aided 35,000 former athletes. This program *cancels tuition and fees with community service hours*. **Louisville**

> The National Consortium for Academics and Sports has assisted more than 33,900 former student athletes in returning to school to complete their degrees at its 280 institutional members.

alerts former athletes – via their video board at football games – about various programs' assistance. And athletes fortunate enough to enter the NFL often benefit from the *NFL's Player Tuition Assistance Plan*.

Athletes Seeking Trademarks

Like their counterparts in the pros, more college football stars are starting to snatch-up trademark rights to their names, nicknames and fan slogans. The NCAA generally forbids its players from cashing in on their athletic success, but by gaining legal ownership of phrases tied to their personal brands, players can pave the way for lucrative licensing deals in the future and can prevent others from exploiting their names.

Ohio State University running back Ezekiel Elliott applied for five trademarks, including rights to use his nicknames *"Zeke"* and *"Eze"* on merchandise. Elliott also filed for trademarks to use *"Hero in a half shirt"* and *"In crop top we trust"* on apparel and for the restaurant name: *"Zeke's Crop Top Bar and Grill,"* a nod to the junior's preference to roll his jersey up like a crop top. At **Mississippi State University**, quarterback Dak Prescott applied for the trademark on his name, along with *"Dak Attack"* and *"Who Dak,"* phrases that fans have waved aloft on game-day signs. Others to pursue trademarks while in college include Johnny Manziel and Jameis Winston, both *Heisman Trophy* winners. Before transferring to **TCU**, quarterback Kenny Hill's family sought a trademark on *"Kenny Trill"* but later abandoned the application. With a trademark in hand, college athletes will be one step ahead when they start pursuing licensing deals after school. Specifically, the athletes are asking for the legal right to sell a wide range of merchandise branded with their names, from jerseys and hats to toddler onesies. Landing those rights can also be a defensive maneuver against so-called trademark poachers. If athletes don't secure trademarks, anyone else can apply for ownership at a cost of about $200. To wrestle it back, athletes can face long and costly court battles. Manziel famously claimed the trademark to *"Johnny Football"* in 2013 amid a legal battle with a company that had been selling T-shirts using his nickname. At **Mississippi State**, Prescott faced a similar situation when a man started making T-shirts with his name. Although experts say the practice is growing, it's mostly limited to a small group of big-name athletes. Officials at the universities of **Florida**, **Oregon** and **California** indicated they hadn't heard of any students interested in pursuing trademarks. Recently, the NCAA lost a court ruling that found students are entitled to compensation when their likenesses are used commercially. It stemmed from a lawsuit filed by former **UCLA** basketball star Ed O'Bannon. The NCAA is appealing. The judge in that case is now considering whether to grant class-action status to other current and former athletes who are suing the NCAA and aim to abolish the league's prohibition against competitively paying players. Many universities, meanwhile, have stopped selling jerseys with the numbers of current players, in part because of legal concerns.

Auburn University (Football): *Toomer's Corner*

All sports fans are aware of the event that led to the destruction of **Auburn's** 130 year-old, famed oak trees (the culprit was arrested in 2011 and received a three year split sentence and was also ruled to pay the university restitution of $796,731.98). But many fans do not realize how **Auburn's** bitter rival helped with the restoration effort. *"Tide for Toomer's"*

raised in excess of $50,000. **Auburn** celebrated the last rolling of the original trees after their spring football game. How appropriate. And before the replacement trees were healthy enough for their turn in the spotlight, **Auburn** accommodated this tradition in a unique way – four wires connecting three concrete poles were installed to accommodate the toilet paper. The wires which were separated by a series of AU symbols that held them together met in the middle and formed a "V" over the famous intersection at the corner of College Street and Magnolia Avenue. This solution was in place for a short while, but only after the city of Auburn ran numerous tests to ensure their temporary solution would work. The 35-foot-tall replacement oak trees were planted in Samford Park at *Toomer's*

Corner on Valentine's Day 2015. What a perfect way for all Tiger couples to spend the most romantic day of the year. For the planting, roads around *Toomer's Corner* were closed and there was a special viewing area for fans. And, as tradition dictated, beginning again in 2016, victories were followed by toilet paper being tossed. But

are only **Auburn** victories celebrated? When **Clemson** defeated **Auburn's** arch rival for the *2017 College Football Championship*, how did **Auburn** students celebrate? They rolled *Toomer's Corner*. And another wonderful fact about the live oaks at *Toomer's Corner*: Concurrent with the two replacement oaks being planted at *Toomer's Corner*, a third live oak was planted elsewhere (at a secret location?) on **Auburn's** campus, just in case one of the newly planted trees didn't survive. So the third oak is viewed as currently on the injury-reserve list. But have you ever given any thought to what happened to the trees that were poisoned? Of course they were removed. But then what? An artisan woodworker heard about the trees and contacted a long-time collector of his work. This collector was also an **Auburn** alum and a university trustee. Their idea: *to create a large bowl that would stand as a symbol to the oaks' majesty* and perhaps even salve the loss felt by the extended **Auburn** family. University administrators loved the idea and approached leaders at ***Auburn's*** *Museum of Fine Art*, who also

loved the vision. A 26.5" diameter, 15" tall bowl, with a little bark left on top to better connect to the original trees, was crafted. The art work is titled, *"Matt Moulthrop: Auburn Oak."* The work was so successful that Moulthrop was commissioned by the university to create two series of bowls from different sections of the trees to be given to major donors to **Auburn's** capital campaign. The artist is a **University of Georgia** undergraduate with a graduate degree from **GA Tech**, so he teases with his friends that he has *diplomatic immunity* working with **Auburn** on this project.

Auburn (Football): *Players Recognized at Graduations*

It's a wonderful thing that many college athletes actually graduate from college. And, as their name is called, and they walk across the stage in their cap and gown, they are students first. But their name recognition often causes spontaneous acts of various kinds. Many of you will remember the *Iron Bowl* in 2013 when *Chris Davis returned an **Alabama** missed field goal 109 yards for the game-winning score, as time expired*. So when Chris graduated in 2014, it is no surprise that his ovation from the audience was said to be the loudest ever heard at an **Auburn** graduation.

Autism Speaks

Tom Herrion, a DI assistant basketball coach created — from his home — an *organization that allows college coaches to support research for autism*. Coach Herrion's son has autism, so this is clearly a labor-of-love. Now, during a specific week during basketball season, *over 225 DI coaches wear the blue puzzle-piece pins associated with Autism Speaks*. Tom is joined in the organizational effort with another coach — Pat Skerry. Pat's son also has autism.

Aztec Bowl (Football): *Mexico versus USA*

The *Aztec Bowl* is probably the longest standing bowl, for small colleges, that you have never heard of. It began in 1954 and has been played intermittently since. The current  version (XLII) was held in 2016, and Mexico defeated the USA 17-14. All games have been played at locations in Mexico except for the 1957 game which was played in San Antonio. Mexico dominated many of the early games, so the USA responded by not sending one college team, but a team of all stars. Since then, *the USA leads 12-3 in the series.*

Basketball Team Managers' Games

You have likely not heard of a *basketball tradition that involves team managers*: those students that wash the dirty uniforms, code film, and prepare water and folding chairs for the timeouts. In gyms across the country, usually late on the eve of a DI game, and usually with nobody watching, *team managers* – of the two teams that will be competing the following day – *play each other in friendly scrimmages*. But it's actually much more than that. As you would expect, many of the managers played basketball in high school, and still view themselves as quite competitive. But the real beauty of this tradition was aided by the website *KPI Sports* (run by a former **Michigan State** manager). *KPI Sports* tracks over 350 scores from over 165 colleges and 27 conferences, and uses a weighted system to *establish rankings of these managers' teams*. The site also provides a shadow schedule. The website was established with the intent of organizing a post-season tournament, and a related *Twitter* account now has over 1,250 followers. ESPN announcer, Jay Bilas, is a big fan of the games. Games are often played on the home courts, since the managers are trusted with keys, and can use the lights, scoreboards, and locker rooms. Members of a team's support staff – including graduate assistants, video coordinators, strength coaches, etc. can participate, although assistant basketball coaches – who often are former college players – cannot. Games are frequently video-taped so that they can be analyzed for areas for improvement. **Maryland's** games

often included a highly talented ringer, Juan Dixon, the program's career leading scorer, who at the time was a special assistant to the head coach. Teams must play at least five *Manager Games* to be selected into the post-season tournament field. The top 64 teams by *KPI* to have met the minimum of five *Manager Games* by *Selection Sunday* qualify for the *Manager Games Postseason Tournament*. The teams are bracketed into four regions of 16 teams each using *KPI Rankings*. Conference matchups and geographical rematches are encouraged to increase the chances of playing. Teams can move up or down one seed line in the interest of geography. The *Manager Games Postseason Tournament* bracket overlaps *March Madness*, and the finals are held in the same city as the *NCAA Championship*.

Baylor (Basketball): *Creative Uniform Choices*

Many football and basketball teams – especially those sponsored in a big way by an apparel company – have a tradition of mixing-and-matching various uniform combinations. As an example, **Oregon** goes an entire football season and never wears an identical

uniform combination to one previously worn that season. But in 2013, the **Baylor** men's basketball team took it one step further: ***Baylor** asked Adidas to print "Sic 'em Bears!" – **Baylor's** slogan – on the front of the jerseys.* The NCAA was consulted and indicated that the slogan would not be allowed. Per NCAA rules, only the school name or traditional nicknames like *"Bears"* are allowed on the front of game uniforms.

Baylor (Football): *Bezos River Commute to the Stadium*

The **University of Tennessee** has the *Vol Navy*, and **Washington** has their famous *Sailgating*. And with those colleges' two stadiums opening in the early 1920's, they have each had almost a century to build their game day experiences. But both are now joined by **Baylor** that recently began a similar tradition of *fans commuting to a football game on their boats*. About forty vessels ranging from speedboats to inflatable rafts dock alongside **Baylor's** *McLane Stadium*. Eighteen dock slips were recently developed with two reserved for the university's use, and the other sixteen sold to fans. More than one-hundred fans vied for the slots, but they were sold based on the university's Foundation donor point-based system. But fear-not, there is also ample room for boaters nearby on a first-come basis. By virtue of the new stadium's site, the pregame *"March of the Bears"* now goes over a footbridge with the *Brazos River* below it. So fans on their boats now enjoy very close proximity to the players.

Beer Sold at College Games

For many years, there was *a tradition at almost every college that alcoholic beverages were not sold on campus*. Events off campus (i.e., when local teams like **Kansas** and **Missouri** play in Budweiser's back yard) were often

exempt. But what about on-campus alcohol sales? The answer is of course, *"it varies."* At **Cincinnati**, beer has been sold for years at practically every on-campus athletics event, and even includes green beer on *St. Patrick's Day* at baseball games. **Cincinnati** isn't an anomaly, as many cities (e.g., Houston, Memphis, and New Orleans) that have professional franchises view the issue quite differently than colleges located in small-town America. The NCAA does not typically sell beer at its championships (with an exception being for luxury suites). And in 2016 beer sales were allowed for both the baseball and softball *College World Series*. That's a long way from 1963 when Walter Byers (the head of the NCAA) told the *College World Series*, "If there's beer, there will be no baseball." But now the governing body consciously doesn't intervene. Conferences can decide, and many leave the issue up to individual schools. Currently *about 40 schools allow on-campus alcohol sales*. **West Virginia** began beer sales at football games in 2011. Wonder if that affected the periodic couch-burnings? **Minnesota** actually lost money during their first year of sales in 2012. **Arizona** began beer sales at off-campus baseball games. **Texas** added beer and wine sales at a handful of sports. And even **SMU**, in 2014, began on-campus sales. If students aged 21 and older enter a venue and want to participate, they get a wristband with three pull-tabs, with one torn-off for each beer they buy.

Big 10 Trophy Games

The Big 10 has never been at-a-loss for *Trophy Games*. Almost every time two schools play each other, a trophy passes hands. If it's not a *Slab of Bacon*, it's *Paul Bunyan's Ax*. In 2015, **Wisconsin's** streak of winning nine consecutive *Trophy Games* came to an end in a game with **Iowa**. So the Badgers continue to share the streak with **Iowa**, **Nebraska**, and **Minnesota**.

Boston College (Football): *Live Eagle Mascot*

The **Boston College** costumed-mascot is named *"Baldwin the Eagle"* a pun derived from the bald head of the eagle and the word *"win."* In 2013, **BC** introduced their first live eagle in 47 years. But the live eagle isn't named *"Baldwin,"* but is named *"Welles,"* in honor of **Boston College** men's lacrosse player and September 11 hero Welles Remy Crowther, class of 1999.

Boston College / Boston University / Harvard / Northeastern (Ice Hockey): *Beanpot Trophy*

The city of Boston has long been the center of the college hockey world, as evidenced by competition between the four area college teams for the *Beanpot Trophy*. The first *Beanpot was held in December of 1952*, but all subsequent competitions have taken place over a two-weekend period in

February, with every game played on the home ice of the NHL's Boston Bruins. All four schools are known for bringing raucous crowds, and the *Beanpot* often results in some of the highest attendance numbers of the college hockey season. **BC** and **BU** have historically dominated the *Beanpot*, but Wayne Turner's overtime goal in the 1980 championship game (the *Shot Heard Round the Beanpot*) gave **Northeastern** its first-ever title and is often considered the tournament's most memorable moment.

Bowl Games Swag

MOST POPULAR GIFTS THIS BOWL SEASON

■ Gift suite/shopping trip	18 games
■ Fossil watch	15 games
■ Ogio bag	9 games
■ New Era products	7 games
■ Oakley sunglasses	7 games
■ Timely Watch Co. watch	6 games

Note: Includes VIP gift packages, in addition to gifts to bowl participants.

For the past eleven years, the *Sports Business Journal* has completed an analysis of the gift packages provided by the *Bowl Committees* to the participating players, and staff. Typically a *Bowl Suite* is where decisions are made, and the participants' choices are often shipped to them later. In addition to the expected headphones, jewelry, back packs, gift cards, sunglasses, etc., there are a few gifts specific to the setting. As an example, the *2013 Famous Idaho Potato Bowl* offered winter coats, and ski gloves, while the *Sheraton Hawaii Bowl* offered beach towels. But my favorite gift continues to be the *Sun Bowl's* – a *Helen of Troy hair dryer*. *Helen of Troy* is a sponsor of the game, but I annually wonder how many of the hair dryers are opted-for. The NCAA has a limit of $550 for the gifts' total value, but conferences and individual schools can

POPULAR GIFTS

GIFT	NO. OF GAMES
Gift suite/shopping trip*	26
Fossil watch	15
Oakley product	8
Best Buy card*	6
Ogio bag	6
Timely watch	6
New Era product	4
Big Game football	4

* The committee that runs both the Russell Athletic Bowl and Buffalo Wild Wings Citrus Bowl provides participants a Best Buy gift card and hosts a shopping trip at an Orlando-based Best Buy. Best Buy's numbers are included in both totals here.

Notes: Includes VIP gift packages, in addition to gifts to bowl participants. Totals do not include vendor relationships with the NCAA Reese's Senior Bowl.

opt-in with an additional $400 each. This proved advantageous as 800 high-end home theater recliners were chosen as part of 2013 *Bowl Packages*. The *2016 TaxSlayer Bowl* had an intern to thank for one of their most unusual gifts: a *personalized bobble-head doll* for each player. I suspect the players opted for the *personalized bobble-head* versus any gift of online tax preparation that *TaxSlayer* might have offered. And while most fans have heard of *bowl-game-swag*, did you know that basketball players also get in on the fun? Not every conference basketball tournament provides gifts, but many do. Per NCAA parity, the value that the basketball players receive is equal to the football players. But with events beyond the conference tournament available, the total for a basketball player in the *Final Four* could total just less than $4,000 in merchandise.

Boxtorow Poll: *Historically Black Colleges and Universities National Championships*

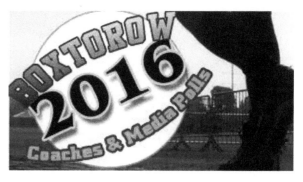

As many sports fans know, the **HBCU's** have their bowl games during the season, and rightly call them *"Classics".* But this group of unique colleges and universities also crowns their own *National Champion(s)* each year. Fourteen times before (in various polls), the **Grambling State** Tigers have been named *National Champions*. And 2016 made it fifteen. The *Boxtorow HBCU FCS Coaches Poll* is now in its ninth year, while the *Boxtorow Media Poll* is in its twelfth year.

Coaches Poll Winners:

> 2016 **Grambling**
> 2015 **North Carolina A&T**
> 2014 **Alcorn State**

2013 Bethune-Cookman
2012 Arkansas-Pine Bluff
2011 Norfolk State
2010 Bethune-Cookman
2009 South Carolina State

Media Poll Winners:

2016 Grambling
2015 North Carolina A&T
2014 Alcorn State
2013 Bethune-Cookman
2012 Winston-Salem State
2011 Winston-Salem State
2010 Bethune-Cookman
2009 South Carolina State
2008 Grambling
2007 Tuskegee

Bradley University (All Sports):
Kaboom, the Gargoyle Mascot

In 2014, after many years with a Native American mascot, then a Bobcat, and even ten years with no mascot, a student vote concluded that a *Gargoyle* should be the new mascot. This is *unique in DI athletics* and pays homage to two campus buildings – each adorned with *Gargoyles*.

Brown: *One for Me*

At **Brown**, officials created a program to leverage peer advising to help student athletes take better advantage of the opportunities available to them. The *One for Me* program encourages incoming freshmen athletes to take at least one course that no one else on their team is taking. **Brown** has an open curriculum (i.e., no core requirements), so athletes can easily find classes of interest to them that may not be of interest to their teammates. At many major colleges and universities, major-clustering is a very real issue. Athletes are often in the same major and many in the same classes together. **Brown's** freshmen athletes are introduced to the program with a letter from an upper-class teammate before they enroll. This teammate shares their personal experience and the value that they have received by participation. One of the school's deans is heavily involved, and hosts a yearly dinner where participants share their personal experiences.

Busted Brackets

Is there any better tradition each March than the *March Madness Brackets* being announced, and testing your ability versus your friends? Who cares that the *odds of a perfect bracket are one in 9.2 quintillion*. That's a nine followed by eighteen digits. But Janice Hough of

leftcoastsportsbabe.com has it right with her recent toast: *"May your troubles last as long as your perfect brackets".*

Butler University: *Bulldog Mascot Walks with Each Graduating Class*

Butler Blue is name of the English bulldog mascot that serves as the official live mascot of **Butler University**. There have been three bulldogs to bear the name, with the current mascot *Blue III*. He assumed his duties in 2013, and immediately continued the tradition of *walking with the graduating class* at their ceremony. Since live mascots are only allowed at *the Final Four* and not at other tournament games, *Blue II* was one of the very few live mascots, if not the only one, to witness *Final Four* games, and he saw two of them.

When *Blue II* passed away, he sent a classic *Tweet*: *"How do I know all dogs go to heaven? Because I'm there now."*

Butler: *Injury Report*

Gamblers, and others, pour-over injury reports about players that might be questionable for the next contest. The New England Patriots – every week for years – has listed QB, Tom Brady as questionable. Brady even laughs when asked about his coaches' gamesmanship. But in the fall of 2016, **Butler University** issued a very serious injury report. Their Bulldog Mascot, *Trip (aka Butler Blue III),* was listed as *"week-to-week,"* based on an ACL tear in his right hind leg. According to *Butler Blue III's* website, his favorite snack is *Hinkle Fieldhouse popcorn.* Hopefully, he got a few handfuls during his downtime.

BYU / Utah / Utah State (Football): *Beehive Boot*

They take their college football seriously in the state of Utah, with a number of programs vying for supremacy over the years. The *Beehive Boot* – a trophy made from authentic pioneer footwear – was created to help settle the issue. This has primarily been a contest between **Brigham Young**, **Utah**, and **Utah State**, as those are the three FBS programs that reside within the state. An FCS school, **Weber State**, was originally eligible to win the award when it was created in 1971, but the Wildcats are no longer factored into the running. Traditionally, the *Beehive Boot* has been awarded to whichever of the three schools had *the best record against their in-state rivals*; in case of a tie, the winner is decided by in-state media outlets. There is some concern over whether this contest will continue in the future, as **Utah** moved into the Pac 12 Conference and is hesitant to schedule both **BYU** and **Utah State** as non-conference opponents.

BYU-Hawaii (Basketball): *Free Ice Cream*

At every home basketball game (men's or women's), if **BYU-Hawaii** scores 100 points or more and wins, their food services provides *free ice cream* following the game to everyone who attends (and is willing to wait in line for their ice cream). This tradition has led to some interesting twists to their games, including chants from the fans of *"Ice Cream"* anytime the team appears on their way to 100 points. Sometimes the chant is *"We want, we want ice cream"* to the tune of *We Will, We Will Rock You* by Queen. They have had opposing coaches go into a stalling tactic to prevent them from reaching 100 and they have had their own coach booed when he told the team to dribble out the clock when they were a basket away from hitting 100. They have also had players (usually reserves who aren't accustomed to such pressure) feel extraordinary pressure at the free throw line with just seconds remaining in the game and a chance for them to put their team to the century-mark with made free throws (they usually fail under the pressure and the chants). The player who puts the team into triple digits is revered as a hero for the night and into the following week.

Cal (Football): *Big Game Bonfire Rally*

Most fans know of the uniqueness of the **Cal** versus **Stanford** *"Big Game,"* and there are many, many traditions that take place on each campus the week of the game. As an example, *since 1892*, the night before the game, on **Cal's** campus, has included a *bonfire*. Except for one recent year when the *bonfire* tradition was cancelled due to a conflict with a Bob Dylan concert. So much for a 125 year old tradition.

Caltech (Football): *Hacked Card Stunt*

In 1961, the **University of Washington** prepared a card-stunt for their team's attendance in the *Rose Bowl*. But fourteen ingenious **Caltech** students, picked locks, posed as reporters, and painstakingly stamped replacement cards so that when **Washington** fans thought they were spelling-out *"Washington,"* they instead displayed *"Caltech."* The second card stunt was to spell-out *"Huskies,"* **Washington's** mascot. But the **Caltech** students had the word spelled backwards for the nationwide TV audience. And for the final card stunt, the intent was a picture of a huskie – **Washington's** mascot. But the **Caltech** students replaced the huskie with a picture of **Caltech's** mascot – a beaver. Ever wonder why **Caltech** has a beaver as a mascot? It's because beavers are *"nature's engineers."*

Caltech: *NCAA Probation*

In 2012, **Caltech**, the school that couldn't succeed at sports if it cheated, *turned itself in to the NCAA for cheating*. One of the country's losingest athletic programs *chose to vacate wins it didn't have, shut down the recruiting it doesn't do and be ineligible for championships it never wins*. In

an announcement as stunning as the ones that brag about a professor discovering the secrets of the universe, **Caltech** said it joined the likes of **USC** and **Ohio State** in NCAA jail by being placed on three-year's athletic probation. Probation from what, no one was entirely sure. *The Beavers aren't on TV, they don't give scholarships, and they rarely qualify for postseason tournaments*. The baseball team vacated all wins during a period in which they went 0-112. The men's water polo team vacated wins achieved while going 0-66. Other famous **Caltech** losing streaks not affected were the 228-game baseball losing streak, and the 26-year, 310 straight losing games for basketball. While other programs often falsely brag that they're winning the right way, seemingly only at **Caltech** do they have the guts to lose the right way. "This is our integrity at stake here," said Betsy Mitchell, who discovered the violations shortly after she was named **Caltech** athletic director in 2011. "It stinks, but we did the right thing, and we're going to take our medicine." You know what stinks? This Pasadena brain boutique is essentially being punished because its classes are so difficult. The NCAA has a rule that *student-athletes must take a full course load to be eligible*. Though **Caltech** students are studying from the moment they set foot on campus, they don't officially take a full course load until the end of the third week of every term because they are allowed to shop the difficult classes before making final decisions. It's hard to blame them. When deciding between, *"Markov Chains, Discrete Stochastic Processes and Applications"* and *"Computational Fluid Dynamics,"* shouldn't one be allowed to sleep on it? One wrong choice could send your term spinning into a maze of all-nighters. "It's really important to know about the class before you take it, the scheduling and the workload, because you have to make sure it fits your other classes," said Albie Lavin, a junior co-captain of the baseball team. When Mitchell took over last summer with the mandate of fostering a stronger connection between the forlorn athletic department and the rest of the university, she took a quick look at the school practices and realized this could be trouble. Her subsequent investigation into the four-year period of 2007-10 uncovered *30 students who were competing for teams for brief periods without officially taking full course loads*. The ineligible athletes weren't stars. They didn't create championships. In keeping with that funky **Caltech** tradition, many of them probably were kids who were just learning the sport and needed a break from splitting the atom. The NCAA never would have found this. The NCAA never would have even looked for this. This wasn't the loud stumbling of a Goliath. This was a tiny trip by Little Red Riding Hood. If anything, you can imagine the folks at the NCAA headquarters hanging up after hearing Mitchell's confession and quietly giggling. "None of that mattered," Mitchell said. "Even though it was very technical, we weren't doing it right, and around here, doing it right is what matters." Her bosses agreed. Her coaches agreed. They knew that the revelations would cause a brief media firestorm, but they didn't care. Mitchell, using the same resolve that helped her once become a silver medal Olympic swimmer, immediately fixed the problem and told her administrators to expect the worst. When the news finally hit, she was visited and offered support by two important athletic boosters – Bob Grubbs, the Nobel laureate, and John Grotzinger, who is working on a rover mission to Mars. "This is about educational athletics versus entertainment athletics," Mitchell said. "We teach through our sports, and we're teaching through this." **Caltech** initially decided to punish itself by placing a 2012-13 *postseason ban on 12 sports, vacating wins achieved by teams using ineligible athletes during that four-year period, eliminating off-campus recruiting for the upcoming school year and paying a $5,000 fine*. That should have been enough, but, of course, the NCAA jumped in with a public censure and three-year probation. One would think officials there could have quietly shooed Mitchell away after she devised their own penalties. But none of us should feel too much sympathy for the **Caltech** athletes, since many potential athletes that can't meet **Caltech's** admission standards view **MIT** as their *"safety school."*

Caltech (Basketball): *Win a Ball Signed by Five Nobel Prize Winners*

At **Caltech's** version of *Midnight Madness*, if a student sinks a half-court shot, they win a *basketball signed by five Nobel Prize Winners*. This was initiated after **Caltech** went twenty-six consecutive years without winning a conference game.

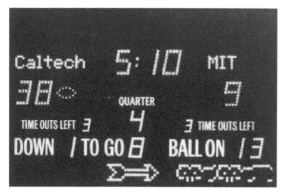

Two colleges that clearly focus more on elaborate pranks (on each other) than they do on athletics are **Caltech** and **MIT**. Their *traditions of planning, and executing pranks*, are legendary, with some of the planning taking up to ten years. Both schools have a set of *pranking ethics*, stating that pranks should be reversible and not cause permanent damage, and emphasize creativity and originality. And at **Caltech**, their assistant vice president of student affairs once indicated, "the grand old days of pranking have gone away, and we'd like to bring those days back." And he ordered local campus security to not intervene in any prank unless they received his approval beforehand.

And not to be outdone, **MIT's** Dean of Admissions has been quoted as saying, "I consider pranks a performance art and I like the concept of inter-institute rivalry." But here are a few that are among the standards in pranking-lore: In the 1984 *Rose Bowl*, **Caltech** students altered the electronic scoreboard – during the game – to show **Caltech** beating **MIT** 38-9. **Caltech** has a cannon on their campus that dates back to 1878, and due to the cannon's

fragility, it is one of the few objects on their campus that is officially designated as *un-prankable*. But do you think that designation tempted **MIT** students. You bet. The **MIT** prank team was comprised of thirty students, of which two flew to the **Caltech** campus, and five drove cross-country. The students posed as contractors, hired a professional shipping company, and even spent $1,000 for specialized rigging to load the cannon to a van for its trip across the USA. On **MIT's** campus, the cannon was placed pointing west towards **Caltech's** campus. But *pranking ethics* require a note explaining the theft, and **MIT** had not complied. My favorite part of this saga is that when **Caltech** students ventured to Boston to secretly retrieve their cannon, **MIT** students somehow found out and were waiting for the **Caltech** students with a friendly barbeque prepared, while blaring music was played from Wagner's *Ride of the Valkyries*, a forbidden song on **Caltech's** campus due to its association with final exams. *Mock newspapers* are also legendary in this

pranking series. One even had a mock advertisement for sperm donations offering more money for **Caltech** students than for **MIT** students. **Caltech** printed a *fake newspaper* that was distributed to incoming **MIT** freshmen that indicated they would be required to take philosophy, and history of literature classes, while science and math subjects were to be eliminated. And for prospective students **Caltech** once had some mugs manufactured and traveled to Boston to give them to high-school seniors that

were considering **MIT**. When the mug held a cold liquid, it displayed the **MIT** logo, but when it contained a hot liquid, the **MIT** logo disappeared and *"**Caltech**: the Hotter Institute of Technology"* appeared. So it is easy to understand why **Caltech's** unofficial motto is *"we do cool stuff, because we can."* **Caltech** is also famous for its *Ditch Day* tradition, in which underclassmen try to outwit elaborate dorm-room locks designed by seniors. One year, students not only picked a tricky lock but took apart the senior's parked car, then reassembled it in his room and reportedly left the engine running. In 1991, when then-President George H.W. Bush delivered a commencement speech at the school, he joked that he might be late to his next meeting because "*some of **Caltech's** finest reassembled Air Force One in the lobby of my hotel.*" But the school's ultimate achievement, hailed as *the best collegiate stunt in history*, is the *Great Rose Bowl Hoax of 1961.* Posing as high school newspaper reporters, **Caltech** pranksters duped cheerleaders from the **University of Washington** into revealing the inner workings of their carefully choreographed halftime flip-card show, in which stadium spectators held up colored cards to form giant words and pictures. The **Caltech** students then stole and replaced **Washington's** flip-card instruction sheets with their own. On the field, **Washington's** band stopped playing and the crowd went silent, according to *museumofhoaxes.com*. Then laughter erupted and the band stormed out. After five years of planning, and a few failed experiments, **MIT** students sneaked into *Harvard* Stadium eight times before the 1983 *Harvard / Yale* game, planted a Freon-driven hydraulic balloon device and wired it into the electrical sprinkler-grid under the field. During the game, they deployed, and then exploded, a black balloon with **"MIT"** written on it. The prank was a massive success and led to a quintessentially 1980s press conference in which the **MIT** students boasted about their efforts, sipped on beer and, evidently, weren't required to wear pants. And one final validation to the **Caltech** pranks: *their efforts are supported by donations from former students.*

Calvin College / Hope College (Basketball): *One of the Best DIII Basketball Rivalries*

This rivalry *began in either 1917, or 1920*, depending on which school you believe. Through the first 185 games, a total of only 88 points separated the two teams. In 2005, the staff at ESPN listed this rivalry as *the fourth-best in college basketball*

and the greatest of all matchups in Division III.

Case Western Reserve / College of Wooster (Football): *Baird Brothers Trophy*

Fishing and football don't ordinarily go together, but don't tell that to **Case Western Reserve University** and the **College of Wooster**. When the Spartans and the Scots meet on the gridiron, the winner claims *one of the most unique trophy traditions in college sports*, the *Baird Brothers Trophy*. This trophy, noted in a 1995 issue of *Sports Illustrated* magazine as one of the most unique trophies in college football, consists of a golden fishing stringer with carved brass fish representing each meeting. The trophy's beginnings *date back to 1984* when Bob Baird, an economics professor at CWRU, and his brother Bill Baird, an economics professor at Wooster, came up with the idea. *The winner of the game gets to keep the stringer for the year and add a new fish for that year's contest.* Each added fish is representative of how the game was played, with the score and winner engraved on the side. The original fish is a

four-inch blue gill symbolizing the narrow last second **Case** victory, 21-14. A big northern pike denotes the Spartans 37-0 victory over the Scots in 1985. Other fish included on the trophy are a flounder, a carp, a walleye, a catfish, a rainbow trout, a sturgeon, a sucker, a crappie, a Muskie, a sheepshead, a gar, a largemouth bass and a smallmouth bass. The Baird brothers originated the trophy in 1984 when **Wooster** and **Case** first met as members of the North Coast Athletic Conference. The brothers, economic professors at the rival schools, were taught by their father to fish at an early age and thought the fish theme would be a fitting reward to the victors. Bob Baird passed away a few years ago, but his brother Bill still carries on the *tradition of presenting the trophy to the winning team* at the conclusion of the game. The two schools have met about 30 times, with **Wooster** currently holding a slight advantage.

Central Florida (Football): *East Side Club*

UCF's stadium features *"The East Side Club"* – a covered lounge and sun deck made to resemble a beach bar. But it doesn't have any sand, just the illusion of it. The area proved so popular that a local company signed a six-figure, multi-year naming rights agreement with **UCF** to put their name on the area.

Chicken Fried Tailgate Song

Any attendee at a Zac Brown Band concert knows that *"Chicken Fried"* is a fan favorite. Apparently, a lot of other people like it, too. In 2015 *Spotify* identified the swinging southern anthem as *the most popular tailgating song.* The streaming service combed through more than 4,000 tailgating playlists and found that *"Chicken Fried"* appeared the most frequently. The song was the first *No. 1 single* for the Atlanta band and has sold more than 4.5 million copies since 2008.

Christmas Lights Supporting Their Teams

In the past few years, I have noticed a trend of college super fans attempting to outdo each other with their Christmas decorations. It only takes one fan being featured on the *Paul Finebaum Show* with their 25,000 lights synced to the **Alabama** fight song to begin an arms-race with other fans. And pity the poor neighbors that might live close by, and not be a fan of the same school. John Storms is the **Alabama** fan in question, but interestingly, he isn't personally an **Alabama** fan. It was a Christmas present to a neighbor, and co-worker that was a huge fan. So another **Alabama** fan decided to surpass John. He synced his lights to a light display that is

synchronized with **Alabama** play-by-play broadcaster Eli Gold's *radio calls from the 2015 Cotton Bowl*. The highlights from the Crimson Tide 38-0 win over **Michigan State** play along with lights on the house. And not to be outdone, an **Auburn** fan created his Christmas lights-show to sync with the radio call of the *Kick-6* game-winning touchdown in the *Iron Bowl* that put the Tigers in position to go to the *BCS* title game in 2014. Other universities that have similar displays by their fans are **Michigan State**, **Oklahoma**, **Texas A&M**, and **Penn State**. And an **Ole Miss** fan takes a special shot at **LSU**, while a **TCU** fan has the score of a recent **Baylor** upset prominently in his lights display.

Churchill Downs Promotion: *Downs after Dark*

Churchill Downs has a tradition called *Downs after Dark*, when on a specified Saturday Churchill Downs is transformed into *College Rivalry Night*. Each fan that enters the track is asked which collegiate team they support, and at night's end, *$10,000 in scholarships are awarded to the winning schools*.

Cincinnati (Basketball): *Midday Madness*

Since 2013 if you're in downtown Cincinnati in October and taking a lunch break around *Fountain Square*, why not watch the **Cincinnati** men and women's basketball teams celebrate the start of the season? They set-up a court right on the square, as part of *Basketball Midday Madness*. Coaches and players are introduced, the **UC** spirit squads cheer and then there is some friendly competition on the court. The hour-long event is free and fans have the opportunity to meet the players and also participate in a drawing for a pair of season tickets for both **UC** men and women's basketball games. I think all urban schools should have similar events.

City Temporarily Changes Its Name

When **Oregon** played **Ohio State** in the *College Football Playoff* in 2015, the small city in Ohio named "Oregon" felt the need to clarify their name – since they clearly could not be viewed as partisan to the **Oregon** Ducks versus their beloved Buckeyes. So the mayor and the city council agreed that the only prudent thing to do was to temporarily re-name Oregon, Ohio to *"Oregon, Ohio: Buckeyes on the Bay, City of Duck Hunters."*

Clemson (Football): *Fan with Tattoo of Dabo Swinney*

Have you ever looked at your body and thought, *"This would be so much better if I had Dabo Swinney drawn on it?"* Neither have I, but there was one **Clemson** fan who indicated on social media in 2015 that "If **Clemson** make it to *College Football Playoff*, I'm getting a Dabo tattoo. If we win, I'm getting a banner under it that says Champions." Well, **Clemson** made the *College*

Football Playoff, and the fan was a man of his word. I wonder what he did the following year when **Clemson** won-it-all?

Clemson: *Fan Waves at Passing Cars*

His name is W.T. Wooten. And he is a wonderful man with an exuberant spirit. When asked how old he was, he answered with a wry grin, "nearly 100." And he spends 5-6 hours a day, EVERYDAY, standing at the fence at the *Six Mile Assisted Living* facility waving his **Clemson** hat and pom poms to cars passing by. In 2014, the gentleman came to **Clemson's** attention so they arranged for the Tiger mascot to visit him and give him lots of **Clemson** gear.

Clemson (Baseball): *Omaha Challenge*

In the fall of 1998, head baseball coach Jack Leggett conceived a first-of-its-kind offseason competition to test his players and build team unity. With reference to the *College World Series*, he coined the competition the *"Omaha Challenge."* With this tradition's longevity, it is an often-imitated event throughout the country. What once was a set of drills limited to the weight room has turned into a challenging yet fun compilation of events ranging all over **Clemson's** picturesque campus. The team-building and camaraderie is evident as the baseball players passionately endure the following 11 competitions:

> *Tug of War - Jervey Weight Room*
> *3x200 Relay - Indoor Track*
> *3x400 Relay - Indoor Track*
> *3x600 Relay - Indoor Track*
> *Cone Shuttle Run - Indoor Track*
> *Freestyle Swim Relay - McHugh Natatorium*
> *Medley Swim Relay - McHugh Natatorium*
> *Rope Race - Memorial Stadium*
> *Omaha Regatta - Lake Hartwell*
> *Football Toss Relay - Indoor Football Facility*
> *Obstacle Course - Indoor Football Facility*

First-place teams for each event received 100 points, second place 75, third place 50 and fourth place 25. There are four teams with one captain per team. Those captains have a draft to choose players they think will be well-rounded in the wide array of events.

Coaches Beat Cancer

Some of the nation's best-known coaches participate in an online auction that allows *charitable fans to spend 24 hours with them*. The winner gets dinner, a round of golf, and / or whatever else the high-profile coach chooses to do. Bids start at $10,000 and, of course, all proceeds go to charity.

Coast-to-Coast Men's Basketball Event

In December of 2018, a very unique type of rivalry will be established. **Michigan State**, **North Carolina**, **Texas**, and **Florida** have all agreed to *play each other consecutively in New York, Chicago, and Los Angeles*. Teams will fly to cities together and take part in cultural activities along the way.

Coker College / Central College (Baseball): *Senior Players Graduate by Walking Down the 3rd Base Line*

Since college baseball's playoff season often conflicts with spring graduation dates, baseball coaches at several colleges have become very creative with a way to have their senior players not miss their graduation ceremony. In 2013, **Coker College** won the *DII Southeast Regional* title, and advanced to the *DII Baseball Championship*. After the victory, 132 miles from **Coker's** campus, *fifteen senior members of the team walked down the 3rd base line to receive their diplomas*. **Coker's** president and provost had officiated over **Coker's** normal graduation the day before, so they decided to bring the graduation to the baseball players. Some of the **Coker** players put on caps and gowns (with their cleats). And in 2015, **Central College** baseball players had a similar experience. While their college hosted commencement ceremonies, at an adjacent venue **Central** was hosting a *Super Regional* games. But due to inclement weather the schedule was impacted. **Central** played much earlier in the day, and was eliminated. As a result, the seniors were able to make their graduation. They walked into the ceremony in their uniforms and were greeted with a standing ovation.

College of Wooster: *Bagpipers*

The Fighting Scots offer *scholarships for bagpipers*, and these musicians *often escort senior athletes* into competition on *Senior Day*. And they always *accompany their football team as they take-the-field.*

College World Series: *Dogpile*

The *dogpile* – at the pitcher's mound – after a series is clinched – has been a staple at the *College World Series* for many years. *Baseball Prospectus* traced the roots of the phenomenon to Major League Baseball in the 1960s. The publication credits the 1962 Yankees for turning their *World Series* winning celebration toward the field and for throwing equipment in the air. Before the widespread TV broadcast of baseball, most championship teams in the post-World War II era simply ran off the field after the final out was

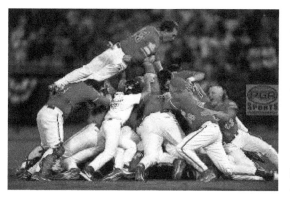

recorded. The 1963 Los Angeles Dodgers' celebration featured players who jumped into a circle of teammates, possibly for the first time. In 1982, the Cardinals won the *World Series* and fell to the ground in a heap much like the modern-day *dogpile*.

Four years later, the *dogpile* reached full chaos mode with the Mets, as reliever Jesse Orosco hurled his glove after the final out of the *World Series* before a gang of teammates tackled him. Players have often been injured in *dogpiles* after winning *Super Regionals*, and have been unable to play in the *College World Series*. But that never stops the *dogpile* at the conclusion of the *College World Series*.

Concordia University (Intramurals): *Synchronized Swimming*

Concordia University performs choreographed *synchronized swimming programs in child-sized pools*. What fun!

Cutting-the-Nets

Every sports fan is familiar with the tradition of *cutting-down-the-nets* after a basketball championship. But did you know, after hockey's *Frozen Four*, the winner traditionally *cuts pieces of the goal's netting*, as a souvenir for each player and coach.

Dartmouth (Hockey): *Tennis Balls Thrown on the Ice*

Yes, it sounds as absurd as it is, but when **Dartmouth** scores its first goal of the game against **Princeton**, the crowd *throws tennis balls onto the ice*. The tradition began in 1998, when a student at **Princeton** threw a tennis ball at **Dartmouth's** goalie after he gave up a goal. The strange moment was not forgotten, and now Big Green fans throw tennis balls on the ice after their team scores its first goal while playing **Princeton**.

Dartmouth (Football): *Robot Tackling Dummies*

In 2015, the **Dartmouth** football team added some *unique practice players: robots.* Yes, you read that right. They're the *Mobile Virtual Players (MVPs),* free-standing, remote controlled, padded dummies. The *MVPs* are designed to create game-like scenarios while reducing the risk of injury

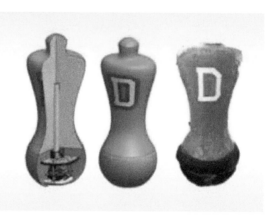

(by lessening the body-on-body contact necessary for tackling drills). The *MVPs* allow the players to get more, and safer, tackling repetitions. The company that makes the robots won the *"Training the Athlete"* category in the second annual *1st and Future* competition, a collaboration between the NFL and the Texas Medical Center. The competition recognizes startups focused on driving innovations by advancing sports technology and athlete safety.

Dear World Social Experiment

A few innovative colleges are participating in a new tradition called *Dear World.* This social experiment was created in 2009 by Dr. Robert Fogarty. Participants write on their skin with dry-erase markers words that mean something to them, then a photograph is taken of the word(s). *Dear World* has taken over 50,000 portraits from around the world, and views that the portraits often are the first line in a story that brings people closer together. College Athletic Departments use *Dear World* as a vehicle to *create a more trusting environment that strengthens bonds among teammates beyond the game.* This process provides an opportunity for teams to connect and share intimate moments that set the course for the entire season – often helping accomplish team goals. Before the beginning of the 2014-15 basketball season, coach K engaged with *Dear World.* Over the course of a weekend in the summer, Dr. Fogarty presented past portraits, and explained the stories behind them. Stories included athletes battling ALS, Boston Marathon survivors, etc. Each **Duke** player wrote one word or a phrase on their skin and were then photographed. The following day, as the photos were revealed, each player stood with his photograph and opened-up about the story behind it. Throughout that season the players pointed to *Dear World* as a pivotal step towards their team goals. Whether it contributed, or not, **Duke** did win the *National Championship* seven months later. Coach K's

words written on his skin were, *"pursue moments."* And when he described what he meant by this phrase to his team, he read them a letter that he composed to his good friend. It reads:

Dear Jimmy,

*You and I became brothers during the last four or five months of your life. You knew that you were dying of cancer. You were in **Duke** Hospital and we spent a few nights every week together.*

We had many moments.

The very best moment though was when you said, "I'm gonna die, but I'm gonna win."

I asked you, "What do you mean?" And you said, "I want to beat cancer. After I die, when we've finally beat cancer I want to be there."

I was with you when you died. And I never looked at our relationship as having a last moment. I always looked forward to the next moment.

I don't remember the last thing I said to you, Jimmy.

And the reason I don't is because I thought you would live forever.

Love your friend,

Mike

Die-Hard Fans

When a huge event like *March Madness* kicks off, you might expect the bleachers to be filled with alumni and students from the competing colleges. In fact, only *about a third of die-hard college sports fans are alumni of their teams' universities*, and another third never attended college at all, according to a 2015 **Duke University** study. The research by Charles Clotfelter, a professor of public policy, economics and law at **Duke's** *Sanford School of Public Policy*, draws upon an unusual source for its conclusions: *obituaries*. Clotfelter's article, "Die-Hard Fans and Ivory Tower's Ties That Bind," was published online by *The Social Science Quarterly*. "Accounts such as these, written to celebrate the life of a loved one, suggest that the decedent's interest in this college team was no casual thing, but rather a noteworthy source of identity," Clotfelter writes. "To refer to these individuals merely as fans of college football or basketball is surely inadequate. These were true believers." *Some*

fans even asked in their obituary that attendees wear the colors of the deceased's favorite team to the funeral. To find these die-hard fans, Clotfelter picked 26 colleges with unusual team names, such as the *Crimson Tide* or the *Jayhawks*, and *searched online obituaries for team references.* His research group collected 1,300 obituaries, 50 for each team. They found testimonies to the fans' affection for their teams, including:

- o *"Throughout his adult life, [he] was a dedicated **Ohio State** football fan. He owned a scarlet and grey 'Buckeye Van' which he drove to the home games. The license plate on [his] van read 'SACK MI'."*
- o *"She will be watching March Madness from the heavens, where she will be cheering on the Blue Devils of **Duke** and her beloved coach K."*
- o *[He] was an independent thinker in all aspects of his life. This was no more evident than in his remaining the only **Michigan** Wolverine fan in a large family of Buckeyes."*
- o *"She enjoyed family traditions, knitting and **Penn State** football."*

Clotfelter compared the fans' obituaries to a random sample of obituaries from the same states. Both sets contained information such as gender, age, occupation, military service, college attendance, religious affiliation, civic and volunteer activity and state of residence. *Die-hard fans were rare, representing only about 2 percent of published obituaries of adults.* They included three times as many men as women. Compared to others featured in obituaries, they were more likely to be white, to be  mainline Protestants and to participate in coaching. In terms of their education and professions, the die-hard fans were a diverse group. Even though a sizeable minority of the ardent fans never attended college, as a group die-hard fans were twice as likely to have attended college as the general population. Many die-hard fans held blue-collar jobs, but 22 percent were in professional occupations such as law, medicine or engineering. Most die-hard fans lived in the same state as the college they supported, but not all. Fans of **UCLA**, **Connecticut** and **Texas A&M** were tightly clustered near those campuses. **Notre Dame** and **Nebraska** fans tended to be widely distributed across the country, perhaps because of the winning histories of their football programs. Clotfelter found no significant link between the academic reputation of a college and the size of its fan base. Die-hard fans represent an authentic link between universities and everyday people, Clotfelter said. Fandom is "a sign of the people's affection, and a source of

pride, even a kind of patriotism," he said. Clotfelter also explored the fans' political party registration by looking at state voting records. The ardent fans were 5.5 percentage points likely to register as Republicans than similar adults, but there was no difference in the rate of registration as a Democrat between fans and the control group. All fans were more likely to be affiliated with some party than to have no affiliation. Few scholars have studied big-time college sports' ultra-loyal fans, Clotfelter said. Fans are significant to universities as customers, followers and stakeholders. Fandom can offer social capital benefits similar to civic volunteerism and other engagement, he said. Being a fan can provide a sense of ownership of the university that can extend to financial and political support. "It's my belief that commercial sports are a core function of universities such as these, even if it is not in their mission statements," Clotfelter said. "Being a fan represents an authentic cultural tie. To call big-time college sports commercial is accurate but incomplete. It's the truth, but not the whole truth."

Drake University: *Beautiful Bulldog Contest*

Each year for the past 40+ years, as part of the **Drake** Relays, a *"Beautiful Bulldog" Pageant* has been held. It is a tongue-in-cheek event that kicks-off the week of *the Relays*. The contest began as a way to find a real dog to represent the school's mascot, but now it involves any English bulldog that chooses to enter the lottery for the fifty entrants that will be considered.

East Carolina: *Ghost on the Wind Poem*

This poem is read, *dramatically*, as a welcome message *prior to the start of **ECU** home sporting events*:

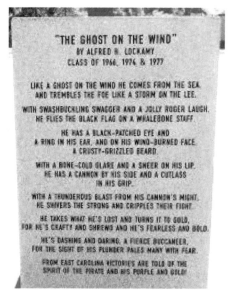

The Ghost on the Wind (Alfred H. Lockamy 2005)

> Like a ghost on the wind
> He comes from the sea,
> And trembles the foe
> Like a storm on the lee.
> With swashbuckling swagger
> And a Jolly Roger laugh,
> He flies the black flag
> On a whalebone staff.
> He has a black-patched eye
> And a ring in his ear,
> And on his wind-burned face,
> A crusty-grizzled beard.
> With a bone-cold glare
> And a sneer on his lip,
> He has cannon by his side
> And a cutlass in his grip.
> With a thunderous blast
> From his cannon's might,
> He shivers the strong
> And cripples their fight.
> He takes what he's lost
> And turns it to gold,
> For He's crafty and shrewd

And He's fearless and bold.
He's dashing and daring,
A fierce buccaneer,
For the sight of his plunder
Pales many with fear.
*From **East Carolina***
Victories are told
Of the Spirit of the Pirate
And his purple and gold!

Electronic Signatures Now Accepted for National Signing Day

The *National Letter of Intent* is a document used to indicate a student athlete's commitment to participating NCAA colleges and universities. The *NCAA Eligibility Center* manages the daily operations of the program while the *Collegiate Commissioners Association* provides governance oversight of the program. Beginning in 1964 with seven conferences and eight independent institutions, the program *now includes 676 Division I and II participating institutions*. There are designated dates for different sports, and these dates are commonly referred to as *"Signing Day."* Division III institutions are specifically banned from using the *National Letter of Intent*, or any similar document that is not executed by non-athletes at those institutions. The letters of intent were *traditionally faxed* by the recruited student to the university's athletic department on a *National Signing Day*, and many schools still refer to *"receiving the fax."* But as we all know, fax machines are so last-century. So believe-it-or-not*, the NCAA now allows electronic signatures.* Recruits can take a picture of their signed form and email it. **UCLA**, and other schools, now use the *SignNow* software that provides an accurate timestamp and ensures that the school receives the signed document, as soon as it is executed.

Fans Storming a Football Field (or Court) after a Victory

It's seen less-and-less these days, but we all remember witnessing fans storming onto a field after a particularly great win. But it isn't always after a big win, or a win at all. At **Clemson University**, everyone is encouraged to go down to the field after every game. But **Clemson** is certainly the exception in this regard. At the 2015 annual spring meeting for the SEC, the league passed a rule that *substantially increased the fines for fans' post-game celebrations* that violate the league's on-field

and on-court policy. First-time violators of the rule now face a $50,000 fine – 10 times more than the previous cost for first-time offenders. An SEC school's second offense is now $100,000 and third-time offenders face a fine of $250,000, the same amount violators will be billed for each subsequent offense. And the SEC commissioner indicated they may also apply additional penalties as necessary, and can apply similar penalties regardless of the sport. For the prior decade, the SEC had fined its schools $5,000, $25,000 and up to $50,000 for first, second and third offenses respectively. But the SEC concluded that $5,000 wasn't much of a deterrent. In 2014 when **Ole Miss** upset **Alabama** at home, the fans stormed-the-field. And, as a result, **Ole Miss** received the maximum fine of $50,000 fine from the SEC. The athletic director joked on *Twitter* that fans should help foot the bill, and that's exactly what happened – very quickly. *Boosters were eager to pay the fine, as well as the expense for the replacement goalposts.* For each donation of $5 or more donors received a thank-you letter from the athletic director. Also, a 3-inch piece of the goalpost was available for $500, and a 6-inch piece was the reward for a contribution of $1,000. In 2016 when **Auburn's** basketball team upset **Kentucky**, students rushed-the-court for the first time in the arena's history (of six years). And **Auburn's** athletic director said that he would happily pay the $100,000 fine.

Final Four Floor

What does it take to make the courts used each year in the finals of the men's and women's *Final Four*? *One-hundred twenty five workers, 500 maple trees (from Michigan), and 122 days*. For the past eleven years one company has produced the floors, using NCAA customized designs. While the floor could be sanded-down and used approximately five times, *it is only used once*. That's because *the winning team gets to take it home*. **Florida** turned theirs into their home court, **Louisville** has the center logo hanging in the lobby of their arena, and at **Kentucky** they used it for the locker room floor. And many schools carve-up small portions to provide to fans, and large donors.

Fishing

I often like to learn more about club sports that are sponsored by various universities. Many athletes competing at the club-level are highly skilled, and rightly-proud of their accomplishments. Each year an estimated *610 college bass fishing teams* in the United States participate in competition. The major college bass fishing tournament series are the *FLW Outdoors College Series, Carhartt Bassmaster College Bass Fishing Series, Cabela's Collegiate Bass Fishing Series*, and *The Fishlife Collegiate Tour*. Since bass fishing is a club sport, the NCAA isn't involved. So college anglers can have individual sponsorships and win cash in non-collegiate events while concurrently representing their schools. Some of these athletes earn close to $50,000 during their college years. The first known college bass fishing tournament took place at Lake Monroe, Indiana on April 18, 1992 between **Purdue University** and **Indiana University**. **Purdue** won the tournament by three pounds. Some of the historically most successful college bass fishing teams are **Auburn University**, **Bethel University** (which provides scholarships), **University of Florida**, **Virginia Tech**, **University of Georgia**, **North Carolina State University**, and **Louisiana State University**. College bass fishing is a growing college sport and in recent years, some schools have even started varsity programs, such as **Adrian College** in Michigan and **Campbellsville University** in Kentucky. These schools are both the first varsity college bass fishing programs in their state.

Florida State University (Football): *Renegade Makes a Road Trip*

When *fans periodically vote for their favorite football tradition*, always among the winners is *Chief Osceola and his horse, Renegade*. I have witnessed the iconic flaming spear being thrown into the ground as *Renegade* rises on his hind-legs. It is quite a moment. But to witness this tradition in person, must you visit Tallahassee? In 2014 when **FSU** played in the *BCS National Championship* game at the *Rose Bowl*, *Renegade* made the 2,300 mile trip by van. But where would *Renegade* stay while in the metro Los Angeles area? Why not with the mounted-patrol horses owned by the LA Police Department? Los Angeles authorities are accustomed to visiting celebrities, so they were happy to accommodate *Renegade*. But my favorite part of this trip is that 10,000 alumni / fans paid $65.00 each to *tailgate with Renegade*. And I was also unaware that someone other than *Chief Osceola* has planted the flaming spear. *Bobby Bowden did it twice.*

Florida State University (Football): *The Garnet and Gold Guys*

2017 will mark the 20th year of this tradition. Two anonymous students are selected each year – one to be known as *"Gold" boy*, while the other is *"Garnet."* Paint and glitter are their friends, as well as the forty-five minute hose-down

(with dish soap) that happens after each home game.

Flyovers

I am often asked, *"What is your favorite tradition?"* And without hesitation, I always answer that it's *the flyover during the Army / Navy game.* No tradition compares to this one. But have you ever wondered about the coordination required to have supersonic jets (or attack helicopters) pass over a stadium at just the right moment of the *National Anthem*? The anthem is approximately 90 seconds when sung, and once the aircraft start towards the stadium there is no turning-back. Jets often peak at 450mph, and singers need to be prepared, and not surprised. Oftentimes there is an Air Force officer atop the stadium communicating with the pilots. I was particularly sad in 2013 when mandatory budget cuts, associated with the government's sequestration, temporarily grounded all planes. But common sense prevailed, and the events were soon resumed – acknowledging the recruiting benefits, as well as that the pilots' time counts as *"training hours."* At their peak, the Air Force performed more than 1,000 flyovers annually using multiple units, but the high-profile games are the ones to receive appearances from the *Thunderbirds*.

Franklin College *(Women's Basketball):* *Grizzly Grandparents*

As is the case with many traditions, I often wonder why more schools don't have a particular tradition. That's the case with a tradition at **Franklin College**. When the **Franklin College** women's team takes the court – for each home, and a few away games – the players look into the stands to find fifty super fans, each of whom *lives at a local assisted living facility*. These *Grizzly Grandparents* range in age from their late 50's to one special fan, whose age is 105. *They arrive with stuffed grizzlies (the team's mascot), identical T-shirts, personalized cheers, and unwavering support for their team.* The group started in 2007, and was the brain-child of an 87-year-old resident, who was the former Grizzlies' coach. Each *Grizzle Grandparent* "adopts" a player and commits to supporting her throughout the season. At the beginning there were barely enough grandparents to go around, but now the program contains more than fifty, allowing all coaches, and team managers to also be adopted. They are frequently viewed as another set of real grandparents, with birthday cards and home-cooked meals often the norm. The *Grizzly Grandparents* have organized Christmas parties for players and coaches, attended the team's awards banquet and even had a surprise baby shower for their coach. One player recently overheard during a game, "Hey ref! That's a foul! That's my granddaughter!!"

GA Southern: *Eagle Mascot Flies for Graduation*

Prior to home football games, a majestic American bald eagle named *Freedom* soars down from high atop the stadium, flying to meet its handler at midfield, much to the delight of fans in the stands. *Freedom* is so popular that in recent years, his dramatic presence concludes the university's spring commencement ceremony. I wonder if **Auburn** also does this?

GA Tech (Golf): *Earning Your Golf Bag*

Golfers at **GA Tech** must *earn their golf bag*. This can be done in one of several ways, but the most common way is qualifying for an event such as the *U.S. Amateur Championship.*

Georgetown (Basketball): *Kale given to Game Attendees*

In 2015, the **Georgetown** women's basketball team began a yearly tradition called, *"Hail to Kale."* The first 100 fans get free bowls of kale Caesar salad, and gift cards are given away to restaurants in the D.C. area that are known for their kale dishes. And fans at the game are able to *top their pizza with kale.* "We were looking to do something different and kale has been on my mind a lot," said Chris Grosse, the Hoyas' director of marketing. "It's polarizing. *People either love it or hate it.*" Events associated with the annual event are constantly being developed (e.g., *kale eating contests,* and anyone who has the letters K, A, L or E in their name is admitted to the game for free. The school also allows *people who hate kale to sit together* in an area of the arena. The university also hopes to have young fans face each other in a race in kale or lettuce costumes.

Georgia (Football): *Players off the High Dive Platform & Watermelon Party during Pre-Season Practices*

UGA, like many other schools, has tried many traditions to break the routine of pre-season football practices. Coach Mark Richt always surprised his players on some random practice day by taking them to the university's natatorium where peer pressure resulted in *each player jumping from the 10-meter platform*.  And some of the huge lineman could not even swim. Coach Richt always performed his legendry backward dive, and many others on the athletic staff also participated. The SID has been known to jump in wearing his clothes, and members of the media were often shamed into joining-in. **UGA** also has an annual *watermelon party* between the last two-a-day practices during the pre-season.

Georgia: *Uga the Mascot*

In the last 100 years of intercollegiate football, Georgia's Uga has established himself as *the nation's most well-known mascot*. The line of pure white English bulldogs, which epitomizes everything Georgia, has been owned by the Frank W. "Sonny" Seiler family of Savannah, Ga., since Uga I first graced the campus in 1956. Through the years, Uga has been defined by his spiked collar, a symbol of the position which he holds. He was given his name, an abbreviation for the university, by William Young of Columbus, a law school classmate of Seiler's. *Each of the Uga mascots is awarded a varsity letter* in the form of a plaque, identical to those presented to all Bulldog athletes who letter in their respective sports. As determined and published by the *Pittsburgh Press*, the **University of Georgia** is the only major

college that actually *buries its mascots within the confines of the stadium*. Uga's I, II, III, IV, V, VI, VII, VIII and IX *are buried in marble vaults* near the main gate in the embankment of the South stands. (**Texas A&M**, and other schools bury their mascots in close proximity to stadiums). Epitaphs to the dogs are inscribed in bronze, and before each home game, *flowers are placed on their graves*. The memorial plot attracts hundreds of fans and visitors each year. For the past 20 years, Uga's jerseys have been custom-made at the beginning of each season *from the same material used for the players' jerseys*. Old jerseys are destroyed. Uga's on-field home is a permanent air conditioned doghouse located next to the cheerleaders' platform, providing comfort in the heat of August and September. Under most circumstances, starting a new job is a pretty solitary activity. Under no circumstances are you celebrated by tens of thousands of cheering fans, unless you're being inaugurated as president. Or, unless you're *Que*. It's not clear whether *Que* understands his destiny as Uga X. He sits atop the University of Georgia's multimillion-dollar collegiate sports empire, and he was *collared* (the position's version of "coronated") in front of a crowd of nearly 93,000 screaming fans before a football game in the same stadium in which his nine deceased predecessors are interred in one of the end zones.

Georgia (Football): *Spike Squad*

In Section 109 of Sanford Stadium on fall Saturday afternoons, you will find 25 students *dressed in football shoulder pads, with protruding spikes*. Faces are painted, and fun is had by all. **UGA's** basketball coach has joined the *Spike Squad* on at least two occasions – for UGA's victory over **LSU** in 2013, and for the **Alabama** loss in 2015. The *Spike Squad* is joined in the student section by the *Swole Patrol*, a 10-person group that chooses to support the Bulldogs by

painting their bodies in red and black colors while *adorning the emblems and costumes of iconic superheroes*.

Georgia (Football): *Lone Trumpeter*

During the pregame excitement of a home game, the crowd suddenly goes silent, the PA announcer indicates a general direction to look-towards, and all fans begin looking and pointing. A *single trumpeter* from the **University of Georgia's** *Redcoat Marching Band* begins playing the *"Battle Hymn of the Republic"* – but only the first 14 notes. After the 14 notes a moving video montage, narrated by the legendary Larry Munson, gets the crowd pumped-up. The *solo trumpeter* is chosen from the entire complement of trumpeters, with generally only 3-4 chosen for the honor.

Goodyear Blimp

Who doesn't view the iconic symbol of a *Goodyear Blimp* floating over a sporting event as a validation of that event's importance? For sixty-two years the *Goodyear Blimp* has covered sporting events, with the first being the 1955 *Rose Bowl*. Each blimp is in service for about fifteen years, and is often donated upon retirement to a museum. Over the years the capacity has grown from six to twelve, the speeds have increased to about 75mph, and the newest blimps even have bathrooms.

Goodyear Blimpworthy Events

In 2016, Goodyear began a creative marketing campaign called *"Blimpworthy."* This concept personifies the iconic *Goodyear Blimp* and chronicles the hard work, determination and grit it has witnessed while covering defining moments in college football history. The *Goodyear Blimp* first provided stunning aerial views of the 1955  *Rose Bowl* revolutionizing the way fans experience sporting events. More than 60 years later, Goodyear's iconic airships have covered hundreds of the biggest matchups in college football history, offering their own unique perspective of the action on the ground. *Blimpworthy* is highlighted by an advertisement titled *"Witness,"* which gives an authoritative voice to one of the most iconic brand symbols in the world - the *Goodyear Blimp*. Filled with gritty clips from college football history, the ad provides a glimpse into some *Blimpworthy* moments — and the hardworking individuals behind them — that the celebrated airship has witnessed over its six decades covering college football.

Grand Valley State University (Soccer): *Linking Fingers*

Members of the women's soccer team *link fingers* in a pregame *tradition of solidarity* before each match. It must work, as they won the *DII Women's Soccer Championship* in 2014.

Grand Valley State University (Softball): *University President Throws-Out the First Pitch*

Grand Valley State's president *throws-out the first pitch* at each season's home opener. And that may not be unusual for him since he was an assistant basketball coach at the **Coast Guard Academy**, as well as started their softball program, finishing his career there with a 24-4 record. And as president of **Cobleskill State**, he spent some time volunteering with their softball team, and with **Grand Valley State** – on a team trip to Cuba – he found himself coaching first base.

Harding University (Basketball): *A Capella National Anthem*

Many fans, at many stadiums, join-in, as the *National Anthem* is performed by a band, or singers. But at **Harding University**, they have taken the crowd's singing to a whole new level. For basketball games the *crowd sings the National Anthem without benefit of music, or a leader*. While a pep bank is present, and Harding has many accomplished music students and professors, this tradition continues unaltered. It began several years ago when a shy music professor was scheduled to sing, and she asked the crowd to help her out. They did, and the athletic director, who was in attendance, said to the Sports Information Director, "We're doing that again!" Now the PA announcer begins the anthem, and then turns his microphone off while *the crowd movingly sings the song*.

Hartwick College / SUNY Oneonta (Soccer): *The Oneonta Mayor's Cup*

Hartwick College and **SUNY Oneonta** are separated by less than a ten-minute walk, and for over 40 years the city of Oneonta and the two colleges have *jointly held a soccer tournament*. The *Mayor's Cup* claims the title as being *the longest-running DI regular season soccer tournament*. The tournament is now a multi-division tournament covering three days and attracting national powerhouses from both DI and DIII men's and women's teams.

Harvard University (Women's Ice Hockey): *I Wanna Dance with Somebody*

In order to banish pregame jitters, and get their adrenaline going, before each game, players dance to the Whitney Houston tune, *"I Wanna Dance with Somebody."*

Harvard (Football): *Little Red Flag*

The *Little Red Flag* is a small silk flag attached to a walking stick which is *carried by the Harvard football team's most loyal supporter and passed on to each following generation*. The *Little Red Flag* was said to have been created by Frederick Plummer in 1888. He made it to 59 consecutive *Harvard vs. Yale games* and carried the banner with him to each one. The flag was then given to the **Harvard** man (or woman) in attendance at the game that had seen the most **Harvard** vs. **Yale** games in their lifetime.

Harvard (Swimming): *Iron Man Meet*

Many coaches like to use a swim-the-meet set the day after a big meet. In this workout, swimmers go through and swim the entire meet schedule as a way to stretch themselves out and focus on their swims from the day before. The **Harvard** men's swim team, however, takes this concept to a physical and mental extreme at their annual *Iron Man Meet*. Because, you see, every year, a freshman is voted by his teammates to *swim the entire meet schedule … in a meet*. Depending on the meet format that is used in any given year, that comes out to roughly 4200 yards of race-pace swimming in just under 2 hours. Think about that for a second, and try not to cringe. Most swimmers would see such a torturous schedule as a punishment. But to a special group of masochistic freshmen, *there is no bigger honor than to be elected as Harvard's Iron Man*. This is because it is a sign of respect and acceptance by the rest of the team, which is always a huge hurdle for any freshman to overcome. In the words of **Harvard** assistant coach Kevin Tyrrell, "the tradition means a great deal, as the freshman who is chosen has earned the respect of the upperclassmen." As a sign of this respect, after the meet the *Iron Man* is paraded around the pool-deck on a stretcher while *Black Sabbath's Iron Man* blasts from the natatorium's sound system. As far as anyone can specifically remember, the tradition dates back to at least 1996. The list of previous recipients of the honor includes the open water *World Champion* Alex Meyer, and several of the biggest names in the history of **Harvard** swimming. There is also a diver, Henry Winslow on the list, which means he must have made a serious impression on his teammates. Former **Harvard** swimmer Rassan Grant joked once that "there is even speculation that former President and Crimson swimmer John F. Kennedy was an *Iron Man* in the past," though there's no indication that he actually was.

Heisman Trophy

Most fans do not know that the *Heisman Trophy* was created by the *(New York) Downtown Athletic Club* in 1935 to recognize *"the most valuable college football player east of the Mississippi."* After the death in 1936 of the Club's athletic director, John Heisman, the award was named in his honor and broadened to include players *west of the Mississippi*. Heisman had been active in college athletics as a football player, a head football, basketball, and baseball coach, and an athletic director. It is *the oldest of several overall awards in college football*, but who knew there could be such nuance in naming an award winner? The *Heisman* and the *AP Player of the Year* honor the *most outstanding player*, while the *Maxwell* and the *Walter Camp award* recognizes *the best player*, and *the Archie Griffin Award* recognizes the *most valuable player*. Pretty confusing, but the *Heisman* is certainly the most well-known of these trophies. The original trophy is insured for $1 million, and *locked away in a secret location*. But never fear. Jostens – best known for manufacturing *Super Bowl, National Championship* rings, etc. – *makes two trophies each year. One goes to the winning player, while the second goes to his university.* And as you would expect, random versions have been created over the years for ESPN, Nissan, and other corporate sponsors. It takes six craftsmen more than a month to produce the bronze statue. It's actually cast in two pieces: the body and the extended arm. The famous extended arm is

actually welded to the trophy, since that is required to get the exact angle of the arm correct. It weighs around 70-75 pounds, and some winners actually struggle to lift it after it has been presented. Prior to 9/11, oil portraits of each winner were commissioned, but since the *Downtown Athletic Club* had to relocate after 9/11, subsequent winners' oil portraits are actually done with *Photoshop* to make them appear similar to the originals.

High-Five

The *high-five* is a hand gesture that occurs when two people simultaneously raise one hand each, about head-high, and push, slide, or slap the flat of their palm against the flat palm of the other person. The gesture is often preceded verbally by a phrase like "Give me five," "High- five," or "Up high." Its meaning varies with the context of use but it can be a greeting, congratulations, or a celebration. There are many origin stories of the *high-five*, but the two most documented candidates are Dusty Baker and Glenn Burke of the Los Angeles Dodgers professional baseball team on October 2, 1977, and Wiley Brown and Derek Smith of the **Louisville** Cardinals men's college basketball team during the 1978–1979 season. The **Louisville** credit begins at a Cardinals' basketball practice. Forward Wiley Brown went to give a plain old low five to his teammate Derek Smith, but suddenly Smith looked Brown in the eye and said, "No. Up high." Brown thought, "Yeah, why are we staying down low? We jump so high," raised his hand and the *high-five* was supposedly born. *High-fives* can be seen in highlight reels of the 1978–1979 **Louisville** team, and during a telecast of a 1980 game, announcer Al McGuire shouted: "Mr. Brown came to play! And they're giving him the *high-five* handshake. *High-five!*" But did you know that there is a *National High-Five Day*. It's a private initiative to give out *high-fives* and is typically held on the third Thursday in April. According to the *National High-Five Project*, the event began in 2002 at the **University of Virginia** after a group of students set up a booth and gave out *high-fives* and lemonade. In the last few years the *National High-Five Project* began holding events where participants take part in a *"high-five-a-thon"* to raise funds for charity. **Murray State** also has a claim to the origin of the *high-five*. Lamont Sleets, a player at **Murray State** in the late 1970's indicates that his father, Lamont Sleets Sr., served in

High Five Origins

Vietnam in the 1st Battalion, 5th Infantry – a unit nicknamed *The Five*. The men of *The Five* often gathered at the Sleets home when Lamont Jr. was a toddler. They'd blow through the front door doing their signature greeting: *arm straight up, five fingers spread,* grunting *"Five."* Lamont Jr. loved to jump up and slap his tiny palms against their larger ones. *"Hi, Five!"* he'd yell, unable to keep all their names straight. Years later, Sleets started *high-fiving* his **Murray State** teammates, and when the Racers played away games, other teams followed. But if you wonder why **Louisville** is credited more often than **Murray State**, here's why. One of the founders of *National High-Five Day* is a comedy writer, and *he made-up the entire **Murray State** story*. It was all a hoax, a publicity stunt. The comedy writers concocted the whole story, then scoured college basketball rosters to plug in a name. "We just found the guy and made up a story about his dad," one of the writers said.

Holiday Traditions

Fans that attend college basketball games as the Holiday season approaches may be familiar with some schools' effort to *add levity to a time-out, or the half-time*. A video is often shown of their team's basketball players, and coaches, making *a really bad attempt at singing a Christmas Carol*. If you haven't seen these, they are hilarious. Another *Holiday Tradition* appears to be that Bill Belichick sends *Christmas Cookies to college football coaches*. Not sure how he determines who makes the list, but **GA Tech's** Paul Johnson received the cookies a few years ago, and it appears to be a tradition of coach Belichick's. And when Mike Riley was at **Oregon State**, one of their team traditions was to *"crank like a chainsaw" between the third and fourth quarters of home games*. So coach Riley would often send out photos of *his Thanksgiving turkey having been carved with a chainsaw*.

Home Games Away From Home

Before the advent of ubiquitous broadcasting of every football game, every week, colleges chose to *play some of their home games at sites other than their main campus*. This was for more money (in some cases), more exposure, and was said to help recruiting. **Ole Miss**, **Mississippi State**, **Alabama**, **Auburn**, and **Virginia Tech** were among the programs that played in larger stadiums than their smaller on-campus stadiums. But with stadiums constantly being expanded, playing at a larger stadium seems now to be the exception. Except for 2016's *Battle at Bristol*, where **Virginia Tech** played **Tennessee** at a NASCAR track with *the largest crowd to ever see a college football game*. I imagine that event will be repeated at some time in the future. But the *college maybe most affected* by the home away from home tradition is **Arkansas**. For over eighty-five years they have played football games at both their Fayetteville campus, as well as in Little Rock, the State Capital. Reducing the number of games played in Little Rock started a statewide debate in 1999, when a two year construction project to expand the Fayetteville stadium was begun. So the prior view of increased revenue by playing in Little Rock no longer held-true. So for the past several years, **Arkansas** has only played one game in Little Rock. And some state legislators may have a view that playing in the state capital is still important, and tie their view to financial support. But my favorite home away from home memory is when I was about ten years old I attended a **UGA** versus **Auburn** game played in Columbus, GA. That game was actually played in Columbus for 38 years, but obviously outgrew the capacity of Columbus' *Memorial Stadium*.

Immaculata University (Baseball): *Stuffed Ape*

The baseball team isn't monkeying around by *keeping a stuffed ape at all practices and games*. The animal illustrates a key lesson: If athletes can control their *"ape" – attitude, perspective, and effort* – the rest will take care of itself.

Indiana (Football): *Slip-n-Slide*

An annual tradition – that began in 2014 – at the **University of Indiana** is for their football team to finish a random preseason practice with the players enjoying a slip-n-slide, while in full gear. It's a very nice way to cool-off.

Indiana (Basketball): *Martha, the Mop-Lady*

A commercial featuring a *beloved mop-lady cleaning Assembly Hall, while singing the* **Indiana** *fight song*? It's often been said that history repeats itself. For fans of Hoosiers' basketball and *Martha*, that is a very good thing as **Indiana** athletics announced in 2010, after a 20-plus year absence, the original commercial spot would make its return. The commercial (by one of **IU's** principal

basketball sponsors) is shown after the *National Anthem*, and right before tip-off – just as it did in the 1970's and 1980's to get fans into the spirit prior to the game. *Martha's* obvious passion for **IU** Basketball was (and is) infectious and led to her personal following that was like none other.

Indiana (Intramurals): *The Little 500*

"No million dollar, no-cut contracts. No agents, just athletes giving it all they have. The essence of sports." So said sportscaster Brent Musberger about *The Little 500*. The *largest collegiate bike race in the country* and the biggest intramural event on the **Indiana University** campus. Modeled after the *Indianapolis 500,* riders compete in four-person teams in separate races for men and women around a quarter-mile cinder track at *Bill Armstrong Stadium* in Bloomington. The men's race is 200 laps, 50 miles. The women's is 100 laps, 25 miles. Thirty-three teams qualify to compete – *just like the number of cars in the Indianapolis 500 at the Brickyard*. The *Little 500* began in 1951, established as a way to raise scholarship money for students working their way through college. Since then, the *IU Student Foundation* has awarded more than $1 million to deserving undergrads. More than 25,000 spectators attend the race every year. You, too, can go online to the **IUSF** store and buy a *Little 500* tumbler for only $20. The *Little 500* also inspired *Breaking Away*, the 1979 *Academy Award*-winning coming of age comedy-drama about four male teenagers who recently graduated from high school.

Iowa (Wrestling): *Outside Wresting at Kinnick Stadium*

Michigan and **Michigan State** started the tradition of *playing hockey in football stadiums* in 2001, and they have been followed by *over fifty other schools* with wonderful tradition. The most notable venue is *Fenway Park* with the multiple-school-event known as *"Frozen Fenway."* But would this same concept work for college wrestling? Yes. In 2015 the **Iowa** wrestling team defeated top-ranked **Oklahoma State** in the Hawkeye's football

stadium, and *shattered the previous NCAA attendance record for wrestling*. **Penn State's** previous record was surprised by a 3x factor, as 42,287 fans attended.

Iowa (Football): *The Swarm*

At the **University of Iowa**, the football team knows how to make an entrance. As players grasp one another's hands to symbolize strength, unity, and support, they *slowly march through the team tunnel* and run on to the field cheered by more than 70,000 fans, as well as *Herky the Hawk*. This entrance, known as *the Swarm*, was started decades ago by legendary coach Hayden Fry.

Iowa (Football): *In Heaven, There is No Beer / Hawkeye Victory Polka*

The *Hawkeye Victory Polka* is the **University of Iowa** *Hawkeye Marching Band's* adaptation of the *song In Heaven There Is No Beer*. First played in the 1960s, it was very popular among students and was played frequently as if it were another fight song. Controversy, however, surrounded the song, as some claimed it promoted the abuse of alcohol. This led to the banning of the song in 2001, although widespread fan pressure eventually forced **Iowa's** president to bring back the song only a month after it was banned. Sheet music for the song is no longer circulated, so band members must now learn the song by ear. Today, it is played after all **Iowa** Hawkeye victories when the band is present, either home or away.

Iowa State (Basketball): *Creative Distraction for Visiting Players*

Many students at a home basketball game pride themselves in distracting visiting players. Online articles are searched for any small item to be used creatively against a visiting player. In 2014, **Oklahoma State's** Marcus Smart had a reputation as *flopping to draw offensive fouls*. So the **Iowa State** students planned for Marcus' visit. The student section did a *"mass flop"* in the stands at *Hilton Coliseum* when the Cowboys star was introduced by the public address announcer before the game. Fliers with instructions were handed-out in the student section before the game, and *all the students participated*.

Iowa State / Missouri (Football): *Telephone Trophy*

This *series began in 1896*, with the trophy originating in 1959. Before the 1959 game, field testing showed that the telephones the two schools used to communicate with their coaches in the coaches box were wired so that *either school could hear what was going-on on the other sideline*. The problem was fixed before the game, but neither of the two coaches knew that. Northwestern Bell Telephone Company decided to have a trophy made (with ½ of each team's colors) to commemorate the incident. **Missouri's** departure for the SEC in 2012 brought this rivalry to its conclusion, with the Tigers in possession of a 61-34-9 lead in the overall series.

Johnson & Wales (Lacrosse): *Oversized Tricycle*

During a spring break, men's lacrosse players found themselves in a sporting goods store, and being competitive, debated the price of an adult tricycle. Their coach estimated the highest price, and he was so certain about his guess that he said, "I'll buy it, if I am wrong." That's how the team came to *own a shiny blue oversized tricycle with their school's **J&W** logo emblazoned* *on it.* It also has a caddy on the rear in order to carry lacrosse sticks. After each win, *the player of the game earns riding privileges* from the field to the locker room two blocks thru campus, while the balance of the team walks.

Ithaca College (Cross Country): *Tattoo inside Their Lip*

As a bonding rite, some runners tattoo *"ICXC"* (the initials of their school and sport) inside their lower lip. It wears off after several years, but the meaning lasts forever.

Kansas (Basketball): *Ugly Sweater Game*

Much has been said about the atmosphere at *Allen Fieldhouse* when the Jayhawks play, but "festive" isn't a descriptor that usually comes to mind. But in December 2015 thousands of *fans wore holiday sweaters* to the **Kansas University** men's basketball game against **Montana**. Snowmen,

Santa Claus and reindeer all made appearances in fans' stitched game apparel, tallying points for a contest of their own. Fans wore the sweaters as part of an effort led by **Kansas** Athletics to break the current *Guinness World Record* for *"largest gathering of people wearing holiday sweaters."* With 3,473 people participating, **KU** fans more than doubled the old record set at Loughborough University in

Loughborough, United Kingdom, where 1,175 people wore holiday sweaters in December 2014. Upon entering the fieldhouse, those wearing holiday sweaters to the game were given an *"official participation"* ticket, which were used to tabulate the total number of participants to submit to those at *Guinness*.

Kansas State: *Mascot*

Any college with a live mascot likely has volumes of entertaining history that could be written. In 1922, a **KSU** *Hall-of-Famer* asked alumni to consider donating an actual Wildcat to the school to serve as a mascot. So two alumni that were also veterinarians did just that. *"Touchdown I"* was donated to the school shortly after the animal was nursed back to health under their care. The bobcat had an encounter with a porcupine, and his face and throat were punctured by numerous quills. Unfortunately, *Touchdown I* never fully recovered from its fight, dying of pneumonia shortly after arriving in Manhattan. Although the bobcats have served as **K-State's** wildcat mascot since 1922, the animals no longer attend **K-State** games. *Touchdown XI*, the 11th in the line, was kept at Manhattan's *Sunset Zoo*. So the game day mascot is now *Willie the Wildcat*, who first appeared in 1947. In 1997, the current "21st Century" *Willie* was created – one that wears a **KSU** football uniform. This mascot has a *tradition of tackling a member of the KSU cheer squad* (dressed

like an opponent) before the real opponents enter the stadium. It gets the home crowd into the festivities, but in 2013 a tackled student was taken to a hospital for evaluation. I'm not sure if this pre-game tradition continues.

Kansas State: *Band Controversy*

In 2015, at the season opener for **Kansas State University's** Wildcats football team, a *Star Trek* and *Star Wars* themed halftime show went awry when the

K-State marching band attempted to form and animate the *Starship Enterprise* destroying a Jayhawk (the mascot of **K-State's** rivals, the **Kansas** Jayhawks). However, many viewed the misshapen *Enterprise* as more like a giant penis, so the resulting scene resembled one of giant-bird fellatio rather than anything to do with *Star Trek*. As a result, **K-State** paid a $5,000 fine, imposed by their conference and self-imposed a suspension of their band director. **K-State's** president *tweeted* an apology, and the school was required to gain approval for all of their planned halftime shows.

Kansas State (Football): *Bill Snyder's Windbreakers*

Coach Bill Snyder served as head football coach at **K-State** from 1989 to 2005, and then was rehired to the position on November 24, 2008, making him *one of the few college football head coaches to have non-consecutive tenure at the same school*. He has been the head coach at **Kansas State** for the program's 300th, 400th, and 500th all-time wins. In recognition of his contributions to the program, the football stadium at **Kansas State**, *Bill Snyder Family Football Stadium*, is named in honor of him and his family. At of the end of the 2016 season, Snyder's 202 wins were *the third-most of any active NCAA Division I head coach*. Coach Snyder has a personal tradition: *wearing purple windbreakers during games*. You don't view that as a tradition? What if the windbreakers were adorned with the logos of his past bowl games? That's very cool, and certainly a subliminal suggestion to recruits, and others. But in 2014 coach Snyder ran afoul of his conference, the Big 12. The reason? The Big 12 no longer has a contract with some of the bowls that have logos on Bill's jackets, and other bowls have changed their names. On an earlier Saturday, **K-State** played a nationally televised game, and coach Snyder's *Buffalo Wild Wings Bowl* was prominently displayed – although the bowl is now *the Buffalo Wild Wings Citrus Bowl*. And the *Citrus Bowl* phrase was not included on coach Snyder's logo. So coach Snyder being the good guy that he is, opted that year to subsequently wear a rare white windbreaker, without a bowl logo.

Kansas State (Football): *Three-Two-One*

Kansas State isn't known for a fast-paced offense, so they often find themselves having not snapped the ball, late in the time before a penalty is called for delaying the game. So the student section helps them by counting, *"three-two-one"* as the clock is expiring.

Kentucky (Football): *My Old Kentucky Home*

Kentucky's state song, Stephen Foster's *"My Old Kentucky Home"* is a favorite throughout the Bluegrass State, especially on game days at *Commonwealth Stadium*, when fans sing along while the **University of Kentucky** *Wildcat Marching Band* plays the state's most famous song.

Lakeland College (Women's Basketball): *Shake-n-Bake*

Their coach yells the phase – *Shake-n-Bake* – before every game, as a method to fire-up his team. But he added to the tradition by bringing a box of the *Shake-n-Bake* seasoned *breadcrumbs to his locker room*. Now their full court press is called the *Shake-n-Bake*, and as for *the box of the breadcrumbs? It accompanies them to every game.*

Lehigh / Lafayette (Football): *The Rivalry*

150th MEETING

THE RIVALRY

LAFAYETTE vs. LEHIGH

The game is simply known as *The Rivalry*, and it is *the most-played rivalry in the history of college football.* The two teams – with campuses about twenty minutes apart – *first met in 1884.* In the first 133 years the only time the teams did not play was in 1896, when **Lehigh** disputed the eligibility of a **Lafayette** player, and refused to play. In the history of this series, the two have only met on a neutral field twice: in 1891 they played in Wilkes-Barre, Pennsylvania and in 2014, for their 150th game, *they played to a sellout crowd in Yankee Stadium.* I was fortunate to see the game in 2012, when the Yankee Stadium venue was announced. The crowd went crazy!

Linfield College (Football): *End Zone Couches*

When the weather is warm and dry, perhaps the most comfortable seats at historic *Maxwell Field* can be found just outside of the south end zone. Students from nearby dormitories and fraternities

figure if they can't bring the **Linfield** game to their living rooms, *they'll simply bring their living rooms to the football field.* A tradition that began in the late 1960s, the practice of *bringing upholstered furniture to the football field*, is one that remains unique among Northwest small colleges.

Louisiana-Lafayette: *Statue of an Equipment Manager*

Louisiana-Lafayette *is the only school in the country whose lone statue of an athletics figure honors an equipment manager.* The 8' bronze statue is of *Blackjack Landry*, who died in 1998. Landry was a special-needs individual that worked as the university's equipment manager for thirty-six years. He is *the only non-athlete in the school's Hall of Fame*. Alumni not only raised the funds for the statue, but also garnered enough to permanently endow an annual scholarship in *Blackjack's* name.

Louisville (Volleyball): *Men's Swimming & Diving Teams' Support*

The **Louisville** women's volleyball team has a secret weapon – the 39 members of the men's swimming and diving teams. The goal:  distraction. The tactic: *each swimmer wears 26 pieces of clothing and sheds a single item for each Cardinals point.* When **Louisville** scores 25 points, enough to win the set, there's nothing left but the Speedos / boxers. The men have been supporting the women since 2009, and many attendees are certain the volleyball team hasn't lost a home game since this tradition began. *It has to be the Speedos.*

LSU (Football): *Mike the Tiger No Longer Attending Games*

Sometimes long-standing traditions are stopped. This happens for various reasons. An example is that **LSU** announced in early 2017 that *their mascot – a live Tiger – won't attend football games in the future*. **LSU's** *Mike VI*, died in the fall of 2016 after a cancer diagnosis. He, like *Mike V* and *Mike IV*, was donated to **LSU** from rescue facilities, which means the school had to undergo its first search for a tiger since 1956. A lot has changed regarding the treatment of exotic animals since 1956, and **LSU** has evolved its practices and renovated the tiger's habitat through the decades. The school announced in early 2017 that *Mike VII* will join the freshman class in August

2017 after his habitat's renovation was completed. Concurrent with the naming of *Mike VII*, **LSU** also decided to *stop the practice of bringing Mike to football games*. "**LSU** has decided that the tiger will not go into *Tiger Stadium* on home football game days. He will be out in his yard seven days a week," a statement released by the school read. "By having *Mike* in his yard on game days, it ensures that fans are able to see him throughout the day." Though the live tiger mascot has been a part of **LSU** football lore in *Tiger Stadium, Mike VI* made fewer appearances in recent years due to his health issues.

LSU (Football): *White Jerseys*

LSU is one of the few college football teams that *wear white jerseys for home games, a tradition that began when* **LSU** *won its first National Championship* under coach Paul Dietzel in 1958. Since **LSU** won the *national title* wearing white, the superstitious Dietzel didn't want to mess with success and neither did his successor, Charlie McClendon. The tradition was interrupted from 1983 to 1994, when the NCAA started requiring home teams to wear dark-

colored jerseys, but it was revived after coach Gerry DiNardo petitioned the NCAA to change the rule in 1995. *The white jerseys have been part of Tiger Stadium lore since.*

LSU (Football): *The Win Bar*

Most football teams enjoy touching something prior to a game – as they leave their locker room, or enter their field. At **LSU**

a section of goalpost is mounted above their tunnel exit into *Tiger Stadium* and painted with a simple message, *"commitment to whatever it takes for victory!"* This particular section of goalpost spent 30 years in the north end of *Tiger Stadium.*

MacArthur Bowl

In 1959 an anonymous donor funded an elaborate Tiffany & Co. *trophy to honor the college football champions for the next 100 years*. The *trophy* was donated in tribute to General Douglas MacArthur – who gave input to the design. You may have seen it? It's a miniature (highly detailed) replica of a huge stadium. Methods of naming *National Champions* have changed over

the years, and as a result, the *MacArthur Bowl* has adapted. In the *polls-era* prior to 1998, the *National Football Foundation* voted for the champion. Only twice did the committee allow co-champions. During the *BCS* era – from

1998 to 2013 – that champion's name was added, and with the *College Football Playoff*, that champion is also added. The trophy is now kept year-round at the *College Football Hall of Fame*.

Maine (Ice Hockey): *Naked-Five*

During the game, each time **Maine** scores a goal the *Naked Five* (members of a fraternity), *run around the rink carrying a cow bell*. They have *no shirts* and their *chests are painted*. One has *M, the next A, I, N, E.*

Manhattan College (Baseball): *7th Inning Stretch*

In the 1880's, Brother Jasper brought the then little known sport of baseball to **Manhattan College** and became the team's first coach. Since Brother Jasper was also the prefect of discipline, he supervised the student fans at **Manhattan College** baseball games while also directing the team itself. During one particularly warm and humid

day when **Manhattan** was playing against a semi-pro baseball team, Brother Jasper noticed students were becoming restless and edgy as the team came to bat in the seventh inning of a close game. To relieve the tension, Brother Jasper called time-out and told the students to *stand up and stretch* for a few minutes until the game resumed. Since the college annually played the New York Giants baseball team in the late 1880s and into the 1890s at the *Polo Grounds*, the **Manhattan College** practice of the *seventh inning stretch* spread into the major leagues, where it subsequently became the time-honored custom we all recognize today.

Mansfield College (Football): *Night Games*

In 1892 **Wyoming Seminary** played at **Mansfield State Normal** in the *first-ever American football game played at night*. In addition to this distinction,

one school was a college, while the other was a high school. The lighting system brought in (by a company later to be known as *General Electric*) turned out to be inadequate for gameplay. The game itself lasted only 20 minutes and there were only 10 plays. Both sides agreed to end at halftime with a 0-0 tie after several players had an unfortunate run-in with a light pole. Beginning in 1992 – *on the game's 100 anniversary* – a yearly reenactment of the original game is held (with temporary lights provided by *GE*) during an autumn festival known as the *"Fabulous 1890s Weekend."* The reenactment of the game is a *play-by-play version of the actual game* as recorded. Fans who watch the game are sometimes known to correct players when they deviate from the original recorded plays. But now, the temporary lights are no longer needed, as **Mansfield** has installed permanent lights.

Marshall University: *Fountain Ceremony*

In 1970 on a rainy hillside in Wayne County, West Virginia, the lives of 75 people were lost in *the worst single air tragedy in NCAA sports history*. Among the losses were nearly the entire **Marshall University** football team, coaches, flight crew, numerous fans, and supporters. The event marked a boundary by which an entire community would forever measure time ... before or after *"The Crash."* On **Marshall's**

campus the *Memorial Student Center Fountain* was dedicated to the memory of the plane crash victims on November 12, 1972, by President John G. Barker. *Each year on the anniversary of that fateful day – November 14 – a memorial service is held*, which includes the traditional laying of the wreath. Then the water is turned off until the following spring. A bronze plaque bears this simple, eloquent inscription: *"They shall live on in the hearts of their families and friends forever, and this memorial records their loss to the university and to the community."* Each year *the football team takes a trip to the cemetery*, and many athletes are known to visit often on their own.

McDaniel College: *Each Sport Has a Different Logo*

Each of the school's twenty-four sports *has their own specific variant of the school's logo*.

McDaniel College (Football): *Drive-in Tailgating*

For as long as there have been cars, there have been cars overlooking the gridiron at **McDaniel College**. It's just sort of how they do football at **McDaniel**. From Model T's to SUV's, **McDaniel College** has long provided *one of college football's most unique game-day venues*. It is not uncommon to see pickup trucks, beds down-to-the-wheels under the weight of grills, sofas and students, backed right up to the edge of the hill that encircles the field. In a 2011 special, *The Weather Channel* named **McDaniel** the *Number 6 Top Tailgating School in the Nation*.

Memorial Stadiums

Hundreds of years ago, the buildings that we fill to celebrate college football may have been dedicated to the ruler or deity of the land. The time, money and effort put into the construction and maintenance of college football stadiums usually pairs with a tribute to a certain person or group. Sometimes it is a family that has generously helped the school's athletic department grow and sometimes the *"Memorial"* in *Memorial Stadium* is in memory of many people worth honoring. *More than a dozen active college football stadiums have "Memorial" in the name*, with a few paying direct tribute to veterans of the armed forces. Among the most famous are: the *LA Memorial Coliseum* opened in 1923 and home to the **USC** Trojans, *Darrell K. Royal-Texas* Memorial Stadium opened in 1924 and the largest of the *Memorial Stadiums*, **Nebraska's** *Memorial Stadium*, **Clemson's** *Frank Howard Field at Memorial Stadium* – where touching *Howard's Rock* and running down the hill has become *one of the most nationally-recognized pre-game traditions*, **Navy**-*Marine Corps Memorial Stadium* in Annapolis, and *War Memorial Stadium* at **Arkansas**.

Merrimack College (Women's Cross Country): *Left Foot Forward*

When athletes make a very special play, they are often seen banging the location of their heart with their right hand ... since every medical student knows the heart lies to the left of the breastbone. So as homage to the heart's location on the left side of the body, the **Merrimack** cross country team forms a pregame circle with their left foot and left hand inside the circle for the coach's pep talk and prayer.

Michigan (Football): *Announcing the Score of all Slippery Rock Games*

At each **Michigan** home game, a crowd of 110,000 cheer raucously as the stadium announcer gives the latest score of a different game: the ***Slippery Rock*** game. **Michigan** fans have cheered for the ***Slippery Rock*** score for more than a half-century. This tradition began in 1959, and now fans at many large schools enjoy hearing the ***Slippery Rock*** scores. The tradition lapsed for a while when news wires ceased to exist, and the internet had not yet proven to have instant access to scores from every school. But **Michigan's** athletic director remembered the tradition from when he was a **Michigan** student, and re-started it. In 1979 **Michigan** arranged for **Slippery Rock** to play their rival, **Shippensburg** at *the Big House*, and over 61,000 fans attended. **Slippery**

Rock also hosted games at *the Big House* in 1981 and in 2014.

Michigan (Football): *Jim Harbaugh Smashes Buckeyes on Grave*

Since 1997, **Michigan** students have gone on a *"grave walk,"* visiting the tombstones of legendary figures from the Wolverines' past during the week of the school's showdown with the arch-rival **Ohio State** Buckeyes. But in

2015, the students were joined by a figure very much from **Michigan's** present – and what Jim Harbaugh did quickly became the stuff of legend in Ann Arbor. The Wolverines' coach, who played quarterback at **Michigan** from 1983 to 1986, not only spoke to the group about his experiences under then-coach Bo Schembechler, he participated in a ceremony that speaks volumes about his school's feelings toward **Ohio State.** *Harbaugh took a hammer and smashed a buckeye nut that he had placed on a small block – right on Schembechler's grave. The*

organizer of the annual *grave walks* said that he had no idea Harbaugh had joined the 2015 group. "It's **Michigan** magic and tradition all in one spot," he said. Harbaugh also brought along his father, Jack Harbaugh, who talked about having been a coach on Schembechler's staff. The current **Michigan** head coach reminisced about how he had met Schembechler as a child and then played under him. The group also visited the graves of Fielding Yost, another former **Michigan** coach, and Bob Ufer, a longtime radio broadcaster. At the conclusion of the tour, everyone, including Harbaugh, sang the school song, *"The Yellow and Blue,"* and then fight song, *"The Victors."*

Michigan: *The Victors*

The story of one of college football's greatest fight songs *began on Thanksgiving 1898*. That day, **Michigan** beat the **University of Chicago** 12-11 to cap an undefeated season and secure the school's first conference title. To celebrate the mammoth road victory, a music student wrote a fight song that has just about everything: tradition, grandeur and a chorus that you will repeat over and over and over – even if it annoys friends who are **Ohio State** fans:

Hail! to the victors valiant

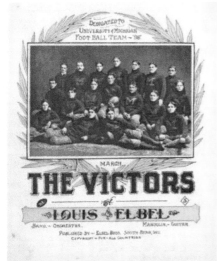

Hail! to the conqu'ring heroes
Hail! Hail! to Michigan,
the leaders and best
Hail! to the victors valiant
Hail! to the conqu'ring heroes
Hail! Hail! to Michigan
The champions of the West.

After having the piece arranged, the music student approached none other than John Philip Sousa with it. The composer, the man behind *"Stars and Stripes Forever"* and a host of other patriotic standards, liked the song so much that he and his band performed it during their stop in Ann Arbor on April 8, 1899. Sousa once said that he considered *"The Victors"* one of the nation's finest military marches and *the best original college song* he had ever heard. Over time, the song's legend has grown. President Gerald Ford, who played football at **Michigan**, preferred *"The Victors"* to *"Hail to the Chief."* In January 2007, the **Michigan** band *played the song during his funeral procession.* *"The Victors"* always seems to stir up emotions and not

always the pleasant kind. In 2012, the *Red Hot Chili Peppers* played a show in Columbus, Ohio, and drummer Chad Smith – who grew up in a suburb of Detroit – decided to have a little fun. After the band's encore, he grabbed the microphone and began singing *"The Victors."* The crowd promptly booed him, and he walked off the stage.

Michigan (Football): *Sportsmanship towards a Fan of Their Rival*

A twelve-year old **Ohio State** football fan was diagnosed with cancer, and viewed his cancer as something that must be beaten. So, *he named his cancer after his favorite team's rival – **Michigan***. When Brady Hoke, **Michigan's** coach at the time, heard about this, he invited the young fan and his parents to be his guest at the next rivalry game. The young fan finished his chemotherapy a few weeks before the game. In another example of these two school's famous rivalry, in 2012 Adidas manufactured a test football for **Michigan** with an "M" on it and embossed with the words: *"Made in the USA – not in Ohio."* A competitor of Adidas (Wilson) is the official NCAA football supplier, and their manufacturing facility is in Ada,

Ohio. And for a wonderful, related *Tweet*, from a few years ago comes this from a bank in Ann Arbor: "We will not be closed for *Columbus Day* tomorrow, because Columbus is in Ohio."

Michigan (Football): *Off-Season Team Trips*

Michigan coach, Jim Harbaugh, likes to shake things up. In 2016, he took his team to IMG Academy, in Florida, for a part of his spring practice. But it wasn't just a nice place for a spring-break-visit. IMG Academy is a premier prep school with tons of DI prospects that **Michigan** would like to recruit. And, as would be expected, since this was in the SEC's backyard, and they had not thought of this idea first, the SEC objected strongly to the NCAA, and the rules for these types of off-campus practices were changed in early 2017. So **Michigan** complied, but took a different approach. For part of his spring practice in 2017, Jim Harbaugh took his entire team, staff, and a few family members *to Rome Italy for eight days* – with the entire trip paid-for by an anonymous **Michigan** supporter. For this trip, coach Harbaugh challenged his players to write an essay about why they should be picked to represent the team and possibly meet Pope Francis at the Vatican. And when coach Harbaugh briefly met the Pope, he took that moment to give him a *personalized Michigan helmet* and ***Michigan*** *sneakers*. To continue the *tradition of these off-campus trips* by **Michigan**, coach Harbaugh has announced his view that *future trips would include South Africa next spring, Japan the following year and Israel after*

that. New Zealand and London may also be in the future travel plans. What a recruiting advantage for **Michigan**.

Michigan (Softball): *Players Simulate Making Pizza*

Whenever a player gets a hit, *she simulates making pizza*. If a single, it's spreading the sauce on the crust. If a double, cheese is sprinkled on top. Knock a triple and toss on pepperoni. Hit a homer and the entire team meets you at home plate while sprinkling imaginary cheese then *taking a bite from the imaginary pizza*.

Michigan / Notre Dame (Football): *Rivalry Breakup*

Michigan and **Notre Dame** claim twenty-two *National Championships* and ten *Heisman Trophy* winners between them, and their *yearly matchup was one of the most traditional of the college football season*. In 1887, **Notre Dame** hosted **Michigan** in what was **Notre Dame's** very first game, and in 1989 they played each other when **Notre Dame** was ranked number one, and **Michigan** was ranked number two. In 2007 the universities announced that they had extended their yearly series until 2031. But built into the contract extension was a clause indicating that either program could end the series with three games notice. But here is where the fun part begins. Both schools agree that in 2012 **Notre Dame** exercised the option to end to the series (due to commitments made to the ACC). **Michigan** viewed that the 3-year clause was *3-years*, while **Notre Dame** viewed it as *3-games*. So the **Notre Dame** athletic director handed the **Michigan** athletic director the written request ten minutes before kickoff of the 2012 game – effectively making the termination two years, and not three. The **Michigan** coach at the time famously indicated that **Notre Dame** was *"chickening-out"* of the series. The **Notre Dame** coach fired back that he did not consider **Michigan** one of

Notre Dame's traditional rivals. So it wasn't unusual that during **Notre Dame's** last visit to *the Big House* that the *"Chicken Dance"* was played frequently over the stadium's PA system.

Michigan State: *Dairy Flavors Reflect the Big 10*

For many years the on-campus dairy at **Michigan State** had the normal assortment of flavors. But a few years ago, as celebration of the campus' founding in 1855, the dairy changed a flavor to the *Sesquicentennial Swirl*. Since the flavor was such a hit, what would be the encore? Why *naming flavors for each of the Big 10 schools*, of course. The *Maize-N-Berry* (for **Michigan**) doesn't sell very well, but visiting fans often go for the *Nittany White Out, Terrapin Toffee Twirl, Huskers Sweet Corn, or Wildcat Crunch*. Most land-grant colleges have dairies and it is not uncommon for the dairies to name flavors with a local touch. As an example, **Wisconsin** has its *Chocolate Chryst* and *Berry Alvarez* flavors. And **Michigan State's** coach is likewise honored with *Dantonio's Double Fudge Fake*.

Michigan State (Football): *Zeke the Wonderdog*

Zeke the Wonderdog is the stage name of a series of *Frisbee-catching dogs* that have performed during halftime shows at **Michigan State University** Spartan football games since the late 1970s. The original *Zeke* was a yellow Labrador owned by a junior at **MSU** in the mid-1970s. **Zeke** competed in the *disc-catching national championships* held at

the *Rose Bowl*. Officials in the **MSU** athletic department noticed *Zeke's* success and in 1977 invited him to perform during a Spartan football game. And a new tradition was born. In 1978, then head coach Darryl Rogers was quoted as saying *Zeke was the best receiver in the Big Ten.* He awarded *Zeke* a football letter, and to this day *Zeke is the only non-human to letter at Michigan State*. The original *Zeke* retired in 1984. After an extended hiatus, in 2002 the **MSU** athletic department held open auditions and *revived the Frisbee-dog tradition*. **Michigan State** is now up to *Zeke IV*, who made his debut in December 2016 at a men's basketball game. However, that's nothing compared to the noise he will ultimately face when he performs in front of the fully-packed football stadium.

Mike Slive: *Personal Note to His Wife Each Morning*

Mike Slive, the former Southeastern Conference commissioner, for more than ten years, woke each day around 4:50am. And before leaving for work, he sat down and jotted a few lines on a yellow legal pad. His personal tradition was *to leave his wife a note each day* – on the kitchen counter, before he slipped off to work – about his work plans for that day (e.g., what excited him for that day, etc.). And he finished each day's note with *"I cherish you."*

Military Academy Nominations / Appointments

MILITARY ACADEMY NOMINATIONS

Almost 175 years ago our lawmakers began a formalized practice of *"patronage"* (i.e., pandering to political favorites). So how are enrollments at our military academies handled? Not very consistently. *There are no standards for nominations; there is just a requirement that each congressional district be represented.* The *Service Academies* refuse *Freedom of Information Act* inquiries, and fewer than one-half of congressional offices release their nomination lists. *Politicians nominate, while the academies appoint*, and nominations do not guarantee admission. Candidates must also meet rigorous academic standards and pass medical and physical fitness tests. *At any given time, each member of Congress, and the vice president can have up to five current enrollees for each of the academies.* For incoming students, members can nominate up to ten students per academy, and can designate a "principal" nomination, who must be admitted if they meet the academies' standards. About one-third of members of congress designate a principal-nomination. They can also rank their ten nominations, although few members of congress do this. Outside of the congressional process, the academies carve-out slots for other groups of applicants. These *include many athletes, the children of Medal of Honor winners, Presidential nominations and nominations from the secretaries of Army, Navy, and Air Force.* With the current value of this education around $500,000, you would expect that some misbehavior might take place. Interestingly, the *USA Today* recently compared nominations to campaign contributions, and found there to be no real correlation – although some parents clearly make contributions in hopes of helping their chances. But in 1934, a low-point may have been reached. A suburban Los Angeles congressman wanted to get his son into **West Point**, so he arranged a deal with another California congressman to nominate his son. In return, he would nominate anyone from that congressman's district. Both nominees flunked their entrance exams, so not wanting their nominations to go-to-waste, they decided to sell the nominations to students that could pass the entrance tests. The conspiracy unraveled and both congressmen went to jail.

Mississippi State (Baseball): *Left Field Lounge*

Fans sit in the back of their pickup trucks and eat Cajun food and students sometimes *give the left fielders hotdogs during the game*. It is rumored that this is one of author John Grisham's very favorite places to visit.

Missouri (Football): *Rock-M*

On the berm overlooking **Missouri's** *Faurot Field*, whitewashed rocks are piled together to form a 90-by-95-foot *block "M," a tradition that began in 1927*. Thirty years later, a group of pranksters changed the *"M"* to an *"N"* the night before the **Missouri / Nebraska** game, but the groundskeeper, with the help of some young boys who gained free admission to the game in exchange for their help, restored the *"M"* before kickoff.

Missouri: *Truman the Tiger*

The **Missouri** mascot since 1986, *Truman the Tiger* is named after former President Harry S. Truman, who was from Independence, Mo. *Truman* is often frequently present at the six columns that are the remains of *Academic Hall*, the first and main building on campus until it burned in 1892.

First-year **Missouri** students pass through the columns during the *Tiger Walk* as they enter college, and graduating seniors pass back through them during the *Tiger Prowl* to symbolize their lifelong connection to *Ol' Mizzou*.

Monmouth University (Basketball): *Bench Celebrations*

Monmouth's bench-players became internet sensations in 2015 when they began *celebrating big plays with rehearsed, choreographed antics*. In their reaction to a huge play on the court called *"the fish,"* one of the bench-players pretends he is a fish, and then dies. Two teammates pick him up, so he's parallel to the floor, and they pose for a fake photograph – just as any great fisherman who had landed a trophy fish would do. They also have *a fake heart attach* (and subsequent CPR effort), *re-enacting a dunk, a touchdown pass, the human scissors*, and many, many more. The thing that I like best about this tradition is that *Monmouth's* coach embraces it

indicating, "I truly think that 18 to 22 year old college athletes should be having fun. What they are doing is not against the other team. It celebrates how our players play." And, to make this tradition even more special, after each (serious) team meetings where strategy for the next game is discussed, *the bench-players have their own meeting to plan their performances*. This tradition has made the bench-players cult heroes on campus, and one of them was recently *asked to deliver the graduation speech for a local high school's graduation*.

Mount St. Joseph (Basketball): *Honoring Lauren Hill*

Many of you remember in 2014-2015 the wonderful story of Lauren Hill. Few will remember the final score of the basketball game between Division III **Mount St. Joseph University** and **Hiram College**, but everyone that heard about the game remembers it. Lauren was a high school senior diagnosed with inoperable cancer, and her greatest goal was to play in a college basketball game. So she enrolled at **Mount St. Joseph** with a specific objective. *But her life expectancy was only a few months*. So her college team chose to begin their practices earlier than normal, and the NCAA allowed an exception for a game with **Hiram** to be played two weeks earlier than the season was to begin. Lauren not only played in her first college game, but she also scored. Typically **Mount St. Joseph's** games may have maybe 100 fans in attendance. But for the game when Lauren would play, *a 10,000 seat arena sold out in less than an hour*. In the locker room before the game, Lauren's coaches and teammates surprised her with gray uniforms made especially for the game. Gray is the color of brain cancer awareness, a nod to the precious gray matter the disease destroys. **Hiram** players warmed up

in gray *Play for 22* (Lauren's number) T-shirts with **Mount St. Joseph** on the front, the same shirts Lauren's mother and father and younger brother and sister wore as they watched the game from behind the team bench.

We Love You buttons and *Never Give up* T-shirts and *No. 22* jerseys filled the arena. The *Cintas Center* was blanketed in an ocean of gray. On this afternoon, everyone was cheering for the same team. The day was not about basketball. It was not about a game. It was a celebration of life and a community coming together to support one girl and two teams as they banded together to beat up on cancer. Lauren raised more than $1.5 million for pediatric cancer research with a Cincinnati telethon for *The Cure Starts Now Foundation*. Lauren played in a total of four games and made five layups. After the fourth game the **Mount St. Joseph** basketball coach announced that she would not play in future games but would stay-on as an honorary coach. In February 2015, she was given an honorary Doctorate of Humane Letters degree by **Mount St. Joseph University**. In March *she was named to the all-conference first team of the Heartland Collegiate Athletic Conference*. "This award is being presented to Lauren in recognition of her courage and outstanding leadership," said conference commissioner Chris Ragsdale. In early April 2015, she was given the *Pat Summitt Courage Award*.

She died on April 10, 2015 at *Cincinnati Children's Hospital Medical Center*, but only after *Wheaties had produced a cereal box in her honor*. Way-to-go, Wheaties.

Mr. Irrelevant

What do **Colorado, Northwestern State, South Carolina,** and **Weber State** all have in common? They each have *two former players that were named "Mr. Irrelevant"*: the tongue-in-cheek name of the 253rd (and last) player selected each year in the *NFL draft*. Although the *NFL Draft* dates back to 1936, the first person to officially be given the *"Mr. Irrelevant"* title was

Kelvin Kirk, pick number 487 of the 1976 draft. Paul Salata, a former NFL player, had the initial brainstorm, and approached Pete Rozelle (who loved the idea). Salata, currently age 90, is still very involved, and personally foots-the-bill for the winner to visit Newport Beach, California for a celebration. When Kirk was selected as the first *Mr. Irrelevant*, he was unsure if he were being made fun-of. But he went along with Salata's plans for the publicity. Except Kirk's flight was delayed and there was a press conference and a parade that must go-on. So Salata recruited a butcher-friend of his that looked like a football player to pose as Kirk. As the fill-in was answering questions by reporters, the real Kirk appeared. Kirk took over and started answering questions and the reporters acted as if nothing unusual had happened. *And so it began*. There is now a *Mr. Irrelevant Week* of fun, with all proceeds going to charity. Due to the media bonus associated with the last pick (in 2017 it was Denver), teams have been known to trade-down to try and obtain the last pick. But as you would expect, the NFL created a rule to stop that. My favorite part of this tradition is that *as the last pick approaches*, and *ESPN*, and others have generally lost interest, *the few fans*

still in attendance often rush-the-stage in mock jubilation. And, of course, there is an immediate photo-op with *a jersey and the number 253 on the back.*

National Association of Basketball Coaches: *Suits and Sneakers Week*

Norm Stewart, former head coach of the **University of Missouri's** men's basketball program, cancer survivor, and member of the *National Association of Basketball Coaches*, provided the vision and inspiration for the *Coaches vs. Cancer* concept. He started the program by challenging fans to pledge a dollar amount for every three-point shot made by his team during the season. The concept evolved into a

nationwide tradition uniting coaches, fans, players, and communities across the country to fight cancer. Since 1993, coaches have raised over $100 million for the *American Cancer Society*. During *Suits and Sneakers Week,* coaches and their staff across the nation wear sneakers with their suits during games to raise awareness and help save lives from cancer by raising funds and encouraging people to educate themselves about cancer prevention, screening, and early detection.

National Champions Visiting the White House

It began in 1865 when Andrew Johnson invited the Brooklyn Atlantics and Washington Nationals, and was mostly an off-and-on tradition until

President Ronald Reagan began taking it seriously. Today many professional athletes choose to make a political statement by not attending, for various reasons. But college students generally don't have this issue. What they often do have is a scheduling reality-check. After **Florida State** won their most recent *National Championship*, the athletic department sent eleven possible dates, only to have each rejected by the White House scheduler. Most football champions visit in April following their championship, but in 1998, the **University of Tennessee** could not arrange a visit until late August. **Boston College** men's hockey coach Jerry York teased **Union College** coach Rick Bennett since **BC** won the 2012 *Frozen Four* championship. "Every time I see him, he asks if we 'had been to the White House' and I had to say 'not yet.' I thought that was going to change—I thought we were next in line," Bennett said with a laugh. When **Union College**, a school of 2,200 students in suburban Schenectady, N.Y., won the *Frozen Four* in April 2014, Bennett thought he had ended the taunt for good. The White House had different plans. Despite a yearlong campaign from the local Congressman to bring the **Union College** team to 1600 Pennsylvania Avenue, the administration refused to admit the team. The Congressman had been in touch with the White House about organizing a visit since Union's April 2014 victory. The final decision was passed along to him, though the administration failed to provide an explanation for the snub. This was a departure from prior years, and the White House refused to provide any reason for ending the tradition of including the *DI Men's Hockey champion* in these ceremonies. President Obama had previously hosted the 2013 **Yale** Men's team and the 2012 **Boston College** squad after their respective championships. President Obama also hosted multiple champions of the 2009-2010 seasons concurrently. **Texas A&M's** track team was one of the teams being honored, and was surprised when the live band played school songs during the reception. When the *Aggie War Hymn* was played, the 28 **Texas A&M** athletes gathered to *saw varsity horns off* on the South Lawn. And what about the run of **UConn's** women's basketball teams? Coach Auriemma and the Huskies visited the executive residence with such regularity that President Barack Obama apparently suggested making the *Hall of Fame* coach a tenant.

National Championship Rings

National Champions receive garnish rings to signify their accomplishment. And, of course, coaches have their rings on display for visiting recruits to see. While this

phenomena *has extended to conference championships, bowl victories, and even for victories over your state's three opponents* (**FSU** in 2016) etc., the gold standard is still the *National Championship* ring. NCAA rules limit the per-item spend to $550, so creativity is required to make the rings flashy enough while staying within the dollar limit. Jostens gets the honor and *often submits as many as 7-10 designs* for the winning university to consider. *Manufacturing is a thirteen step process*, and oftentimes as many as 102 (non-precious) jewels are used on each ring. So how many rings are given? More than you would probably expect. A typical university's order might be for 250 rings – to be given to players, coaches, and key administrators, and often takes three months after a championship before the rings can be distributed. But I wonder why more college *National Champions* don't take the lead from *Major League Baseball's* Chicago Cubs? When the Cubs won the 2016 *World Series* (after 108 long years), the team arranged for *20 ardent fans – ranging in age from thirteen to ninety to present rings to the players*. Videos were submitted, and an example of one winner is a fan that had named each of his children with a Cubs-themed name. This *memory of a lifetime* could so easily be extended to super fans of colleges whose teams have won a championship.

National Championships – Claiming Lost Titles

At **Auburn**, athletic director, Jay Jacobs, once advocated retroactively bumping up his football program's *National Championship* total. "It's right there, nothing but facts," Jacobs said. "It's awful hard to argue against facts."

He's not the only one. *Claiming lost titles* has become a laughable, outlaw cottage industry. For years, **Alabama** and **Notre Dame** have listed championships outside the accepted boundaries. Everybody just kind of winked because they were **Alabama** and **Notre Dame**. Then, suddenly, it seems to have gotten ridiculous. Recently **Texas A&M** – even **Minnesota** – gave themselves championship makeovers. Just don't mess with college football tradition. *Tradition dictates that the legit championship era didn't begin until the AP poll debuted in 1936*. Part of the **Auburn** frenzy is based on a book, *Auburn's Unclaimed National Championships*. Jacobs attempted to clarify himself, but the narrative remained. Someone, somewhere believes it's worth digging up **Auburn's** game film from 100 years ago. In the *wire-service era* (1936-1997) *National Championships* are mythical enough without cooking up more unicorns. Also, the NCAA has nothing to do with crowning major college football champions. *FCS has its own playoff* administered by the association. But since 1936, things have been largely subjective at the highest level. If you're confused, don't even look at 2004.

That year the NCAA website lists a title vacated by the *BCS* and ignored by the coaches' poll. **Auburn** was one of four *"Champions"* from 1993. That despite being ineligible for the *SEC Championship* and a bowl because of NCAA improprieties. *There are 39 polls / indexes on the NCAA website naming champions all the way back to 1869.* It's silly enough to believe that **Princeton** is recognized as a *"Champion"* for beating **Rutgers** in that first game almost 150 years ago (so says the *National Championship Foundation*). It's another to argue about it. Former **Lafayette** coach Parke H. Davis retroactively proclaimed (in 1933) that **Rutgers** and **Princeton** shared the title. And you thought split *National Champions* was a thing in 2003 (**LSU** and **Southern Cal**)? **Arkansas'** off-the-books 1964 claim has more legitimacy than most. That year **Alabama** was consensus *National Champion* only because, back then, the *Associated Press* and *United Press International* polls ended after the regular season. *They didn't take into account the bowls.* The Hogs ended up being the nation's only unbeaten team that year. Meanwhile, Bama got beat in the bowl game. Hopefully, the playoff era has put an end to the unclaimed titles era. Four teams, two semifinals, *one Champion*.

Naval Academy (Football): *March On*

We are familiar with the *March On* done by both **Army** and **Navy** before the **Army** / **Navy** game. This show of joint patriotism is wonderful to

experience, but the *March On* is *also done by each of the Service Academies prior to every home game.* As an example, the naval officers-in-training depart from the **Academy** about an hour before kickoff, marching down Annapolis' Taylor Avenue, then hang-a-right, and straight into the stadium. From there they take their seats. Really? I think they stand the entire game.

Naval Academy (Football): *When Navy Beats Army*

At the **Naval Academy**, wins over **Army** earn *"Carry-On"* for the remainder of the semester for first year students known as *plebes*. This means they no longer have to adhere to strict physical movements like squaring off corners while walking on the campus grounds, and are free from *"Come Arounds"* which is the slang term for the twice-daily, 30-minute indoctrination sessions consisting of interrogations by the upperclassmen on all aspects of required professional knowledge, and physical exercise as punishment for incorrect answers. After a **Navy** win, plebes also get to suspend *"Chow Calls"* which means standing in a pre-arranged spot in the company area and yelling at the top of their lungs the menu for the noon meal, the professional topic of the week, and major events on the yard, while their senior classmates watch and eagerly wait for a mistake. A **Navy** win also calls for *the ringing of two bells* on the steps of *Bancroft Hall*. One is the ship's bell from the aircraft carrier *USS Enterprise*, World War II's most decorated ship. *On game day it is rung continuously*, from the time the final score of the game is known until the team returns to Bancroft Hall. The other bell that is rung only if **Navy** defeats **Army** - is the *Japanese Bell*. *The tradition began in 1900*, after **Navy** had beaten **Army**, 11-7. The team's captain rung the bell to communicate the winning score.

Naval Academy (Football): *Tecumseh, the God of 2.0*

The *"Tecumseh"* statue on **Navy's** campus in known as the *"God of 2.0,"* which is *the grade needed to pass at the Academy*. Prior to the **Army / Navy** game, the students *paint the statue and render left handed salutes*. Normally, a salute is rendered with the right hand but in sports a win is recorded in the left hand column of a ledger, hence *the left handed salutes for good luck.*

Naval Academy (Football): *Lei worn by Coach during Army / Navy Game*

In 2008 **Navy's** coach, Ken Niumatalolo, received a gift from *Tutu Betty*, a lei-maker in Hawaii. The lei that she gave him represented his Hawaiian heritage, and *contained eleven strands of leaves – with eleven symbolic of the eleven players on the field at one time, and a knot – which symbolized the coach. Tutu Betty* had no idea that coach Niumatalolo would wear the lei, of all times, during that year's **Army / Navy** game. **Navy** won that game, and since the lei was perceived a good-luck charm, each successive year *Tutu Betty sends the coach a fresh lei* before the **Army /**

Navy game, and *he continues to wear them*. But with eight consecutive wins wearing the lei, **Army** upset **Navy** in 2016. Will coach Niumatalolo wear the lei for 2017's game? My bet is that he will.

Nazareth College (Women's Soccer): *Inspirational Quotes in Players' Socks*

The women's soccer team starts each game *with an inspirational quote*. Players take turns finding the material, and after it's shared in the pregame huddle, each player receives a slip of paper with the saying and puts it in her sock. *This tradition began 23 years ago.*

NCAA DII Sports Festivals

In 2004, the NCAA began experimenting with having multiple *Championship* events concurrently in one city. The first *Festival* was a huge success, and the

Festivals have continued since. *Festivals* are now held for the fall and winter sports and *in excess of 1,000 athletes often converge on one city.*

NCAA Organization

Traditions exist at each level of the NCAA, and the NCAA's current organization (of three divisions, and subdividing DI football into 2 more groups) encourages unique opportunities for traditions to exist. The NCAA was established in 1906 and for three decades there was no need to change anything. But in 1937 there were 193 institutions and the percentage of small schools dictating to the large schools just wasn't an effective model. But nothing of importance happened until *1973, when the NCAA established Divisions I, II, and III.* Prior to that, there were only 13 *National Championships* – all for men's sports. Now traditions abound at every level, and the *National Championships* are in the hundreds.

NCAA DII Championships Include Community Engagement Events

I can't imagine members of *Final Four* teams attending local community engagement events, as they are rightly focused on the games during their brief visit. But DII of the NCAA has a different focus. In most years, as many as 2,500 student athletes, participating in about 25 championships *participate in local community engagement events.* In 2014, almost 6,000 youth, veterans, and others were impacted by these athletes. *Team Impact* creates partnerships between universities and children that are sick. More than 250 NCAA schools, representing 35 states, participate. *Team Impact's* ultimate goal is to *match every kid facing a life-threatening or chronic illness, with a nearby university.*

NC State: (Running): *Krispy Kreme Challenge*

The *Krispy Kreme Challenge* is an annual charity event in which participants *run 2.5 miles, eat one dozen doughnuts* (totaling 2,400 calories and 144 grams of fat), *and run back to the finish line, all in under one hour. The Challenge* is held at a few different schools (e.g., **Kansas**, **Kentucky**, **and Florida State**) but is most notable at **North Carolina State University**.

Nebraska (Football): *Tom Osborne Leadership Award*

The *Tom Osborne Leadership Award* is presented annually to a top leader in **Nebraska** or a top national leader with ties to **Nebraska** who also has given back to the community. *Astronauts and former Olympic medal winners have received the award* in the past, but recently the recipient was Greg McGarity. Greg's contribution was in the area of sports nutrition. Since becoming athletic director at the **University of Georgia** in 2010, he has *hired three full-time nutritional experts*.

Nebraska (Football): *Big Red Express*

During the Bo Pelini years, **Nebraska** honored its fans throughout the state. The athletic director, coaches, and members of the athletic department rode the *"Big Red Express"* train across Nebraska, making stops in various towns to greet Husker faithful.

New Hampshire (Hockey): Fish Toss

For four decades and counting, the **New Hampshire** *Fish Toss* has driven Wildcat fans, well, wild. Following **New Hampshire's** first goal of the game, *a fish is thrown on the ice*. Should the Wildcats somehow go scoreless through three periods, *the fish is later thrown on the university president's front porch*. Not to worry. It's rare that **UNH** doesn't score and that the president's porch stinks. What invariably happens is this: after **New Hampshire** scores its first goal, heads turn and all eyes in the *Towse Rink at the Whittemore Center Arena* focus on the

opponent's goal. As if on cue, up and over the boards comes a flying fish, now gliding across the ice. The Wildcat crowd erupts. *The tradition took hold back in the early 1970s*. So says Bob Norton, a former **New Hampshire** assistant coach. "It goes back to when we were playing a Division II team, and our program had gone way past theirs. I remember they (Wildcat fans) threw out this dinky thing and they called it a *Division II fish*." "I guess," Norton said, "they were trying to tell them they weren't worthy of a first-rate fish." Nope. This was a guppy, or a minnow, not Moby Dick. But the fine art of fish-tossing became a big hit. A local fraternity, *Zeta Chi*, took it upon themselves to fling the fish after **New Hampshire's** first goal. It was a symbolic gesture, *the opposing goalie fishing the puck out of the net*. **UNH** fans ate it up, and still do. These days, Wildcat head coach Dick Umile likes to tell this fish story. In the early 1990s, the home team in college hockey received a penalty if fans flung objects on the ice. "At all these different rinks," Umile said, "people were throwing things – tennis balls, newspapers – and it was really holding up the game. It's the **Maine** weekend, and the cops won't let the kid in with the fish." "I'm in the office before the game, and the students come to get me," he continued. "So I go down there, get the fish from the cops, and as we're walking in with the fish in the bag, the kids say, 'But coach, we're going to get a penalty!' "I say, 'Don't worry about it. We'll kill the penalty. *Just throw the fish.'"*

North Carolina (Basketball): *Scheduling Games in Home Towns of Players*

Dean Smith began the tradition, and Roy Williams has continued it (at both **Kansas** and **UNC**). Early season games, or sometimes practices, are held in the home town of one of **UNC's** players. *Juniors, or seniors, are honored, and many times, very small towns are involved.*

North Dakota: *Selling Merchandise Associated with Team's Prior Mascot*

North Dakota was known as the *Fighting Sioux* from 1930 until the university retired the nickname in 2012, ending a seven year battle with the NCAA. **North Dakota** had been one of eighteen institutions the NCAA singled out in

2005 for American Indian mascots it deemed hostile or abusive. *All were prohibited from hosting NCAA postseason tournaments.* The university appealed, lost and chose to fight in court. The dispute dragged on, with the state *Board of Higher Education* and the *Legislature* weighing in. Ultimately, in June 2012, **North Dakota** voters overwhelmingly chose to phase out the nickname. Nearly four years after retiring the *Fighting Sioux* mascot due to criticism from Native Americans, **North Dakota** found itself back in the business of selling *Fighting Sioux merchandise*. The reason is that the settlement agreement

with the NCAA over the nickname *required the school to keep the Fighting Sioux trademark*, and the only way to do that is to continue to show the mascot's use (i.e., with sales of related items). So a limited series of items hit-the-shelves, and to no one's surprise, sold-out within hours. Even though

North Dakota scrubbed the *Fighting Sioux* name and Indian head logo from its uniforms, communications, website and booster club, *approximately 2,500 Sioux logos remain throughout their hockey arena*, since the arena's benefactor ordered that the old logos remain. And the NCAA's rule about prohibiting onsite championships really doesn't matter, since almost all tournaments are now held off-campus. But for the outside of the hockey arena, one concession was made: the name on the building now indicates, *"Home of **North Dakota** Hockey,"* instead of *"Home of the Fighting Sioux."* Outside the arena there remains a statue of *Sioux chief, Sitting Bull*, and in addition to the numerous NCAA championship banners hanging from the ceiling, there is also one indicating, *"You're in Sioux Country."*

Northeastern: *Jock-the-Vote*

In 2013, **Northeastern** started a *Jock-the-Vote* campaign, encouraging **Northeastern** students to register to vote. *Athletes spread the word about the importance of the youth vote*. They also

created a video promoting the campaign and explaining the benefits of casting a vote. The **Northeastern** ice hockey athlete that began the program hopes to expand the program nationwide. As part of this effort, she distributed tool kits to various universities' *Student-Athlete Advisory Committees*.

Norwich University (Men's Soccer): *Claw Machine*

The **Norwich University** men's soccer team has *one of the most unusual traditions* that I have come-across. Their coach came to Norwich in 2006, and at that time, the assistant that he hired had a three year old son. Before each bus trip for a road game the two coaches went to a local grocery store to pick-up some snacks for the ride. This machine had a *claw machine*, and each

time the coaches visited the grocery store to buy snacks, they played the *claw machine* – to win a prize for the three year old. But, as luck would have it, **Norwich** went 18-3-1 and 19-3-1 and won their *Conference Championship* for the first two years associated with the *claw machine* toys. They even won an NCAA first round game. Could their team's success be linked to the *claw machine* toys (which accompanied the team on the road trips, before being given to the three year old)? Of course it could. Successful clawing, of course, isn't always possible, so the two coaches had to hone their skills at various other machines in their area. Their basic rule was they could not stop until *at least one toy was won*. And sometimes what was spent far exceeded the value of the cheaply-made toys. *Team captains often were responsible for carrying the toys from the team bus to the games*. After the games – win, or lose – the toys went home to the three year old. Except once, when **Norwich** was upset in a *Conference Championship*, and as a result lost an NCAA bid. After that game the toy ended up in the trash next to the team's bench. Over the years the two coaches *have won over 200 toys*, and since the three year old grew older and is no longer interested, the toys are now donated. The tradition waned over the years, as did the team's record (*any correlation?*). So in 2011 when the team started their season at 1-5, the two coaches decided, *"We have to play the Claw."* They did, and acquired a rare *Green Lantern* stuffed toy. And the *Lantern* lit-the-way to a turnaround season. They clawed their way back to a 12-10 finish and advanced to their *Conference Championship* match.

Notre Dame (Football): *Trick-Shot Monday*

In 2011, **Notre Dame** footballers Mike Golic, Jr., Jake Golic, Kapron Lewis-Moore, and John "Johnny G" Goodman decided to *film themselves trying to bounce a ping pong ball off their general surroundings*

in the locker room into a cup of water after a Monday practice. The resulting made-shot, along with the spirited celebration immediately following it, were placed on *YouTube* by the **Notre Dame** football communications / marketing department, and the rest was history (if the history you're learning about includes popular **Notre Dame**-related *YouTube* videos). Now, fans love spending a couple minutes each Monday during football season – a day of the week typically spent tired and depressed because the weekend just ended – basking in the creativity and anticipation and goofiness of various members of the **Notre Dame** football team.

Notre Dame: *Local Hotel Duplicates Traditions*

In each hotel room in a *local South Bend hotel*, there is a large framed picture of *Touchdown Jesus*. And in the hotel's lobby is a sign that says *Play like a Champion Today*. Business people slap it on their way off to work.

Notre Dame: *Leprechaun*

The **Notre Dame** *Leprechaun* is *one of the few live mascots without a costumed-head*. And as such, certain challenges exist. *Leprechauns* are considered part of the cheerleading squad and must tryout each year. But their tryout is fairly unique. Since they are viewed as gregarious, those trying out are placed into difficult situations. As an example, they are asked to visit a local bar and pretend they are there to fire-up the crowd while watching a **Notre Dame** basketball game ... and all the bar's attendees are not fans of the local team. The *Leprechaun* became **Notre Dame's** official mascot in 1965 but in the past twenty-four years (the tenure of the current cheerleading coach) there have been only two women to audition, and neither was selected. The **Leprechaun's** suit is, of course, custom-made, but *the shoes are furnished by Under Armour*.

Notre Dame (Football): *Pot of Gold Recruiting*

In 2014, the *"Pot of Gold" Recruiting Campaign* returned to **Notre Dame**. The football program sent 477 different recruiting letters to their top prospects – *one for each former player who had been drafted to the NFL after having played for* **Notre Dame**. *Some of the letters were dipped in 24-carat gold powder*, which is the same gold the school uses on its helmets.

Notre Dame (Basketball): *Bookstore Basketball*

Officially, it's known as the *All-Campus Bookstore Basketball Tournament*. But it's better and more widely known as simply *Bookstore Basketball*. That's the annual outdoor basketball tournament held on the **Notre Dame** campus each spring semester. It's also *the largest 5-on-5 basketball tournament in the world*. A little history: In 1972, two **Notre Dame** guys decided the school needed a third sports season to follow football and basketball. And *Bookstore Basketball* – so named because the tournament finals were originally held on an asphalt court behind the **Notre Dame** bookstore – was born. Almost anyone was eligible to play: **Notre Dame** students, faculty, staff, employees, even priests. Especially Monk: Rev. Edward A. "Monk"

Malloy, a tall, lanky, ardent hoopster who later became **Notre Dame's** 16th university president from 1987-2005. Early on, the idea was to stack your team with athletes, since varsity athletes were eligible to play. *In the spring of 1978, 13 of the 14 players on Notre Dame's varsity basketball team that reached the 1978 Final Four entered Bookstore Basketball. So did 60 members of Notre Dame's 1977 National Championship football team*. Now, there's only one varsity basketball player allowed per team. Also, female students and staff from nearby **Saint Mary's College** and **Holy Cross College** are welcome as well. So are **Notre Dame** coeds, who play with gusto. Early *Bookstore Basketball* team names included *Dolly Parton & the Bosom*

Buddies. Twice Down the Court and I Wish I Could Breathe. Leon Spinks and the Tooth Fairies. Forfeit and Bye. And countless others that were rejected for being too obscene. In 2012, *Hoops We Did It Again*, one of nearly 700 teams participating, rallied to nip SWAG 22-20. The Championship game was played outdoors in pouring rain. No one minded. They couldn't wait for *Bookstore Basketball* 2013 to arrive.

Bookstore Basketball players who have been on the cover of *Sports Illustrated:*

> *1986 Mark Bavaro*
> *1990 Derek Brown*
> *1987 Tim Brown*
> *1977 Ross Browner*
> *1974 Tom Clements*
> *1978 Terry Eurick*
> *1984 Gerry Faust*
> *1979 Vagas Ferguson*

1989 Lou Holtz
1980 Rocket Ismail
1988, 1990 Bill Laimbeer
1990 Rick Mirer
1982 (2), 1985, 1989 (2), 1990 (2), 1992 Joe Montana
1988 (2), 1989 (2) Tony Rice
[Date unknown] Bobby Taylor

Bookstore Basketball players who have won the *Heisman Trophy*:

1987 Tim Brown

Notre Dame (Lacrosse): *Player-Bagpiper*

In 2015, **Notre Dame** junior Eddie Glazener's final warm-up before an NCAA Lacrosse *Semifinal Game* took  place in a tunnel at Philadelphia's *Lincoln Financial Field*. It was there that Glazener played a few bars of *"Amazing Grace"* to prepare for what he finds the most nerve-wracking part of his game day. His role as a starter in the Irish defense was of paramount importance, but it came after his performance as a bagpiper in a **Notre Dame** Lacrosse ritual that has taken place *for 20 seasons*. Glazener was the latest in a line of *uniformed Irish lacrosse players who have piped their teammates onto the field with the inspirational anthem, "Scotland the Brave,"* the best-known piece of music for the instrument. Like nearly all his athlete bagpiper predecessors, *he had never played the instrument before*. "After I play the bagpipes, sometimes I feel like I got the toughest part out of the way," Glazener said. Of the seven Irish lacrosse players who have been pre-game pipers over the 20 years, *only* *two*, including Glazener, *have done it as a full-time starter on the team*. That the musical commitment might be a distraction does not concern Kevin Corrigan, in his 29th year as Irish head coach. "They get themselves in the frame of mind they need to do both," Corrigan said. "I don't lose any sleep over it." After all, what better way to *wake up the echoes*, fire up your teammates and put fear in your opponents than the chilling chant and drone of an instrument that is part of both the Scots and Irish cultures?

NYC Colleges: *Home Games*

Manhattan has many challenges, not the least of which is space for athletic events. So, as a result, many of the local colleges have *unique traditions when it comes to where they play their games.* When the **City College of New York's** women's soccer team practices at 6:00am in the fall, their coach heads to a subway stop to pick-up the ladies and shuttle them off to *Randall's Island* in the middle of the East River, and then afterwards to class on the Lower Manhattan campus. When inclement weather forces **St. Johns** tennis team to reconsider where practice is held, they opt for the site of the *US Open* in Flushing Meadows. **Manhattan College's** Jaspers (first team to initiate the *7th Inning Stretch*) hold their baseball practices nearby their campus but *play their home games an hour north of the city.* **NYU's** men's volleyball team doesn't play on their Manhattan campus, but on their Brooklyn campus – a 20 minute subway ride away. But my favorite is **Hunter College** on Manhattan's Upper East Side. For their cross country team, they only have to walk two blocks west to practice on the scenic trails of Central Park.

Oberlin College (Men's Soccer): *The Hustle Suit*

If you are honored with being able to *wear a specific red polyester warmup suit* at **Oberlin**, it's a big deal. A key player is chosen by the previous winner for the honor. *It started in the 1980's* and has continued since. The award goes to the player whose effort galvanized the team by his play. The *Hustle Suit* is the embodiment of respect among teammates. But in a wonderful twist, the recipient of the warmup suit *must keep-it-own until the next morning*. I wonder how often it gets laundered.

Occidental College: *Latin Cheer*

Several yells have been used at athletic events in **Occidental's** history, but the most popular one to continue to the present is *Io Triumphe*, introduced to **Occidental** *in 1905* by Frank P. Beal, class of 1907, of Albion, Michigan, where the yell was used by **Albion College**. According to **Albion College** history, the words *Io Triumphe* were probably borrowed from the Latin poems of the Roman writer, Horace. Both Roman troops and citizens used the phrase to mean literally *"Hail, Triumphal Procession"* or less formally, *"Hurrah, O Triumph."* At **Albion College** it was believed that parts of the yell were inspired by Euripides' play, *Iphigenia in Tauris*. Through the years *Io Triumphe* has moved beyond being used solely at athletic events to formal occasions, particularly those initiated by the alumni. By itself, *Io Triumphe* is used as a salutation or cheer by alumni:

> *IO TRIUMPHE!*
> *Io Triumphe! Io Triumphe!*
> *Haben, swaben, Rebecca le animor,*
> *Whoop-te, whoop-te, sheller-de-vere-de,*
> *Boom-de, ral-de, I-de, pa*
> *Honeka, heneka, wack-a, wack-a*
> *Hob, dob, bolde, bara, bolde, bara*
> *Con, slomade, hob-dab-rahi.*
> *O! C! RAH*

Ohio State University (Marching Band): *Script Ohio*

Most everyone knows that the **Ohio State** marching band spells out "Ohio" in script before each game – both home and away. To *"Le Regiment de Sambre et Meuse,"* two-hundred twenty five band members and two drum majors perform as *the world's largest brass and*

percussion band. For the *Homecoming Game* each year, *former band members are invited to participate*, and there are often nine-hundred marching – from freshmen to those *in their late nineties*. Most people do not know that the **Michigan** band takes credit for first performing *Script Ohio*. When the Buckeyes hosted the Wolverines in 1932, the **Michigan** band spelled "Ohio" diagonally across the field. They didn't actually draw it out as script; they just ran to the formation. So, of course, **Ohio State** disagrees that this tradition was begun by their rival. The sousaphone member that gets the honor of *"dotting-the-I"* is *forbidden from practicing this maneuver until their fourth year begins*. In their fourth year, *they are guaranteed an I-dotting honor*. That is if they make the band's roster. The band requires that each of their two-hundred plus members try out each year, and practice for approximately thirty hours per week. When Urban Meyer was hired, his first official meeting was to meet the football team. His second was to meet the band's director, and begin a relationship. And *after each game, coach Meyer goes to the band, salutes them, and shakes the hand of their director*. The band is so famous that during games that approach Halloween each year, kids in the stands will dress like band members. Some members are known to have been cut two, three, or more times, with an estimated 50% of the band indicating that they did not make the unit at least one year they tried-out. And of the two-hundred twenty five members, *only one-hundred and ninety perform on any given Saturday*. The remaining thirty-five alternates can challenge any remaining band member in hopes of taking their spot. And

I thought scout teams for football were competitive. But with the band's notoriety comes the expected satire from other bands. In 2013, the **Michigan** band performed a *"Script Oh No."* In 2014, the band director was fired for a perceived sexualized culture existing within the band. One example at that time was a tradition known as *"Midnight Ramp,"* where students *marched in their underwear* under the supervision of the band directors and staff.

Ohio State University (Football): *Buck-I-Guy*

John Chubb, better known to fans as *"Buck-I-Guy"* wasn't born inside *the Horseshoe*, but he was born only two miles away. And it is fitting that he was born on a Saturday, since about every fall Saturday since then, he has spent at *the Shoe*. When inducted into *ESPN's Fan Hall of Fame* in 2015, he quoted Lady Gaga, indicating that he was *"born this way."*

Ohio State (Football): *Quick Cals*

When Urban Meyer came to **Ohio State** he began a tradition called *Quick Cals*. Twenty-three minutes before every home kickoff, in the south end zone, the Buckeye players do fast, upbeat pregame exercises while facing the students. *And the students participate by doing the identical drill.* "We started a new tradition, *to show the relationship between our student body*, the best student body in America, *and our football team*," Urban Meyer said.

Ohio State (Football): *Babies Get National Championship Blankets*

After **Ohio State** won the *National Championship* in 2015, **Ohio State's** *Wexler Medical Center* combined the celebration of a new life with that of a new *Championship.* Each baby born immediately after the Buckeye's *Championship* received a *National Championship* blanket.

Ohio State University (Football): *Mirror Lake Jump*

Ohio State's campus buzzes each November as the football team gets set to battle rival **Michigan** (or *The Team up North*, as **OSU** likes to call them). Off the field, there is one tradition that the students love to participate in every year: *the Mirror Lake Jump*. And yes, it is very cold in November in Columbus, Ohio. On an announced school night before the game, undergrads jump into the freezing cold lake in celebration while chanting inappropriate phrases about **Michigan**. In 2013, the school tried to regulate the event, and as you would

imagine, the student body mobilized to thwart **OSU's** efforts. Among the major changes, students are now required to show their student ID to get a wristband, which they must wear during the jump. The surrounding area is fenced off, resulting in only one entrance and five exits. The jump is not a university sanctioned event, but **OSU**, and Columbus authorities, are astute enough to add police and medical presence near the lake.

Ohio State University (Football): *No Blue Worn at the Athletic Center*

Coach Urban Meyer does not allow visitors to wear blue at the Woody Hayes Athletic Center because it is one of the colors worn by chief rival, **Michigan**. And NFL scouts are no exception to the rule. Recently at least two scouts visiting the Buckeyes practice were given **Ohio State** shirts to wear over their blue ones. Coach Meyer's message was even passed through players, some of whom yelled at the scouts *that blue was not a color welcomed on OSU's campus*. The NFL scouts were surprised and offered that, "if that blue shirt rule is going to be enforced, they should let us know." Coach Meyer obviously takes this rivalry very seriously, while Coach Harbaugh at **Michigan** might be taking a different approach. He discontinued the infamous *"Countdown Clock"* that showed the days, hours, and minutes remaining until the next **Ohio State** game (**Ohio State** still has their *Countdown Clock*).

Ohio State University (Football): *Tearing Down a Goal Post*

After **Ohio State's** victory over **Oregon** in the *College Football Playoff*, thousands of fans converged on *the Horseshoe* with the intent of tearing-down the goal posts. But local police using tear gas turned them

away. So the fans did what any self-respecting fan would do – they *went to a local high school and tore-down those goal posts, instead*.

Ohio State (Football): *Governor's Proclamation*

Before a recent **Ohio State** versus **Michigan** game, the governor of Ohio issued a proclamation aimed at **Michigan's** head coach. The proclamation banned pleated khakis, as *"a garment only appropriate for Jake from State Farm."*

Ohio State (Football): *Pants-Shaped Pin*

Many sports fans know that **Ohio State** players and coaches receive *a gold pin in the shape of football pants* following a victory over *That Team up North.* There is an interesting story behind this tradition. The **Ohio State University's** football program was founded in 1890, and the most important game of the regular season, obviously, is the annual matchup with **Michigan**. *The first game between the Buckeyes and the Wolverines was held on October 16, 1897*, with **Ohio State** losing. One of the traditions that has developed from this rivalry is the distribution of *pins in the shape of gold pants to the players after a win over the Wolverines*. The tradition developed in response to the dominance of **Michigan's** program in the early days of the rivalry, with just six wins for the Buckeyes, and two ties, in 30 games from 1897 until the end of the 1933 season. Francis Schmidt became the head coach of the Buckeyes prior to the 1934 season, following his very successful five-year tenure at **TCU**. When Schmidt accepted the head coaching position, the local media had many questions about how Schmidt expected the Buckeyes to fare against the rest of the Big Ten, and particularly their most bitter rival. Schmidt was never afraid of the Wolverines. He replied with a saying that was prevalent in Texas at the time, saying, *"They put their pants on one leg at a time, just like the rest of us."* Schmidt is generally credited with popularizing this now-common phrase outside of Texas. The statement, establishing Schmidt's belief that **Michigan** wasn't at all invincible, prompted two local businessmen to form what is still known as the *"Gold Pants Club,"* and to create a tangible expression of the sentiment expressed by Schmidt in the form of *gold lapel pins shaped like football pants. Each player and coach on an **Ohio State** team that beats **Michigan** receives the Gold Pants*, inscribed with the player or coach's initials, the date of the victory, and the score of the game. The largest margin of victory in the history of the rivalry came the first year after the commencement of the *Gold Pants* tradition, as

the Buckeyes won that year's matchup 38-0. Sadly, in 2011, coach Jim Tressel was forced to resign after several of his players were found to be in NCAA violation for selling memorabilia. Quarterback Terrelle Pryor sold his *Gold Pants Pin.*

Oklahoma (Football): *Mex, the Mascot*

Most sports fans know that *Boomer & Sooner* are the current **Oklahoma** mascots. But like many colleges, **Oklahoma** had a different mascot prior to the current one. In 1914, during the *Mexican Revolution*, Mott Keys, an army

 medic stationed along the border near Laredo, Texas, stumbled onto a litter of abandoned terrier puppies on the Mexican side. Keys adopted one of those pups and took him back home to Hollis,

Oklahoma, after completing his duty. Before long *"Mex,"* as Keys named him, would become *the most famous dog to Sooners fans everywhere.* Keys enrolled at the **Oklahoma**, and his experience as an army medic landed him a gig on the **OU** football training staff. *Mex* would go to the games, too, donning a red sweater with a big red letter *"O"* on the side and famously barking whenever the Sooners scored a touchdown. *Mex* also was charged with keeping stray dogs and cats from roaming onto *Boyd Field* in the middle of games. It wasn't until 1924, though, that *Mex* went down in Sooner lore. On a road trip to **Drake University**, *Mex* was accidentally left behind when the Sooners switched trains in Arkansas City, Kansas, to head to Iowa. Without their good-luck mascot, **OU** fell to **Drake** 28-0. The following day, a headline in the *Arkansas Daily Traveler* said: *"Crushing Defeat of (Sooners) is charged to Loss of Their Mascot Here."* The Sooners offered a 50 cent reward to anyone who could find the dog, and *Mex* was soon located pacing the train station platform in Arkansas City. *Mex* became so beloved that when he died

April 30, 1928, *classes at **OU** were canceled for three days in his honor*. He was buried in a small casket somewhere under *Owen Field*, where the Sooners still play today.

Ole Miss (Football): *Chucky Mullins Bust*

Before every home game, for luck, ***Ole Miss** players touch the bust commemorating the late Roy Lee "Chucky" Mullins*, a defensive back for the Rebels who sustained a paralyzing neck injury in 1989. But more interesting than the **Ole Miss** players touching the bust, is *a personal tradition of Brad*

Gaines. Brad was the **Vanderbilt** fullback that Chucky tackled that fateful day. *For more than 20 years, three times a year – on Christmas Day, the anniversary of the accident, and the anniversary of Chuckie's death – Brad makes a three-hour drive to visit Chucky's gravesite*. After the accident, buckets were passed at **Ole Miss** games to raise money and the school said that it collected more than $1 million for a trust fund for Chucky. *The bust of Chucky* also contains a plaque that says, *"Never Quit,"* and each year a *defensive player wins an award named for Chucky and wears his number 38*

throughout the season. Each year when the award is presented, *Brad Gaines attends*. Chucky died two years after the accident.

Ole Miss (Football): *Fins-Up*

The *"Fins Up"* gesture is a relatively new **Ole Miss** tradition that began in 2008, when the Rebel defense, led by senior linebacker Tony Fein, adopted the name *"Landshark"* and began *celebrating big plays by putting a hand to the forehead in the shape of a shark fin*. Fein, an Army veteran who served a one-year tour in Iraq before arriving in Oxford, died in 2009, but his legacy at **Ole Miss** continues.

Oregon (Football): *Untraditional Uniforms*

Oregon's athletic spokesperson often is quoted as saying, "It is **Oregon's** *tradition to be untraditional* when it comes to our athletic programs." Since beginning their well-known partnership with Nike, **Oregon** *never duplicates (in a given year) a prior game's exact look*. But how many schools – in a *National Championship* game – could wear uniforms that did not contain any reference to their school colors? It was roughly two decades ago that Nike co-founder and chairman Phil Knight and his top design lieutenant both former **Oregon** track and field members, *set out to make* **Oregon** *the coolest team in college sports*. The plan worked, thanks to the devotion of  the company – which designed **Oregon's** new "O" and gave it cutting-edge technology and looks – and the team itself, whose style of play revolutionized the game. For the *National Championship* game in 2015, the equipment team's first task upon arriving in Dallas for the game was putting the players' nameplates on the lockers. They go through locker nameplates and organize them by position groups. Quarterback Marcus Mariota's *name went on the first locker closest to the door, as is* **Oregon's** *tradition*. After the names go up, the jerseys come out of the bin. They *do not, as is mentioned above, feature the school colors of green and yellow*. It's a rarity, but it's not a first for **Oregon**. The year before against **Arizona**, the Ducks wore a similar white, silver and gray combination and wore all white and silver against **USC** in 2010. *The two looks for the college playoffs were actually determined the previous spring in a meeting attended by Nike officials, the equipment manager, and **Oregon's** head coach. **Oregon's** tradition is to not be traditional, and their uniforms follow that direction.* But sometimes there are disagreements. Chip Kelly was against doing a pink jersey for breast cancer awareness because he felt it was unfair to single-out just one cancer cause. After talking about ideas with players and Nike, **Oregon's** equipment manager orders blank uniforms for the following season each October. *He sits down with Nike again in February to mix and match the combinations, which are completely schemed out by the time the spring game rolls around.* When the season begins, **Oregon** doesn't receive all the equipment at the same time. In a typical season, each **Oregon** player *will receive seven different helmets, seven different jerseys, six different pairs of cleats and five different pairs of sneakers. Count the pants, the warm-ups, the chinstraps and the 50 different styles of facemasks and there's nearly 20,000 pieces of gear that the team barcodes and scans into a system.* What also must be done is to calculate how much each look is going to cost the school. *Nike gives **Oregon** $600,000 in cash in a typical year, $2.2 million in equipment and another $185,000 to spend as the equipment manager wishes, but even that isn't enough.* That's why Knight himself writes checks one or two times a year for special uniforms, like when the team wore a retro uniform to celebrate the 20th anniversary of the 1994 **Rose Bowl** team. Helmets have a different designer, and are dipped in chrome paint and painted white, green, or yellow to create the wings look. They cost about $650 each. Equipment managers place the *"O"* in the middle on the back of the helmet. Being *part of Nike's research and development team* is just as valuable to **Oregon** as the cost of these items. Nike designers frequently come to practice to test out cleats. One version might be the 30th iteration of a particular shoe. Another might be the 90th. Little tweaks are made with player feedback before the shoe can hit the market. When a shoe is ready, **Oregon** players might get it first, which sometimes causes a problem. Players immediately want to wear it because it's cool, but they may have an ankle issue or it's not the proper shoe for them. There are truly custom items, too. Riddell also did something special: *Mariota's facemask spells out "8-0-8," which is the area code for Honolulu, where he grew up*. The equipment team also has to remember player preferences. Some wide receivers like to get new gloves days in advance so that they can be broken-in. The cool factor associated with all of **Oregon's** gear isn't lost on its potential future. Almost all *recruits get an equipment room tour, even though making custom jerseys or giving them anything has long been off the table*. When a student position on the equipment staff comes open, there will be at least 40 applications, and after interviews, the equipment manager will narrow it down to 10 and the finalists will get a look during spring ball. Those who get the spot get a scholarship: in-state tuition and books, worth about $10,000 a year. With Nike's help, **Oregon** has not only revolutionized the college football uniform game, but also changed the scope of the job done by the people behind the scenes that continue to bring it all together.

Oregon (Basketball): *Pit Crew*

Each year, **Oregon** basketball and their student section, the *Pit Crew*, gain national recognition. And when *March Madness* concludes the college basketball season that doesn't stop the *Pit Crew*. Every year in the spring the

Pit Crew hosts a *3-on-3 basketball tournament* for students. Nike recently took the *Pit Crew* under its wing, *issuing a specially-designed shoe for the Pit Crew*. I'm just guessing here, but I bet the *Pit Crew* may be the *only student-fan-group with their own line of shoes*. "We're treating them like another team down there," said Tinker Hatfield, Nike vice president of innovation design and special projects. But not every *Pit Crew* member received a pair of the shoes, in part because the initial run for the 2011-12 academic year totaled 500, and there were approximately 1,000 *Pit Crew* members. As a result, *Pit Crew* members *had to earn them*, by adhering to standards, attending a certain number of games and agreeing to a code of conduct. But in a very cool-move, 10 pairs of the shoes were up for grabs in a raffle during **Oregon's** version of *Midnight Madness*.

Oregon: (Football): *Phil Knight's Locker*

Some donors get free game tickets, others might get a building or hall named after them. Some might get a chance to sit in on meetings or news conferences. *Phil Knight gets a locker in the Ducks' locker room* ... as well as everything just mentioned. Knight, who has donated more than $150 million to the **Oregon** athletic department and endows 27 professorships, was a runner at the school before co-founding Nike. "It is symbolic as much as anything," a university spokesman said. "I've never known him to use it." But an even greater perk in my mind went to Phil when **Oregon** won their *March Madness Regional* in March 2017, and qualified for the *Final Four*. During the traditional ceremony to *cut-down-the-nets*, the players insisted that Phil be given the scissors and join-in. And good for him, *he didn't hesitate*.

Oregon (Football): *Speed School*

I'm not sure if they still have this tradition, but for years **Oregon** had a *Speed School* for their football players. You think that athletes are gifted with speed, or not. But **Oregon** feels differently. No matter the speed of the players, many participate in the *Speed School*. There they learn the biomechanical techniques that allow them to adjust to the warp speed of **Oregon's** offense. The sessions are weekly and are recommended for all new players, regardless of their position. The *school* is all about technique, not fitness. And just how far has **Oregon** come since the early 1980's? During that period, the **Oregon** athletic director had to stage a bingo game at halftime of basketball games to raise funds to paint the inside of the basketball arena. That must have been before Nike & Phil Knight got involved.

Oregon: *Four-Sport Athlete*

I am certain that many college athletes play more than one sport, and often excel at each. But in 2013, I heard about what I believe to be a *unique athlete*. Liz Brenner was a student at **Oregon** (a major DI school, and competitive in every major sport), but not quite like most students. She was *the lone collegian among three finalists for the 2013 Sullivan Award, which honors the nation's top amateur athlete*. And, she was *a finalist for Sports Illustrated's female college athlete of the year*. But what makes Liz special? *She is a four-sport athlete*: an All-American volleyball player, in track & field she

Congratulations Marcus

throws the shot put and javelin, and qualified for the NCAA Championships, in basketball she played in 20 games and averaged almost ten points a game, and in softball she played for the Ducks when they advanced to the *College World Series*. I find her schedule and her well-rounded abilities quite amazing.

Oregon State (Football): *Congratulating Team's Rival*

The game between **Oregon** and **Oregon State** is called *the Civil War*, but **Oregon State** put aside its dislike of its in-state rivals to congratulate **Oregon** quarterback Marcus Mariota who won the *Heisman Trophy* in 2014 The Beavers placed an ad in the next day's *The Oregonian* – as well as published a digital ad – to congratulate Mariota.

Palestra

In 2017 I made my first trip to *the Palestra* in Philadelphia. This "gym" made its *debut 90 years ago*, and to its credit *hasn't changed much* in the interim. It is truly one of the meccas of college athletics, having *hosted more college hoops games than any other venue in the country* – and every college fan should try to see a game there one day. In its prime, *the Palestra* held intercity games with the *Big-5 universities* in town: **Penn** (on whose campus the building resides), **St. Josephs**, **Temple**,

Villanova, and **La Salle.** But with seating only about 8,500, many of the games are now played elsewhere. In the summer of 2007, *ESPN Classic* broadcast a one-hour documentary on the historic arena, entitled *"The Palestra: Cathedral of Basketball."* This feature-length documentary traced the evolution of college basketball through the rise of the arena. NBA great Bill Bradley, *Naismith Hall of Fame* coaches Chuck Daly, Jack Ramsay and John Chaney, John Feinstein, and many others were interviewed. The arena draws coaches and competitors it normally would not. In order to experience the building, and its history, *at least seven NBA teams practice there on a*

yearly basis. **UNC** coach, Roy Williams, once scheduled **Penn** so that he could coach there and in 2017 Tom Izzo worked with **Penn State** to have a **Penn State** home at *the Palestra* so that he could coach there. It's maybe *the only venue to have a mascot:* his name is *Yo-Yo*, he's homeless, and he somehow showed-up at every game for years. And another tradition at *the Palestra* is that the public address announcer credits both the scorer, as well as the player making an assist.

Penn State (Football): *Football Eve*

Football Eve is a giant pep rally held every year, in Beaver Stadium, before the first home game (unless it is a neutral site game). The event often debuts the annual pre-game video that will be used to excite the crowd throughout the year. For a recent *Football Eve*, participation was expanded to include representatives from every **Penn State** sports team. The *"One Team"* approach has become much more than a motto for their coaches and teams.

Piedmont College (Women's Basketball): *Routines during Pregame Free Throws*

Many teams rotate shooters, for practicing free throws, as part of their pregame drills. At **Piedmont College** the women's basketball team *has a different routine for each shooter*. There could be arms waving like a bird flying, palms slapping the floor, a series of claps, or various dance moves.

Pittsburgh: (Football): *The Pitt Script*

When Johnny Majors became **Pitt's** coach in 1973 he redesigned **Pitt's**

uniforms, including their helmets. He liked **UCLA's** script on their helmets, so asked a designer to do something similar. The result was *the iconic script lettering for "Pitt" on the helmets*. The helmet logos lasted 24 seasons, only to be replaced by an insignia known as *"Dino Cat,"* then a block-letter logo. But congratulations to

Pitt, for in 2015, they *recognized the importance of this tradition, and brought the script back to the helmets*. And it certainly doesn't hurt that sales of related items at the university bookstore, and online, are up significantly, and that a further incorporation of the logo is happening with all other university teams.

Pittsburgh (Football): *Heinz Red-Zone Pouring of Ketchup*

In 2001 two large electric signs – in the *shape of Heinz ketchup bottles* – arrived at **Pitt's** new football stadium after a four-day cross-country journey from Nevada. The devices, 35 feet long, 9 feet high and 6 feet deep and weighing several tons each, were hoisted into place atop the *Sony Jumbotron* scoreboard. The bottles are horizontal at the top of the scoreboard, with their caps

facing inward. When the Panthers are driving for a touchdown and get within the *"Heinz red zone"* – the area between the 20-yard line and the goal line – *the two bottles tilt downward, the caps flip up and red LEDs (simulating ketchup) flow downward*. This simulation flows into the *Jumbotron*, and sparks further animation. The truckers transporting the bottles across America also had some fun. Truckers were saying on their CBs, "Now that's a big-ass bottle of ketchup – where are the fries and the hamburger to go with that ketchup – how do you keep that thing refrigerated?"

Pittsburgh / Penn State (Football): *Rivalry Game*

Most every school has at least one main rival, and they look forward to that rivalry game each year. Some schools have several legitimate rivals and, as a result, play numerous rivalry games each year. So I found it extremely strange that during the 2016 football season, there were **Pittsburgh** players that were playing in his fourth year, but *had yet to play in any rivalry game*.

Pittsburgh's main rivals were **West Virginia** (the *Backyard Brawl*) and **Penn State**. **West Virginia** stopped playing **Pittsburgh** when they joined the Big 12 in 2012. And **Penn State** had also not played **Pittsburgh** in the past sixteen years, probably as a result of Big 10 scheduling restrictions. So when **Pitt** did recently play **Penn State** they made the most of it, winning 42-39.

Playing Games outside the USA

The NCAA *sanctions many games outside of the USA*. Games have been played in Ireland, Germany, the Bahamas, Austria, France, Australia, Italy, Tanzania, and even on Aircraft carriers. Many basketball teams take foreign trips. It's a cultural experience, and most of the participating athletes have never been outside of the USA. **Michigan's** *Fab Five* wasn't excited about traveling outside the US, but coach Fisher dragged them off to Italy anyway. Now, playing outside the US is a rite of passage, and even a recruiting tool, for college basketball teams. Basketball teams are *allowed one trip every four years*, and *about 60 programs head out of the country each year*. But what other perks are involved? Why 10 extra practice days, of course. Coaches choose to take their teams all over the place. Europe seems to be the bread-and-butter location, with good touring opportunities and ample competition. In 2016, coach Pitino of **Louisville** scheduled coach Pitino of **Minnesota** (his son) for a game in Puerto Rico. *The two teams traveled together and a new tradition for each school was established*. The first game played outside the United States occurred on October 23, 1874, when **Harvard** defeated **McGill** (of Montreal). In addition to the early Canadian games, several teams competed in the *Bacardi Bowl* in Havana, Cuba until it was discontinued after the 1946 game. The first game played after the NCAA created the rule regarding schools playing outside the US only once every four years was in 1976 when **Grambling State** defeated **Morgan State** in the *Pioneer Bowl in Tokyo*. Subsequent games were played in Tokyo until 1993. Since 1977, regular season games have also been played in Australia,

Bermuda, Germany, Ireland, Italy and the United Kingdom. Several international games have been proposed from time-to-time that were never actually played. In 1989, **USC** and **Illinois** were scheduled to open their season in the *Glasnost Bowl* at Dynamo Stadium in Moscow. However, the game was canceled and moved to the *Los Angeles Memorial Coliseum* due to the logistics of undertaking a college football game in the Soviet Union. In 1996, the *Haka Bowl* was scheduled for play in Auckland, New Zealand, but its certification was subsequently revoked by the NCAA due to financing concerns. In 2013, bowl games were proposed for both Dublin, Ireland and Dubai, United Arab Emirates, but neither has yet been certified.

Pranks:

Pranks have their own special place among college sport traditions. The more clever and creative they are the better. Throughout history, California schools have led the way, with many of the great pranks chronicled in the book about campus practical jokes, by Neil Steinberg, titled *"If at All Possible, Involve a Cow: The Book of College Pranks."* Among the  first pranks dates to 1899, when **UC Berkeley** students stole **Stanford's** ceremonial ax after a baseball game, touching off over a century of dueling shenanigans between these two schools. In addition to back-and-forth ax-napping's, the capers include *tweaking Palo Alto freeway signs to say "Stanfurd,"* disrupting **Cal's** halftime marching band with *tiny motorized cars* and *unleashing mice in each other's campus libraries*. In 1982, after **Berkeley's** football team beat **Stanford** with a wild last-second kickoff return that involved five laterals, **Stanford** retaliated by replacing **Cal's** student newspaper with an impostor edition that *claimed NCAA officials had overturned the touchdown and made **Stanford** the winner*. At another game, **Cal** fans hacked into the stadium sound system and announced: *"Penalty, excessive arrogance; Stanford sucks!"* Southern California has a similar prank rivalry. It began in 1941 with **USC's** *theft of a 295-pound victory bell* from cross-town rival **UCLA**. The subsequent battle of stunts includes planting *20,000 gold-and-cardinal-painted crickets in **UCLA's** library, kidnapping **USC** fans and chaining them to fire hydrants – and numerous sneak assaults on statues of Tommy Trojan and **UCLA's** Bruin Bear*. On another occasion, in 1958, **UCLA** pranksters *rented a helicopter and tried to dump manure on Tommy. But the escapade backfired* when the helicopter's rotors sucked some of the aromatic gunk back onto the passengers. Church-affiliated colleges and commuter campuses also pull their share of pranks. At **Concordia University Irvine**, a Lutheran school, dorm residents recently lined a quad with sandbags, and then *filled the area with water and goldfish*. At **Cal State Fullerton**, science professors have seen their *offices bricked up, filled with beach sand or decorated with a life-size plaster dinosaur head that spewed gas flames from its mouth*. Chemistry professor Richard Deming once opened his office door and found *all the furniture* – including a sofa and lighted Christmas tree – *hanging upside down from the ceiling*. Such elaborate stunts are rare today, thanks in part to political correctness, post-9/11 anxiety and fear of lawsuits, school officials say. *"The golden age of college pranks was the 1950s,"* said author Steinberg, who traces the phenomenon back to colonial times. In 1998, a group of five **Cal** students *"liberated"* the **Stanford** Tree mascot from the **Stanford** campus. Mr. Black, Mr. Green, Mr. Orange, Mr. White, and Mr. Yellow, the pseudonyms the five students used in their correspondence following the event, set off an interesting chain of events following the initial theft. *Police and school administration treated the event as a major incident, and police treated the event as a felony. The Tree was paraded in front of cameras blindfolded*, much like a hostage might be, and letters where written by the five supposedly from the Tree, talking about *how wonderful the world outside the **Stanford** campus happened to be*. Eventually, after pressure from the administration of the two schools, and heat from law enforcement, the five decided to return the mascot to avoid any more serious repercussions. After its return, *the Tree was shredded at halftime of the game between the two rivals, due to contamination*. When online messaging first became popular, a star **USC** point guard started receiving text messages and pictures from a cute **UCLA** coed named Victoria. Except Victoria wasn't real, and was actually **Cal** students. So, as expected, when **USC** played **Cal**, the **Cal** students had great fun *chanting "Victoria, Victoria,"* as well as the **USC** *point guard's cell number*. **Duke** students once *stole Michael Jordan's jersey which was hanging from the rafters of the Dean Dome, and hung-it in Cameron Indoor Stadium*. An architect who graduated from **Virginia Tech** was commissioned to do a stadium addition to rival **Virginia's** stadium. So he claims that he shaped the area into a *"T,"* to give it the **Virginia Tech** *(VT)* logo, and a view from above seems to verify this. **Army / Navy** pranks are also legendary. The *most intense rivalry in college sports has seen pranks dating back over 100 years*. There have been *cannons dumped into rivers, uniform thefts, email blasts, painted messages, flybys, stale cheese, flour dumps and helicopters dropping ping pong balls on cadets in formation*. One of the oldest, and simplest, is still the best. **Army** *first stole **Navy's** goat mascot, Bill, in 1953*.

Since then, the goat has been taken on a number of occasions. It's been *found tied to a post near the Pentagon or appearing in a New York Times ad reading, "Hey **Navy**, do you know where your kid is today?"* **Navy** got even in 1991 and *stole **Army's** mule for the first time*. **Harvey Mudd College** is close in proximity to **Caltech**, so how do they get their time in the limelight? When *your college's mascot is a concrete brick with arms and legs named Wally the Wart*, it is imperative that you win the *Victoria's Secret*

"Pink Collegiate Collection" contest so *Wally's* image can grace some fashionable lingerie. Or at least that's what students at **Harvey Mudd College** thought when they heard about the contest in 2009. The contest website was set up so that *people could cast only one vote a day*, which put colleges with large student bodies at an advantage. But the site's flawed security put colleges with a high quotient of tech wizards who like to pull pranks at an even greater advantage. A group of Mudders went to work and *wrote a computer program that bypassed the CAPTCHA and automatically cast a vote every two or three seconds*. Suddenly **Harvey Mudd College**, *with fewer than 800 students, was at the top of the list, with over a million votes*. But that wasn't enough for the pranksters. They *rigged the voting so*

that the schools in second through fifth places spelled out the acronym *WIBSTR*, which stands for "West Is Best, Screw the Rest," the motto of a *famously wild dorm at **Harvey Mudd***. Not surprisingly, they were disqualified from the contest, and *Wally is still waiting for his underwear opportunity*. When Steve Noll was a junior at the **College of William and Mary** in 1972, he and his friends loved college basketball, but they hated the fact that the *top honor for players involved being named to All-America teams by national sports journalists*. The students were just as unhappy that their own school's top player, guard Mike Arizin, would never make one of those teams. Noll and three friends decided *to correct the situation themselves*. They formed the *Association of Collegiate Basketball Writers* (even though none of them had ever penned a word about sports) and they invented the *Leo G. Hershberger Award*, which *they named for a cigar-smoking New York City sportswriter who never existed*. The four spent hours poring over player stats to select their team of honorees, which included, of course, Mike Arizin. They *designed an official-looking certificate, and stationery bearing the slogan "Serving the Sport."* When every detail was perfect, they told the *Associated*

Press about the award, and soon *the news was in every major paper in the country. Then the pranksters shut their mouths. For forty years.* They didn't reveal the award was a hoax until 2013, on the eve of the *Final Four* tournament. Most of the winners said they were surprised but amused to learn that the award was a fake – and Mike Arizin decided he was *"sort of flattered."* A long-running rivalry between **Harvard's** two school papers, the *Crimson* and the *Lampoon*, came to a head with this 1953 prank. Crimson staffers played one of their favorite pranks by *stealing the Lampoon's Ibis*, the large bird statue perched on top of their office. But this time, *they sent a letter to the Soviet consul in New York to report that the editors of the Lampoon wish to offer the Ibis as a symbol of friendship, billing the bird as "sort of an American peace dove."* The *Soviets accept*, and *the Ibis is handed off to a confused U.N. delegate in a formal ceremony*. Not wanting to be outdone, the *Lampoon retaliates* with a letter of their own. With help from then-editor John Updike, *they write to Joseph McCarthy, insisting the prank clearly proves the Crimson's communist leanings and calling for a full investigation.* Since their first meeting in 1898, the Wolverines and Spartans have had one of the longest running and most intense rivalries in Big Ten history. This rivalry became an issue of vandalism during their 2014 football season, however, after the **Michigan State** Spartans defaced **Michigan's** *block "M" by spray painting "SU" in green paint next to it*. The **Michigan** Wolverines did not take the offense lightly. They later combated the Spartans' "paint job," the following season, by adding one of their own to **MSU's** *Magic Johnson Statue*. The Wolverines *spray painted a large yellow "M" on the chest of the statue*. A very entertaining rivalry is the one between

the **Duke** Blue Devils and **North Carolina**. In early 2013, **UNC** stole **Duke's** costumed mascot, *decapitated it, and placed its head in a stake on Chapel Hill*. The beheading may have been "payback" for **Duke's** 1998 *theft of Michael Jordan's retired **UNC** jersey*. Later in 2013, UNC struck again, this time taking advantage of **Duke's** religious origin. Students at **UNC** went to every chapel on **Duke's** campus and *placed the sheet music to their fight song in all of the hymnals*.

Presidential March Madness

Many presidents have been very pleased to have their *March Madness* picked revealed to a national audience. President Obama took this tradition to a higher level by working with ESPN to *pick his bracket*, and provide his analysis, during a live broadcast, and *he picked not only the men's bracket, but also the women's bracket*. When ESPN wished to continue the tradition and asked for President Trump's selections, *the White House respectfully declined*.

Purdue University (Football): *Breakfast Club*

At **Purdue University**, *Breakfast Club* is a home football game tradition: Wake up early, dress in costume, and head to the local bars surrounding the campus. It's a *tradition built on outlandish costumes, and of course, the early morning beverages*.

Radcliffe (Crew): *Team Name not Harvard*

There's the **Radcliffe** Crew. No, not **Harvard** Women's Crew. **Radcliffe** Crew. Clad in black and white and well-read all over. Not – repeat, not – clad in crimson. From the *GoHarvard.com* athletics website: *"Why Are We Called Radcliffe Crew?* The question is common and understandable – if we *apply to, take classes and graduate from Harvard*, why are we called *"Radcliffe*

Crew?" To best answer the question, it is important to understand the unique and deep history of **Radcliffe** and **Harvard** Colleges, and the beginning of *Radcliffe Crew*. **Radcliffe College**, founded in 1879, *was the female counterpart to the all-male Harvard College*. A series of steps toward merging into one coed institution began in the 1960s, when **Radcliffe** students were first allowed to take classes at Harvard. This process was finally completed in 1999 with *the transformation of **Radcliffe** from an undergraduate college to the **Radcliffe** Institute for Advanced Study, a graduate center for interdisciplinary scholarship; meaning that all current undergraduate*

*students apply to, take classes at, and graduate from, **Harvard**. **Radcliffe** Crew,* the oldest women's rowing program in the Ivy League, was organized in the fall of 1971 by a group of enterprising **Radcliffe** athletes. The progress of the newly-formed team was phenomenal and in 1973 **Radcliffe** won the *National Championship* and represented the United States in the *Eastern European Championships* in Moscow. In 1974, the *Eastern Sprints League (EAWRC)* was formed, and in 1974 and 1975 **Radcliffe** won consecutive *Sprints* titles.   In 1976, two years after **Harvard's** Department of Athletics took over administration of **Radcliffe** athletics, *the captains of the women's teams took a vote on whether they should remain Radcliffe in name and continue to compete in black and white or be called Harvard and compete in crimson.* When the voting was done, *only women's rowing had chosen to remain **Radcliffe***. The respect gained for women's athletics at **Harvard** by the early **Radcliffe** crews carried over to the 1976 vote and is maintained today by the **Harvard** women who race for **Radcliffe** in black and white. Our team is proud of the determined women who began our program and proud of the women who continue to race and win, as we always have, under the name *"Radcliffe Crew."* "The rowers said no, that's how we started and we're going to hang onto that," said **Radcliffe** *Varsity Heavyweight* coach Liz O'Leary, who started her coaching career at **Radcliffe** – not **Harvard** – in 1986. In 2003, O'Leary won the *Varsity Eight* and NCAA team *National Titles.* "Black and white are our colors, not crimson," O'Leary said. "So yes, *tradition is an important part of rowing here."* And thus they remain **Radcliffe** Crew. Totally Rad. First, still and always.

Regis University (Women's Lacrosse): *Individualized Memes for Each Player*

Groups of players – pairs, or teammates playing the same position – come up with an individualized greeting for each player before their games. Some choose *special handshakes, while others pretend to sword fight with their lacrosse sticks.* There are also *airborne chest bumps, and various other choreographed routines.* With twenty-three players on the roster, the combinations are many, but the overall intent is to build solidarity.

Rhode Island School of Design (Various Sports): *Scrotie*

Scrotie is perhaps the most ridiculous mascot ever embraced by a student  *body.* The *giant walking penis* is awaited by spectators at every university sporting event, and the costume makes sense considering that the teams at the school are also crudely named after male genitalia. The basketball team is known as *the Balls* and the hockey team goes by the name *the Nads.* The names passed through university administration and have become *a part of school tradition.* The basketball cheerleaders even go by the name the *Jockstraps, since they support the Balls.*

Rice (Football): *Coaches' Table*

Years ago, coaches drank coffee daily at *Ye Olde College Inn* where **Rice** coaches & visiting coaches *carved their names in a table*. The original table and a duplicate (used for current signatures) are on display in the *Owl Club*.

RIT (Hockey): *Hockey Festival*

The **Rochester Institute of Technology** partners with two local teams: the *Rochester Americans and the Rochester Red Wings*, for a ten-day *hockey festival* each December at the Class AAA Red Wings stadium. RIT plays on a specially constructed rink for the occasion. Many high school and amateur games are also held during the festival.

Robert Morris University (Video Gaming): *Athletic Scholarships for Video Gaming*

In 2014, **Robert Morris** became *the first school to offer athletic scholarships to its varsity video game team*. This seemed so bizarre that *Sports Illustrated* awarded this its *"Sign of the Apocalypse."*

Rose Bowl (Football): *Lawry's Beef Bowl*

A few days prior to each year's *Rose Bowl*, the competing Big 10 and Pac 10 teams also compete in a unique way. For 65+ years, the teams have met in *Lawry's Beef Bowl* to see *which team can consume the most prime beef*. Winning teams typically consume between 600-700 pounds of beef. But interestingly, the winner of *Lawry's Beef Bowl* has gone on to take the *Rose Bowl* 70 percent of the time.

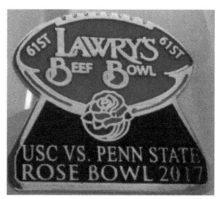

Rutgers (Football): *Rutgers Cannon*

Many colleges have cannons, and some of them even work. **Rutgers** was founded in 1766 and was named for a colonel in George Washington's army. That military connection might be the reason that the class of 1949 chose to buy a cannon *to commemorate the 80th anniversary of the very first college football game played – a 6-4 **Rutgers** victory over **Princeton***. The **Rutgers Cannon** was originally operated by the school's ROTC, but it stopped working

about 30 years ago. So why not have some *Revolutionary War re-enactors* save the day? They got it working, and now operate it at games. *At least five cannon shots are fired at each game*: three before kickoff, one at halftime, and one at the game's end. And that's if Rutgers doesn't score. So with every point (including PATs), the cannon is discharged. Each blank cartridge has four ounces of black power wrapped in aluminum foil. The cannon produces a flame up to 40' long, so everyone is discouraged from walking in front of it.

Rutgers (Football): *First Game Statue*

Unlike fans at other colleges, **Rutgers** alums and fans have a singular, touching tradition, much like the Scarlet Knight football players themselves. Before every home football game, the team *walks the walk*: *the Scarlet Walk* and, for good luck, touches the *First Game Statue*. It commemorates *the first college football game ever played* between **Rutgers** and **Princeton** on November 6, 1869. Amos Alonzo Stagg was just six years old then. But nearly a century-and-a-half later, *a tradition before every **Rutgers** home game honors the very first collegiate game*. Thanks, *Jersey Boys*.

Sage College (Softball): *Simulating a Roller-Coaster*

To remind themselves to have fun before a game starts, the team stands in single file in front of their bench, and then *a senor leads them in a routine of up-and-down arms like a ride at Six Flags*. And, of course, they add sound effects.

Saint Joseph: *Hawk Mascot's Constant Wing-Flapping*

You've seen them cavorting at most every

college sports broadcast on TV. They get passed through the stands on the hands of rowdy fans. They wrestle and tease the opposing team's mascot. They sometimes even toss goodies into the stands for the pleading crowd. In other words, college mascots have a very active and – seemingly – fun life. Maybe not. As most college basketball fans know, *the **Saint Joseph** Hawk mascot never stops flapping-his-wings*. From the time he leaves the locker room until the time he returns, he is flapping. Even during *the National Anthem*, with one wing over his heart, the other is slowly flapping. There have been thirty-six Hawks since the mascot's debut in 1956. And for many of them *their personal tradition is to return to a new Hawk's very first home basketball game, where they form a ceremonial line – from the most senior to the most recent – and pass along the Hawk's costumed head until it reaches the current mascot*. The head goes on, and the arms go-up, not to stop until sometimes three hours later.

Saint Joseph (Basketball): *Double-Dip / Ultimate Double-Dip*

When **Saint Joseph's** wins a basketball game, a single dip of ice cream is often ordered, by students, after a game. If **Villanova** loses on the same night, it calls for a second color of ice cream, and is known as a *Double-Dip*. A cherished tradition by many of the die-hard Hawk fans, the *Double-Dip* is a victory that is twice as sweet. The *Ultimate Double-Dip* occurs every time the Hawks beat the Cats.

Saint Joseph (Basketball): *Bracketology Class*

Joe Lunardi, very well known for his personal knowledge (and predictions) of teams to be included in *March Madness*, as well as their seeds, teaches a *Bracketology Class* at **Saint Joseph's**.

Salisbury University / Eastern University (Men's Lacrosse): *Shots of Honey before Each Game*

Honey provides natural energy, but why stick with this tradition? Why if it helps with a winning streak, of course.

San Jose State (Football): *Assistant Coach Dances*

Alonzo Carter is currently the running backs coach at **San Jose State University**. But Carter, in his earlier life, was a backup dancer for rapper MC Hammer. He worked for the rapper in the 1980's and 1990's, and even went on tour with him. During 2017's spring practice, Carter *put his dance moves on display* for his players *when the team played "Can't Touch This" over the stadium speakers*. The official football team *Twitter* account posted the video, and it was quickly  re-*Tweeted* by *Sports Illustrated*, *Bleacher Report*, and MC Hammer himself. Hopefully he will continue this personal tradition in the future.

Service Academies Adjusting their Military Duty Schedules

All sports fans are aware that if you attend one of our *Service Academies*, immediately after graduation, you enter the related branch of service. Roger Staubach and David Robinson are probably the two best known athletes to begin their professional careers after fulfilling their military obligations. But *that tradition changed for a short period of time*. A 2016 policy change by the *Department of Defense* allowed athletes that signed a contract with a professional franchise to defer the five years of service that is required. In fact, they could even meet their commitment with service in the Reserves. Previously, *Service Academy* graduates had to spend at least two years on active duty before applying for a waiver for the balance of their commitment. Over the years, several dozen academy graduates have reached the NFL, and this change in policy likely would have allowed for more participation at the next level. But the 2016 policy was changed in early 2017 to revert back to the prior policy. So the current rules are that Service Academy graduates must fulfill their commitment prior to considering opportunities with professional franchises. Elite Air Force receiver, Jalen Robinette, was affected by this policy-change reversal. But another star athlete was asked his opinion about the policy change and replied, *"I am a cadet and will be a commissioned officer first and foremost. I will serve until I am allowed to play."* Hooah, Oorah and Hooyah to all members of our *Service Academies*!

Simon Fraser: *Only NCAA Member not Allowed to Host a Championship*

In 2007, the NCAA *began allowing colleges from outside the USA to participate as members*. DII embraced the idea and enthusiastically accepted **Simon Fraser University's** application. **Simon Fraser** is only a few miles, or kilometers actually, into Canada just north of the Washington state border. **SFU** is just over 50 years old, and has competed on American soil since their founding – in NAIA, prior to joining DII of the NCAA. But this arrangement does present a few unique challenges. Oftentimes, DII schools with outstanding records are allowed to host NCAA Championships, but since it might be difficult to ensure proper travel documentation into Canada for large numbers of athletes and staff, **Simon Fraser** *is not allowed to host a championship on its campus*. The next frontier is Mexico, with their border towns. Several universities (**CETYS Universidad**, **Monterrey Tech**, and **University of Nuevo Leon**) have begun the initial steps. Their membership will require a DII vote, but hopefully leaders will view this as an opportunity to build overall relationships between the USA and Mexico. If Mexican schools are given membership, safety will be a main priority. Since Mexican officials acknowledge the drug violence in northern Mexico, they have indicated that Mexican home games can be played on the American side of the border, as long as the danger is deemed unacceptable in Mexico. But the ultimate goal is to allow American athletes to compete in Mexico.

SMU: *Peruna, the Shetland Pony*

SMU's official mascot *was named after an early 20th-century patent medicine, Peruna Tonic, which was popular for its kick. Peruna* is a black stallion Shetland pony that attends all home football games. *Peruna* once kicked the **Fordham** mascot (a *Ram*) in the head and killed it. To my knowledge, this is *the only mascot to have killed a rival mascot.*

Sonic's School Spirit

America's sports mania has come to this: *football team logos stamped into burger buns*. In 2013, the *Sonic* fast food chain unveiled plans – with universities in Oklahoma, Texas, and Louisiana – *to steam team logos onto burger buns*.

South Carolina (Football): *Cockabooses*

A *tailgating tradition* began in 1990 at South Carolina's *Williams-Brice Stadium*, when a developer hatched a scheme to buy up twenty-two cabooses and a patch of land with plans to lease the mini properties as primo game day real estate. The first twenty sold in forty-eight hours, and, since

then, very few have been up for re-sale, and those that have resold recently went for about $300,000. Owners can customize the interiors, but cannot change the exteriors at all. My daughter and I invited ourselves into one of the *Cockabooses* a few years ago, and *the owners could not have been more gracious*.

South Florida (Softball): *Protruding Zippers*

For the sake of superstition, two players that have since graduated would walk up to any player with their zipper protruding on their jacket, and *tuck-it-in*. The coach even played along by intentionally lifting his jacket zipper to get the girls' attention.

Southern Illinois (Intramurals): *Cardboard Boat Regatta*

This popular event originated in 1974 at **Southern Illinois University**. Now *Regattas* are enjoyed by more than 1,500 participants and more than 100,000 spectators across the USA each summer, and more communities join the *Circuit* each year. Colleges known to participate are **Notre Dame**, **Central Michigan**, and of course, **Southern Illinois**.

Southern Mississippi (Football): *SMTTT*

If you're a **Southern Miss** fan, you know their standard end to a conversation. *One fan will say, "Southern Miss," while the second fan says, "to the top."* And since there is a dictionary that publishes text message abbreviations for 300+ phrases, there must be people that use them. But don't count former **Southern Miss** football coach, Todd Monken among them. When he arrived for work in 2012, he was inundated with texts that said *"SMTTT."* He had to ask, and be told, about **Southern Mississippi's** *catch-phrase*. During his tenure at **Southern Miss**, he had foot-high letters on a shelf overlooking the stadium that read *"SMTTT."*

Spring Game Hijinks

When Steve Spurrier was coaching at **South Carolina**, he had an irreverent attitude towards the spring game. His *tradition was always to have a pass to someone coming off the sidelines*. The officials played-along, and the person catching the pass was very often a celebrity. Many schools allow celebrity coaches to participate in their spring games. As an example for the 2017 spring game, **Ohio State** had Lou Holtz and Phil Knight coaching the two teams. At **Nebraska's** sprig game, *fans of all ages take the drug-free-pledge on the field*. They pledge to remain free from drugs, alcohol, and tobacco. Prior to **Clemson's** spring game, the *Clemson Son Bowl* takes place. It features former **Clemson** players taking part in a flag football game. The 2013 version featured ten former NFL players, and twelve former all-ACC players. At **Northwestern**, after the spring game, a *dizzy bat race* is held. Players spin around a bat ten times, run ten yards, and then eat a hot dog. The main goal of the event is to not be sick. In 2017, **Arkansas** actually requested that their fans *not attend* their Spring Game. Unusual? Not really. A major weather event was forecast, and lest anyone think this was a ploy by the Razorbacks to avoid showing some secret formations, the truth is that the game was actually broadcast on the *SEC Network*.

Stanford (Football): *Telephone Number to Order Tickets*

Most sports fans know of the rivalry between **Stanford** and **Cal**. It is often called the *"Big Game,"* and entire books have been written about it. These two schools obviously have some very bright and creative students. But I wonder who came up with the idea for **Stanford's** telephone number to purchase tickets? The number is *1-800-BEATCAL*. That's a classic.

Stanford (Football): *The Most Interesting Offensive Line in the World*

Year-after-year, the **Stanford** offensive line relishes in calling themselves *the most interesting offensive line in the world*. The reason? They have a very diverse array of personalities and academic majors. Here is an example from 2016: *biomechanical engineering, environmental engineering, philosophy, Japanese*, and one lineman with an unusual major combining *science, technology, and society.*

Stanford: *Band Irreverence*

Their official name is the *Leland Stanford Junior University Marching Band*, and they do love to be different. And are they! If the band director isn't suspended at some point during the season, it might be considered an under-achieving year. Many people may not realize this but the **Stanford** mascot is the *Cardinal*, while the **Stanford** *Band's mascot is the Tree*. And **Stanford** has a traditional cheering squad, while *the band has their own version (5 Dollies). How many bands have their own mascot and cheerleaders?* Probably not many. In 1997, the band mocked not only **Notre**

Dame, but Irish people and Catholics in general, including a reference to the *Irish potato famine*. There was so much outrage after that performance that the **Stanford** *athletic director apologized.* Another time they did a halftime show titled, *"Why Must the Irish Fight?"* In the 2016 *Rose Bowl* they *made fun of Iowa, cow-tipping and FarmersOnly.com, and as a result drew the ire*

of the Iowa state legislature. A bill introduced in the Iowa Senate would have prevented any of the state's three state universities from playing **Stanford** until they publicly apologized to Iowans for the unsporting behavior during the 2016 *Rose Bowl*. ESPN producers cut-away from the halftime performance. But Iowa hasn't been the only opponent singled-out by the **Stanford** *Band*. In the 2014 *Rose Bowl*, while playing **Wisconsin**, the band performed an *"Ode to Cheese,"* and the *Oregon governor once tried to prohibit the band from entering the state.* The **Stanford** *Band* traces its origins back to the heady days of the '90s, the 1890's, when John Phillip Sousa was all the rage and kids ripped music from each other with gramophone records. Founded in 1893, the *band* marched in step, in straight lines, with dignity and reverence. *Contemporaries would describe the band's performance as either "boring" or "our school has a band?"* Nevertheless, the **Stanford** *Band* continued to support the **Stanford** *Indians* for six decades with its in-step line formations, its dignity and its reverence. As the turbulent nineteen-sixties hit America, the *band* was doing fine with their beloved Director Jules Schucat at the helm. *Then everything changed.* In 1963, a reorganization of the music department resulted in the dismissal of Director Schucat, and the loyal and enraged *bandsmen* went on strike in protest. The *band* refused to perform at the first two football games of the 1963 season. When the University hired Schucat's replacement,

Arthur P. Barnes, he wasn't exactly met with open arms. Barnes, a graduate student pursuing his doctorate in the musical arts was able to get the *band* back on the field by cutting a deal with the students: *the band would start playing at football games again and Barnes would allow for the band to be*

student-run. This compromise was the beginning of Arthur P. Barnes' significant legacy with the **Stanford** *Band*. As the turbulence of the nineteen-sixties hit the **Stanford** campus, the fledgling organization absorbed the decade's irreverent attitude and society-threatening rock-and-roll music. Over the course of the decade, the *band* threw out its military uniforms and marching style and substituted with *tacky red blazers, white fishing hats and a scatter (or scramble) style of field show performance*. Armed with the weapons of student autonomy, rock-and-roll music and bad fashion sense, the *band* was ready to take on the world. The *Leland Stanford Junior University Marching Band* has been entertaining America ever since with its *cutting-edge musical arrangements, irreverent humor, and high energy performance style*. In the past 50 years, the Band has roamed the streets of South Beach, rocked out in New Orleans, crashed Baltimore, danced in Washington D.C., road-tripped across the Midwest, been looked at quizzically in China, romped about Down Under, mystified Texas, performed for the Queen of England, scrambled on national TV in five *Rose Bowls* (and lots of other bowls, excluding of course the coveted *Salad Bowl*) and built a killer robot out of cardboard. The *band* is the shining example for scatter

bands across the country regarding how to entertain thousands with rock and roll and liquid excitement, and even the strictest, tightest, most perpendicular marching bands standing at attention have to crack a smile when the *One, the Only, Leland Stanford Junior University Marching Band* runs screaming onto the field. The core of the *band* is the *band staph*, of which there are currently 27, plus *the Tree* and the *five Dollies*. Attendance by others is completely voluntary, so the number of people at any event varies, but for football games they often scatter with 100 to 150 participants. Approximately 40 *band*-folk cheer on the women's volleyball and men's and women's basketball teams for every game. *For each school year, the band claims to have more events than they do school days.* They have about 70 songs in any current repertoire, and never play the same song twice in any one day. They claim to have made 14 albums, but I don't know if that is true or not. A couple of *band* members played outside of *OJ Simpson's Trial* in 1994. And what tune did they play? Why *"She's Not There"* by *the Zombies*, of course. Each time a new *Tree* steps into the spotlight, an original costume is born. Sarah Young, who won the right to don *the Tree* costume most recently, debuted her creation at the first home football game of the season. *As is tradition* for a new *Tree*, Young conceptualized the idea and then constructed the costume by hand over the summer. For

the newest iteration, she chose a weeping willow design, noting, "There has never been a willow before, so I wanted to represent the new generation of *Trees*, both as people and as costumes."

Swarthmore / Ursinus (Rugby): *Prom Dress Rugby*

Swarthmore & **Ursinus** play an annual match of *Prom Dress Rugby*.

Teams' Support after Tragedies

There are many examples of athletic teams supporting other teams after a tragedy that affected one, or both teams. It's a tradition that wonderfully continues, even though the circumstances that generate the traditions are sad. One day after the bombing of the *Boston Marathon*, **Boston University** was scheduled to play **Bryant University** in softball. A **BU** player asked her coach to reach out to **Bryant's** coach to coordinate a moment of silence. *Both teams wore blue and yellow Boston Marathon ribbons in their hair.* When the public address announcer called for the moment of silence, the players from both teams spontaneously linked hands. Also related to the *Boston Marathon* tragedy, is *"Row for Boston."* A **Harvard** rower suggested the annual *Muri Cup* and *Women's Beanpot* race on the Charles River be dedicated to the bombing's victims. *Crews from six Boston-area colleges wore identical shirts, with oar designs of each school, which when viewed together formed the word "Boston."* In Alabama, babies are taught to say *"Roll Tide" or "War Eagle"* at the same time they learn, *"Mommy"* or *"Daddy"* – or maybe earlier. The entire state counts the days – each and every one of them – until the annual, season-ending *Iron Bowl* is played. And then they start over again. But what about when a monstrous, unforgiving band of killer tornadoes dragged their funnel spouts through parts of the south, including Tuscaloosa, home of the Bama campus. Then almost nothing, most

of all a football game, seemed too important anymore. Forty of the 236 Alabamans who lost their lives lived in Tuscaloosa, and more than 300 people in the city are unaccounted for early-on. *Soon after the storm, a 70-person* **Auburn** *contingent including* **Auburn's** *head coach, players and administrators traveled in two waves to the Birmingham area – a Bama stronghold – to assist with the relief effort. They weren't dressed to the nines in* **Auburn** *gear. They didn't burn up their Twitter or Facebook accounts with updates. It was just 70* **Auburn** *folks trying to help those in need.* "Toomer's for Tuscaloosa" was established to raise funds and provide a human chain of support and relief for those tornado victims whose stories of loss made you want to sit on a curb and cry. *In a show of solidarity, the Tigers' baseball team wore state of Alabama stickers on the back of their batting helmets the weekend following the tornadoes.* And when the **Auburn** and **Alabama** baseball teams played each other the following weekend at **AU**, a collection fund was established and Auburn fans happily reached into their wallets to help. *"Roll Eagle and War Tide."*

Tennessee (Swimming & Diving): *Ghosts in the Rafters*

Seniors on the swimming & diving teams climb to a catwalk by way of the diving platform and *sign a beam at the top of their natatorium*, thus becoming a *Ghost in the Rafters*. They often add nicknames, years, and clever quips.

Tennessee (Swimming / Diving): *Home Water*

A swimming / diving tradition that has proven to be a favorite of **Tennessee** fans is the ritual that takes place prior to away dual-meets and Championships meets. Prior to the opening event, a **Tennessee** swimmer *will pour a bottle of water from their home pool into the opponent's water*. The tradition, started by coach Ray Bussard, excites both fans and foes alike.

Tennessee (Football): *Skeletons inside Neyland*

One summer when Phil Fulmer was a student at **Tennessee**, his job was to paint *Neyland Stadium* – from the concession stands to the benches on the sideline – and it afforded him a nuanced appreciation  of *one of the country's most celebrated venues*. "I've seen every nook and cranny of it," said Fulmer, who was the Volunteers' coach from 1992 to 2008. From the locker rooms to the press box to the classrooms below the stadium, Fulmer knows *Neyland* as well as anyone. But was he aware that **Tennessee's** anthropology department is located inside *Neyland Stadium* in rooms that once served as the players' dormitory? *There are more than 1,000 skeletons curated inside Neyland Stadium*. Bodies are donated to the department, which then studies how they decompose at an off-site facility known colloquially as *"The Body Farm."* The skeletons are then cleaned inside *Neyland*, where they are used to develop tests that help law enforcement identify the remains of unknown individuals. Of course, while there aren't ghouls hidden in the depths of the stadium, the field did hide some relics of the past, and they were unearthed in the mid-1990s. For nearly 30 years, **Tennessee** used artificial turf to cover the field at *Neyland*, but then grass was installed. When the digging began, **Tennessee** found giant sinkholes beneath the stadium caused by the turf's poor drainage – caverns filled with an assortment of items from Neyland's early years. *Bottles, and other items that dated back to the 1920s when the stadium was built, were found.* And while the bodies are curated in Knoxville, at Ole Miss – under their medical school campus – there are currently over 7,000 bodies actually buried. Due to the high cost to exhume and rebury each of these bodies, Ole Miss has decided to have this work done internally. I wonder if the next Phil Fulmer is excited to be involved in this?

Texas: *Colored-Lights on the UT Tower*

The 27-story *Main Building* – the *UT Tower* – is bathed in orange-colored lights that stand as a beacon to the Longhorns' success. Orange lights first flooded the Tower in 1937. In 1947, guidelines were created for using the orange lights. *A Number "1" on all sides highlighted by orange lights signals that the university just won a National Championship (in any sport).* The full Tower glowing orange alone represents a victory over **Texas A&M**, commencement, and other occasions the president deems appropriate. *The Tower top bathed in orange symbolizes other victories or a conference title in any intercollegiate sport.*

Texas A&I: *Javelina*

Texas A&I's mascot for years was a live *Javelina* (related to a swine). In 1929 the university president was bitten by the mascot. The *Javelina* was found to be rabid and the president underwent treatment for rabies. *To my knowledge this is the only example of a school's mascot giving a university president rabies.*

Texas A&M: *Fish Camp*

Many schools have various forms of freshman orientation, but few do it quite like **Texas A&M.** Sessions are held over four days at an offsite camp, where over 1,000 upperclassmen volunteer in some way to help the incoming freshman. A huge part of this experience is learning the unique **Texas A&M** traditions and yells. In fact this camp is also known as a *Freshman's First Tradition*.

Texas A&M (Football): *Bats in the Stadium*

Texas A&M is a very special place. Their traditions are among my favorites. *The 12th Man, Midnight Yell Practice, the Bonfire* (now held off campus), *Reveille,* "Howdy," etc. But they

also have one you may be unaware of. They have a *tradition of housing, and actually supporting bats that live in the stadium.* Mexican free-tailed bats. Since the stadium opened in 1927, much of its existence has also been accompanied by the presence of the bats who found shelter in the stadium, often in its upper decks. An estimated 250,000 bats lived in the crevices of *Kyle Field* and the stadium has long been a *"bat-friendly"* zone, with signs posted in the stadium alerting fans to their presence. The Mexican free-tailed bats, which are the official flying mammal of Texas, are vigilant in controlling insects, with the population eating anywhere from 50 million to 150 million insects a night. The large population of bats was difficult to clean up after, though, with bat guano appearing throughout the stadium and requiring an estimated $150,000 per year in cleanup costs. How many bats remained after the recent, extended renovations to *Kyle Field* is unclear, but the number is expected to be highly diminished from before. During construction of the new *Kyle Field*, **Texas A&M** took measures to prevent bats from re-entering the stadium, which led to the mammals taking shelter in other places, like dorms or the campus natatorium, which had to be temporarily shut down this spring after numerous bats made their way in.

Texas A&M: *Five Monuments Honor Their Traditions*

In 2014, as *Kyle Field* was being renovated, the university unveiled *five statues that honor their wonderful traditions*. There is a 12-foot, 1,700-pound bronze monument of the student – E. King Gill – that was the origin of the *12th Man* tradition. There are also statues dedicated to the *Fightin' Texas Aggie Band* and *the Corps of Cadets* with their symbols on top. Students removed the cover from the *War Hymn* monument. The 40-foot-wide piece displays 12 students locked in arms *sawing varsity's horns off*, located purposefully on the 50-yard line of the stadium's east side, *the side that will always belong to students*. Arms locked together, *sawing varsity's horns off is one of the most unique and thrilling college traditions in college football.* And lastly, there is a *Yell Leader*

monument. Each of the five statues embodies individual student values on the side of the stadium that will always belong to them.

Texas A&M -Kingsville: *Tortilla Tossing*

In 2010, **Texas A&M-Kingsville** banned the tradition of tortilla tossing at football games. The opening coin toss? Fine. Tossing touchdown passes? Better by the home team. But *tossing tortillas*? No more. According to a newspaper report in *The Corpus Christi Caller-Times*, while no one knows who started the tradition, *tortillas had been flying for decades*. Students at other universities, including the **University of California-Santa Barbara** and **Texas Tech**, flirted with the idea of *tortilla tossing* in the stands. Both schools stopped it when officials threatened to penalize the home team. "Over the course of the past year, I wrestled with a difficult issue related to the spirit of the institution," **Texas A&M-Kingsville** president Steven Tallant said in a

2010 statement *outlawing tortilla tossing*. *The Caller-Times* roundly agreed in an editorial headlined "**A&M-Kingsville** is right to ban tortilla tossing." It began: "Before the first kickoff of the 2010 season, **Texas A&M University-Kingsville** President Steven Tallant made an excellent call. On August 19 he *banned tortilla tossing* at Javelina football games, a quasi-tradition of questionable origin and unquestionable lack of decorum. Tallant *based his decision on three issues*, according to his official statement: *safety, a waste of food, and offensiveness*." On the safety issue, he noted reports of spectators hit by frozen tortillas. He also pointed out that someone could slip on a slippery tortilla and fall, and that tortilla tossing can provoke fights. Tallant said the waste of food is inconsistent with the stewardship he expects of students, and insensitive to families in need. Refraining from the tortilla tossing won't feed those families but at least it will remove the impression that the students don't care. The university president also took care to explain why the practice would offend: "Many people, both Hispanic and non-Hispanic, have told me they are offended by this practice. They consider it a racist gesture, and even if some people in our community do not agree with this opinion, we need to *be sensitive to those who are offended by throwing tortillas*." Tallant *discussed the topic of tortilla tossing at student roundtables and with the student government before making his decision*. "I know that some people, especially some student groups, are disappointed by my decision to ban throwing tortillas," Tallant said in his message. "I understand their disappointment, and I hope everyone understands that I didn't make this decision lightly." Obviously he didn't. He showed tolerance and patience. He is also offering an alternative. The school handed-out free *Spirit Towels* at the following year's first home game September 18. Another good call.

Texas Tech (Football): *Masked Rider*

This tradition began in 1954 at the *Gator Bowl*, when Texas Tech's coach realized that his team was the only Southwest Conference university without a mascot. So, just before the game, the coach persuaded a student to *don a masked rider's costume and roam the sidelines on a horse*. As a result, the underdog Red Raiders defeated **Auburn** 35-13. Since that fateful day, fifty-one other student riders on fourteen horses have filled the role.

Texas Tech (Football): *Saddle Tramps Wrapping Statue*

Saddle Tramps (**Texas Tech's** student group) form a big circle on the field before each football game, ring cowbells, and chant, *"go-fight-win."* Also, before every home football game the *Saddle Tramps wrap a statue of Will Rodgers & his horse, Soapsuds, with red crepe paper*. Will Rogers and Soapsuds have also been wrapped up in black crepe paper to mourn national tragedies.

Trinity College (Squash): Unbeaten Streak

Trinity's men's squash team *won 252 consecutive matches*, including 13 *National Championships*, between 1998 and 2012.

Trinity College (Football): *Team's Battle Cry*

Trinity College's mascot is bantam rooster, and their football stadium – officially named *Jesse / Miller Field* – is known as *"the coop."* And this, of course, inspired the team's battle cry: *"NO POOP IN THE COOP!"*

Trophy Games

Nothing so clearly screams college football as *Rivalry Week*, when *giant axes, territorial cups, and ruby-adorned Gaelic war clubs* crash through our television screens. The traveling *trophy game* distills what's loved most about college football. The teams below have played each other many more years than is indicated, but the *traveling trophies* associated with these games is what is depicted below (as of the 2016 season). You have to love *trophy games:*

Trophy	Team	Team	Years Awarded
Territorial Cup	Arizona	Arizona State	118
Victory Bell	Miami (Ohio)	Cincinnati	118
Little Brown Jug	Michigan	Minnesota	114
Old Oaken Bucket	Indiana	Purdue	92
Illibuck	Ohio State	Illinois	92
Golden Egg	Ole Miss	Mississippi State	90
Keg of Nails	Louisville	Cincinnati	88
Stanford Axe	California	Stanford	84
Floyd of Rosedale	Minnesota	Iowa	82
Victory Bell	USC	UCLA	78
Golden Hat	Oklahoma	Texas	76
Purdue Cannon	Purdue	Illinois	74
Wagon Wheel	Akron	Kent State	72
Iron Skillet	TCU	SMU	71
FOY-ODK Sportsmanship	Alabama	Auburn	69
Paul Bunyan's Axe	Wisconsin	Minnesota	69
Victory Bell	North Carolina	Duke	69
Megaphone	Notre Dame	Michigan State	68
Old Brass Spittoon	Michigan State	Indiana	67
Jeweled Shillelagh	USC	Notre Dame	65
Paul Bunyan	Michigan	Michigan State	64
Silver Spade	UTEP	New Mexico State	62
Shillelagh	Notre Dame	Purdue	60
Platypus	Oregon	Oregon State	58
The Saddle	TCU	Texas Tech	56
Apple Cup	Washington	Washington State	55
Bedlam Bell	Oklahoma	Oklahoma State	51
Bronze Boot	Wyoming	Colorado State	49
Governor's Cup	Kansas	Kansas State	48
Fremont Cannon	Nevada	UNLV	47
Frank Leahy Memorial Bowl	Boston College	Notre Dame	42
Cy-Hawk	Iowa	Iowa State	40
Paniolo Trophy	Hawaii	Wyoming	38
Ram-Falcon	Air Force	Colorado State	37
Textile Bowl	Clemson	NC State	36
Anniversary Award	Kent State	Bowling Green	32
Centennial Cup	Colorado	Colorado State	31
Legends Trophy	Notre Dame	Stanford	28
Golden Boot	Arkansas	LSU	25

Tufts: *Jumbo*

Tufts initial mascot was a stuffed elephant from *PT Barnum*. When the elephant was destroyed in a 1975 university fire, a small amount of his ashes were saved in a *14 ounce Peter Pan Crunchy peanut butter jar. The jar of ashes is passed from athletic director to athletic director in a formal ceremony. Football players often touch the jar for good luck.* Before the fire, students put pennies and other items in the elephant's trunk for good luck during exams. The real Jumbo died while saving a baby elephant from a runaway locomotive. *The stuffed school mascot arrived on the Hill in 1889, and the name and image have been etched upon* **Tufts'** *sports teams, clubs, psyche, school spirit, periodicals, yearbooks, songs, offices, artifacts, campus structures, tchotchkes, and the graduating student body ever since.*

UCLA: *Bruins*

There are myriad bear mascots in college football, varying in color, subspecies and age, among other designations. But when you hear the name *"Bruins"*, one school comes immediately to mind: **UCLA**. Given that **UCLA** is the *Los Angeles branch of the University of California System* and the bear is on the California state flag, it made sense for **UCLA** to adopt an ursine mascot. Initially, **UCLA** teams were known as the *"Cubs,"* while the **University of California at Berkley** went by the *"Bears,"* and later the *"Golden Bears."* But students at **UCLA** resented the little brother status and rejected the *Cubs* nickname in favor of the fiercer *"Grizzlies"* nickname. The *Grizzlies* moniker lasted just two years. In 1926, **UCLA** joined the old Pacific Coast Conference, which already had some *Grizzlies* in the mix – namely, the

University of Montana. **UCLA** agreed to give up the *Grizzlies* nickname, and **Cal** bequeathed **UCLA** one of the variations on their *Bear* nickname: *"Bruins."* The centuries-old Dutch reference stuck, and soon enough *live bears stalked the sideline at Bruins games in the Los Angeles Memorial Coliseum*. They eventually gave way to *Joe Bruin*, **UCLA's** costumed mascot.

UConn (Basketball): *Carrying the Coach off the Court after a National Championship*

Everyone realizes the dominance of the **UConn** women's basketball team. Their accomplishments are unmatched by any team, in any sport. But did you know that the **UConn** team has a *tradition of carrying their coach off the court after a National Championship*? The tradition began in 1995 and Geno Auriemma recently remarked, "Back in 1995 they were overjoyed; now all they do is bitch and moan about how heavy I am. I make it worst because I lie there like a stone. They have fun with it. As I have gotten older, *I embrace more of the traditions that they think are important*."

UNLV (Basketball): *Khem Kong Puppet*

The evolution had to happen. First there were die-hard fans showing up in face paint. And this snowballed to the ubiquitous huge cutout heads you see behind the goals during

basketball games. So what's next? Yep. *3D-heads and giant, articulated puppets*. **UNLV** may have been the first of these (in 2012) with their version of then-**UNLV** forward Mike Moser, dubbed *Mozilla*. When Moser's transfer to **Oregon** forced *Mozilla's* retirement, its creator, former **UNLV** student Sean Clauretie, devised the largest prop yet: *Khem Kong* – a 20-foot-wide puppet, based on forward Khem Birch. If this doesn't distract visiting free throw shooters, nothing will. *Creating the **UNLV** puppet involves about a dozen students*, each with a different responsibility. As an example, one student might do the puppet's teeth – fifteen small pieces of paper that must fold into a pattern, be glued to other body parts, and keep its shape when sprayed with foam. During a game, four people hold it, so practice is required prior to the game.

US Presidents and College Football

Our Presidents are too busy to have personal traditions associated with college sports, but nonetheless *several of our former leaders have interesting connections to college football*. Although Theodore Roosevelt never played collegiate football because of his nearsightedness, his son played at **Harvard**, and frequently took a beating on the field. Teddy expected his son to be strong, but any father could see the brutality of the early football games. So he did something about it. In 1905, he staged a *Football Summit*, to discuss

the facts that *few helmets or face guards were being used, there were no neutral zone between teams, and no limits to how many players could be on the line at once. Football could be fatal and at least 45 college and prep school players died from injuries during the 1904 and 1905 seasons*. So Roosevelt summoned representatives of **Harvard** (whose president had *said that football was more brutal than prizefighting, cockfighting, or bullfighting*), **Yale** and **Princeton** to the White House to talk about the future of college football, and he told them that *unless the game was reformed it would be outlawed* – perhaps by an executive order from TR himself. Partly in response, the *Intercollegiate Athletic Association of the United States* was formed in 1906 and it instituted rule changes, such as allowing the forward pass, which made football safer and more popular. So *President Roosevelt began a tradition of the game being safer*. Way-to-go, Teddy. President Eisenhower played football for the **US Military Academy** at West Point, NY. In the days when players appeared on both sides of the ball during games, Ike was a running back on offense and a linebacker on defense. In November 1912 Eisenhower severely hurt his knee in a game against **Tufts** and his playing days came to an end; he was so depressed that he seriously considered quitting the **Academy**. He recalled years later that "Life seemed to have little meaning. A need to excel was almost gone." Ike's spirits soon recovered and he coached **West Point's** junior varsity football team. After John F. Kennedy transferred from **Princeton University** to **Harvard** in 1936, he tried out for the varsity football team but was underweight at 156 pounds and ended up playing wide receiver on the junior varsity squad. Speaking in 1961 to the *National Football Foundation and Hall of Fame Banquet*, President Kennedy observed: "Politics is an astonishing profession. It has enabled me to go from being an obscure member of the junior varsity at **Harvard** to being an honorary member of the *Football Hall of Fame*." Richard Nixon played football for **Whittier College** in California during 1932-1934 as a substitute tackle. Although his collegiate football career did not go entirely as he had hoped, Nixon remained a devoted fan and as president enjoyed interaction with college teams and their coaches. In 1969 he told the *National Football Foundation and Hall of Fame*: "I look back on football and have many pleasant memories. I just enjoyed playing it, watching it, reading about it over the years." For many people Ronald Reagan's connection to college football involves his portrayal of **Notre Dame's** star halfback George Gipp in the 1940 film *"Knute Rockne: All-American,"* but Reagan was also a college football player in real life. Reagan was a starting guard for the Golden Tornadoes of **Eureka College** near Peoria, Illinois (he also belonged to the swimming and track-and-field relay teams). After graduation from **Eureka** in 1932 he worked as a part-time announcer of **University of Iowa** home football games for Davenport, Iowa's radio station *WOC*. Gerald R. Ford had the most distinguished college gridiron career of any president; he was a member of the **University of Michigan's** 1932 and 1933 and *National Championship* teams. The Wolverines also won Big Ten Conference titles in 1932 and 1933 with Ford on their roster. In 1935 Ford graduated from **Michigan** and played in the *College All-Star Game* against the NFL champion Chicago Bears. He received offers from both the Detroit Lions and Green Bay Packers to try his hand at the professional game, but turned them down. "Pro ball did not have the allure it has now," he recalled 30 years later. "Though my interest was piqued at the time, I didn't lose sleep over the offers." Instead Ford enrolled at **Yale University** Law School, where he graduated in 1941. Herbert Hoover didn't play football for **Stanford University**, but as the football team's business manager he played a crucial role in arranging for **Stanford** to play the **University of California** on March 19, 1892 – one of the first major intercollegiate football games on the west coast. Hoover rented a baseball field in San Francisco for $250 and had 5,000 tickets printed with admission at two dollars each. The tickets were snapped up quickly, but on game day so many extra fans turned out – and paid for admission in cash – that a desperate Hoover grabbed some fellow **Stanford** students to search the neighborhood for pots, pans, buckets and cloth bags that could hold the bills and coins that were part of **Stanford's** share of the receipts. Eventually $20,000 was collected and Hoover, fearful of robbery, did not see the game but instead stayed in his hotel room guarding the money.

UT Chattanooga (Football): *Moc Walk*

While many college football teams have *game day traditions in which players walk through crowds* of cheering fans to get to their stadiums, **UTC's** *"Moc Walk"* is a bit of a different twist. After changing from street clothes into their pads and uniforms, the players are joined by coaches, trainers, managers and other support staff for the *decades-old tradition of walking to their practice field*. Five days a week the Mocs make their way along a *half-mile walk that includes crossing three busy intersections* before reaching the practice field. It's not uncommon for motorists to roll their windows down and yell encouragement to players and coaches or, even ignore a green light and let the padded pedestrians cross.

Utah: *Changes to Fight Song Lyrics*

In 2014, the **University of Utah** decided that certain words in their fight song (written in 1904 by a former coach) were sexist. *Lyrics such as "I'm a Utah man," and "our coeds are the fairest" spiked emotions on campus*, so the university administration acted. Their new version changes "man" to "fan," and now "our students are the finest." And, probably to get alumni on-board, the administration indicated that *anyone could sing either version of the song that made them happy.*

Utica College (Ice Hockey): *New York Sash Teddy Bear Toss*

Teddy Bears are tossed on the ice after the first score of the night. The accumulated *Teddy Bears* are subsequently distributed to *Catholic Charities*, et al. This event has gone on for 15+ years, and generally has about 4,000 fans attending this DIII hockey game. If you bring a *Teddy Bear*, you get in free.

Vanderbilt (Football): *Anchor Drop*

The ***Vanderbilt*** *Anchor* was adopted in 2004 as a symbol of unity and strength and *accompanies the team to all home and away games*. Before each home game, a group or individual is selected to *"drop the anchor"* at midfield.

Virginia Tech (Basketball): *Players Respecting the National Anthem*

Virginia Tech men's basketball coach Buzz Williams was angry with the way some of his players were acting while the *National Anthem* was sung or played before games, so he made them come to the court early one Saturday morning in 2015 to teach them a powerful lesson. Williams had his players stand face-to-face with a group of veterans as he explained why everyone should stand at attention and show respect during the *National Anthem*. "These guys, when they were your age, interrupted their life, they paused their education, they changed their career, and they gave their life," Williams said. "So when the *anthem* is played, we're going to stand like grown men and we're going to honor men like this that gave their life so we could have a chair to sit in." "Those two and a half minutes we're going to give to the people that earned these chairs," Williams said about a row of chairs set up behind the veterans. "Because that freedom allowed us to do what we're doing." "I don't care if you sing," he continued. "But *I want you to know the words*, and *I want you to be respectful of the words*, because *those words represent people's lives*." The veterans, many of whom were in full dress uniforms as they surprised the players, stood proudly at attention as the *National Anthem* played over the speakers to an empty arena. Way-to-go, Buzz.

Virginia Tech (Football): *Touching the Hokie Stone*

Inside the tunnel that the players run thru prior to the game is a stone, from the university's quarry, with the phrase, *"For those who have passed, for those to come, reach for excellence."* Each player touches the stone en route to the field. Some would argue that the *Hokie Stone* contributes to – perhaps even serves as a foundation of – *Hokie*

For those who have passed, For those to come...
Reach for Excellence!

Spirit. The native limestone, mined at the university's own quarry, has defined the campus scene for more than a hundred years. The rocks have become so integral to the aura of Virginia Tech that the Board of Visitors decreed in the mid-1990s that all buildings constructed in the central campus thenceforth must be clad in *Hokie Stone*.

Virginia Tech (Football): *Skipper the Cannon*

The **Virginia Tech** *Corps of Cadets* has been an active part of the student body since the school was founded in 1872. **Virginia Tech** was founded as a military school and remains one of a handful of universities in the United States with an active cadet corps on campus. That rich military history helps explain why there's so much *cannon fire at football games*. For 50-plus years, **Virginia Tech** fans (and opponents) have heard *"Skipper"* booming out during Hokies games. *Skipper* is the name of **Virginia Tech's** working cannon, which fires off a blank *blast each time the Hokies enter Lane Stadium and each time they score at home*. As with all great college traditions, *Skipper* was born out of a fierce rivalry – in this case, with nearby **Virginia Military Institute**. **VMI** and **Virginia Tech** competed in sports for years, and each time **VMI** beat the Hokies, students would fire off *"Little John,"* their college cannon. The **VMI** cadets also would blast *Little John* before each rivalry game, then chant *"Where's your cannon?"* Remember, this was pre-*Twitter*, so chants about cannons were the height of trolling. In 1963, a couple of **Virginia Tech** cadets had had enough of **VMI** shooting off before every game, so they decided to take matters in their own hands. They collected scrap metal from their classmates in the form of brass plates, buckles, fittings, and spent bullet casings from the school firing range. *They found Civil War-era blueprints for a cannon and commissioned a nearby foundry to melt down their scraps.* Next, they located a woodworking shop that specialized in era-appropriate wooden carriages for transporting the new artillery. On November 22, 1963, the cadets picked up the completed cannon and drove it back to campus. During the ride, they heard terrible news: *President Kennedy had been shot and killed in Dallas.* The cadets decided to name the cannon *"Skipper" in recognition of Kennedy's naval background*, and *they first fired it in his honor*. A few days later, at the Thanksgiving Day game between **Virginia Tech** and **VMI**, *Little John* went off as usual. That's when the **Virginia Tech** cadets rolled out *Skipper*, which was massive in comparison to *Little John*. As the legend goes, they never heard *"Where's your cannon?"* chants again – possibly because everyone had gone deaf. Now, *Skipper* inspires Hokies fans and rattles **Virginia Tech** opponents during every home game. A special 10-man *"Skipper Crew"* of cadets is responsible for cannon upkeep and operation, led by a gun captain. The original *Skipper* suffered a fatal blowout in 1982, but the same foundry that built the original cannon created a new model in 1984. The original *Skipper* is still on display on campus, and the new *Skipper* is still blasting off at *Lane Stadium* – although it has undergone a few repairs after malfunctioning during a 2010 game against **Wake Forest**.

Virtual Reality Recruiting

College football teams have used *virtual reality* for training purposes for years. But now, they have *branched into recruiting with this technology*.

Imagine a 360 degree view that puts the prospective athlete into your school's facilities, and game day traditions? They can be transposed into a huddle, and run thru a tunnel onto a field. And, of course, the VR only simulates the very best of

experiences that may be available. And it doesn't count as an official campus visit for the recruit. *But coaches using this tool feel it does convince potential recruits to make that official visit.*

Vulgar Chants

In 2017, the president of **Kansas State** felt it necessary to ask his school's basketball fans to *stop using vulgar chants targeted at the **Kansas** Jayhawks*, calling the chants "personally embarrassing." **KSU** students often chanted an expletive followed by *"KU"* in a variety of songs. And a **University of Missouri** student fan group *was ejected from two consecutive games* in November 2013 for what school officials called a pattern of inappropriate chants. In recent years, **LSU** strayed from a few of their traditions involving their band, since the student body created some profane chants to go along with a number of the band's songs. And although the chants may have been clever, and even somewhat intimidating, they were not showing **LSU** in a very good light. So **LSU** removed those songs from their band's game-day program for a period of time, and reinstated them in 2013 as part of a new *Tradition Matters Campaign.* But the school also felt the need to *create a video reminding students to stay classy with these traditions.* Wonder how that went?

Western Kentucky: *Birthday Party for Costumed Mascot*

For 40+ years, each year on December 1st, Western Kentucky students *celebrate Big Red's*

Birthday with laser tag, bands, birthday cake, etc. Thousands of students attend the party from about midnight until 2am.

Whitman College / Whitworth University: *Battle of the Whits*

These two DIII schools are 150 miles apart, but have an intense geographic rivalry. They are travel-partners in their conference and often stay at the same hotel, eat at the same restaurants, etc. Both schools were established in the late 19th century, so various *"Battles of the Whits"* have taken place over the years. In 2011, one team upset the other after trailing by 18 points midway thru the second half. And predictably, hundreds of students rushed the court.

Wisconsin (Football): *Camp Randall Stadium's History*

CAMP RANDALL STADIUM

On fall game days when **Wisconsin** students do their famous *Jump Around*, I wonder how many of them know the history beneath their feet? Camp Randall Stadium stands tall as an iconic college football venue. The stadium site and its adjacent land, though, are steeped in US military history that far predates the game. *Camp Randall*, a 53-acre property owned before the *Civil War* by the *Wisconsin State Agricultural Society*, transformed into a training center for the majority of 91,000 Wisconsin troops who served in the *Grand Army of the Republic* from 1861 to 1865. Named for wartime Gov. Alexander W. Randall, the site also *housed 1,400 captured Confederate soldiers. About 140 soldiers who died from their battlefield injuries are buried at the northernmost Confederate cemetery in the United States.* Headquarters for Union military operations at *Camp Randall* were located along a hillside on which the stadium's luxury suites today are erected. *Camp Randall housed troops again* *in World War I and World War II*, but its military connection to the 19th century is most remembered. The five-acre *Camp Randall Memorial Park*, east of the stadium, was built in the early 20th century and remains listed in the *National Register of Historic Places*. Its entrance, the *Memorial Arch*, dedicated in 1912, stands as a notable structure on campus. The **Wisconsin** marching band, en route to the stadium from *Union South* on game day, marches through the arch. Football was first played at *Camp Randall* in 1895. Construction of the current stadium began in 1913. Today, it seats 80,321 and provides the Badgers with a home-field advantage that ranks among the nation's best.

Wisconsin (Football): *Cane Tossing*

Believed to have been tradition for over 100 years, third-year law students at the **University of Wisconsin** *run onto the field before the homecoming game wearing bowler hats and throw a cane through the goalposts*. Legend has it that if they catch the cane on the other side, they'll win their first case.

Xavier (Soccer): *Coach's Superstitions*

Xavier's soccer coach has a *few very weird superstitions* that he refuses to deviate-from. He *won't watch the first thirty seconds of any match*, and *he won't watch penalty kicks at all*. And *during a penalty kick*, he has to either *be holding, or wearing, one of the team's heavy rain jackets*. Once a team manager had to sprint to the team bus to find the jacket. He has a water cup that he uses all season. The *cup must always have water in it during a game*. When he *stretches during pre-game, everything must be done to an eight-count, or a number divisible by eight. He also always arrives eight minutes late for pregame meals*. And, following a superstition held by many coaches, he is *always the last one off the bus*.

Yale: *Bladderball*

Bladderball was a game traditionally played by **Yale** students between 1954 and 1982. An event that typically preceded the **Yale** / **Dartmouth** football game, *Bladderball involved rolling a 6-foot inflatable ball onto* **Yale's** *Old Campus where teams from each residential college would fight for possession of the ball.* Teams were allowed to use any means necessary to seize control of the ball, leading to a vicious free-for-all that often spilled into the streets surrounding the campus. In 1982, several participants were injured during *Bladderball* giving **Yale's** president reason to put an end to the tradition after a toll of minor injuries, property damage, near riots, and crazy pranks surrounding the tradition were too much to bear. A revival game was played in 2009 and briefly again in 2011.

Zero-Waste Initiatives

Environmentalism has a front-row seat in collegiate athletics. In 2012, during **Ohio State's** home football game against **Purdue**, the sustainability, athletics, and facilities departments joined together to roll-out a *zero-waste initiative*, and achieved a 94.4 percent diversion rate (from landfills). Similarly the **Colorado** branded its *zero-waste student force* as *Ralphie's Green Stampede* (drawing from the name of their mascot). And, **Arizona State** hopes to achieve *climate neutrality* in building energy by the year 2025. At **Middlebury**, each team is asked to nominate one of its members as *a green liaison*. One of their ideas led to all **Middlebury** athletes *wearing green shoelaces* to raise awareness. **North Texas'** *Apogee Stadium*, which opened in 2011, was *the first sports venue in the US to reach LEED Platinum certification*. Three wind turbines help power the stadium.

Baylor University: *The Immortal Ten*

Baylor annually remembers the *Immortal Ten,* and what is considered to be *the first college sports tragedy.* On January 22, 1927, on a rainy night, 10 men were killed when a bus carrying the **Baylor** men's basketball team to a game in Austin against **Texas** was hit by a train. Twelve others aboard the bus survived. *The 10 casualties were immortalized. Their story is told annually by twilight at **Baylor's** Freshman Mass Meeting on the Wednesday of homecoming week*: How first-year coach Ralph Wolf was taking his **Baylor** team, which had lost to **Texas** 22-15 earlier that month, to Austin for a Southwest Conference game. How Wolf, whose wife was pregnant and nearly due, considered not travelling with the Bears. But with **Baylor** on a four-game losing streak, including three conference defeats, Wolf accompanied his team. Tragedy struck, but Wolf survived. Nearly 70 years later, funds were raised for a memorial to *The Immortal Ten*. It would eventually become a statuary memorial, consisting of four individual statues of players killed in the wreck, and a bas-relief panel of the six other victims. The fund-raising took more than a decade. The estimated cost: more than $280,000. This, for statues or sculptures of men who'd died in the 1920's. The sculptor worked on the project for more than three years, and was determined to sculpt likenesses of the 10 as they looked in 1927. The sculptor frequently attends the yearly candlelight ceremony with his wife. The managing editor of the *Baylor Lariat,* was on the bus and sent a telegram to the *Associated Press* shortly after the accident occurred. "The heart of Baylor University is torn to shreds at this moment … Nothing like this has ever happened before." Back in Waco, the small **Baylor** campus (only about 1,600 students in 1927) was consumed with grief. More than 3,000 mourners attended a memorial service in the auditorium of **Baylor's** chapel building, which also served as the basketball team's court. Flowers and green and gold streamers were everywhere. The balance of the 1927 basketball season was cancelled. The accident would eventually lead to railroad-crossing safety reform. **Baylor's** long-standing tradition of remembering the *Immortal Ten*, and *sharing this story with each year's freshmen class, prior to their homecoming game*, is a wonderful reflection on the fabric of this university.

Clemson (Football): Howard's Rock

Nothing tops *the most exciting 25 Seconds in college football*. That's **Clemson's** entrance before every home game in *Memorial Stadium*, long known as *Death Valley*. It involves *Howard's Rock*, mass transit, an orange carpet, some of the most fervent fans in college football and a tradition born out of necessity. In 1942, the first 20,000 seats in **Clemson** *Memorial Stadium* were built and ready for the season opener. The shortest entry into the stadium was a walk down Williamson Road from the *Fike Field House* dressing room to a gate atop the hill behind the east end zone. There were no dressing facilities in the west end zone, just a large clock whose hands turned, and a hand-operated scoreboard. The Tigers would don their uniforms in *Fike*, walk down Williamson, enter a gate and jog – not charge – down the hill to warm up. There was no *Memorial mania*: no cannons booming, no huge Tiger Paw flag, no *Tiger Rag* played by the marching band, much less over the PA system. It remained modestly like this until the mid-1960's. By then, Frank Howard had become a legend and iconic coach. He was a great coach, and a gruff yet hilarious character. As **Clemson's** athletic director, he once denied a student request to fund a crew program. When told what crew was, Howard growled, "What kinda sport is that, where you sit on yo' ass and go backwards?!" *In 1965*, S.C. Jones, **Clemson** class of 1919, took a trip to California. It included a stop in notorious *Death Valley*, where Jones picked up a *2 and ½ pound rock* of white flint. He *gave it to coach Howard as a gift, from Death Valley, California, to Death Valley, South Carolina*. Howard was duly unimpressed. *The rock sat on the floor in Howard's office for more than a year, serving as a doorstop*. Finally, he told Gene Willimon, the executive secretary of *IPTAY*, Clemson's athletic fundraising organization, *"Take this rock and throw it over the fence, or out in the ditch. Do*

something with it, but get it out of my office." But Willimon only partially complied with the coach's wishes. He saved the rock, and mounted it on a pedestal atop the hill inside *Death Valley* and above the east end zone. It was unveiled on *September 24, 1966*, when **Clemson** hosted **Virginia**. Down 18 points with 17 minutes left, the Tigers won 40-35 on a late 65-yard TD pass from Jimmy Addison to Jacky Jackson. *Players began rubbing the rock for luck on September 23, 1967*, before **Clemson** beat **Wake Forest** 23-6. Before the Tigers ran down the hill that afternoon, Howard told them, *"If you're going to give me 110 percent, you can rub that rock. If you're not, keep your filthy hands off it."* Under Howard and his successor Hootie Ingram, then under Danny Ford, Tommy Bowden and now Dabo Swinney, *Clemson continues the tradition*: After the Tigers finish warming up, they go back into their dressing room under the west end zone stands for final instructions. About 10 minutes before kickoff, it's time for mass transit. Or massive transit, given the girth of Clemson's linemen. The Tigers hop aboard two buses, ride behind the north stands to the east end zone and disembark on the hill. *Then it's show time. The band forms two lines, a gauntlet for the players to run through. But not before rubbing Howard's Rock and hurtling down the hill on an orange carpet. Let the cannon boom. Strike up the Tiger Rag. And the best entrance in all of college football commences once more. Somewhere, Frank Howard's smiling.*

Colorado (Football): *Running of Ralphie*

The *Ralphie Run* at **Colorado** is one of the most dramatic moments in college sports, as the Buffaloes players run out of their locker room tunnel behind a real, live 1,300-pound animal. Live Buffaloes first appeared on campus in 1934, three weeks after a contest to select an official school nickname was completed. But *a live buffalo run as we know it today didn't start until October 28, 1967*, for **Colorado's** homecoming game against **Oklahoma State**. While Ralphie has five trained student handlers trying to control her with ropes, you just never know. And that's why even opposing players know that *Ralphie's Run* is *one of the most notable moments in college sports*. But how is *Ralphie* stopped after her run? When I personally witnessed this wonderful tradition a few years ago, I was surprised to see that after her run, the handlers guide her into a huge net to stop her.

DePauw / Wabash (Football): Monon Bell

This is *one of the oldest uninterrupted rivalries west of the Alleghenies* (since 1910), with the winner receiving the *Monon Bell* (since 1932). On one Saturday each November, **DePauw University** and **Wabash College** meet on the gridiron in *one of college football's oldest and most colorful rivalries*. The two west central Indiana schools have faced each other about 125 times with

Wabash holding a slight lead. The teams not only play for pride but also for possession of the 300-pound *Monon* (pronounced MOE-non) *Bell*, the trophy that goes to the winning team. The two schools are each located on the *Monon Railroad Line* (now L & N). The 300-pound bell was a gift of the

Monon Railroad, taken from one of the railroad's locomotives. *The Bell* has been *stolen at least eight times* from its temporary owners, but the most famous thefts may have occurred in the mid-1960s. In 1965, a **Wabash** student appeared on the DePauw campus *posing as a Mexican dignitary and interested in developing an exchange program* with **DePauw**. While meeting with the University president he asked to see *the Bell*. After learning of its whereabouts, the student returned with friends later and stole it. **DePauw** got *the Bell* back in time for the game which the Tigers won 9-7. **DePauw** students, hoping to keep *the Bell* safely under wraps, *stole it from their own school the week after the game and secretly buried it for 11 months in the north end zone of Blackstock Stadium.* Only a handful of **DePauw** students knew of its location. But an unexpected problem arose prior to the big game. The *ground froze that week* in Greencastle, and *the students were barely able to recover it in time* for the **Wabash** team to claim it as the game ended in near darkness. The *Monon Bell* game is more than just a game. The week preceding the annual contest has included shared activities between the two schools, such as concerts, debates, an intramural all-star football game, an alumni football game the morning of the varsity contest and other events. In 1985, Jim Ibbotson, a member of the *Nitty Gritty Dirt Band* and a 1969 graduate of **DePauw**, arranged and recorded *The Ballad of the Monon Bell* which was written by 1968 **DePauw** graduate and football player Darel Lindquist. The media have long understood the special nature of *this famous small college battle*. In addition to *Sports Illustrated's* extensive coverage in 1973, *CBS-TV's* Charles Kuralt did a feature on the game during his *Sunday Morning* show in 1979, *ABC-TV* aired it as a regional telecast in 1977 and *The Christian Science Monitor* praised it in a 1981 feature. The November 13, 1987, edition of *USA Today* highlighted the rivalry in a feature story in its sports section and in 1988 the *CBS Radio Network* aired a feature on the rivalry throughout the nation. The 1998 contest was covered as a feature in *The Wall Street Journal* and the 1999 contest was featured on *Fox Sports Net's* weekly show, *The Slant*. The centennial game also was featured in the November 22, 1993, issue of *Sports Illustrated*. The game is regularly telecast live to combined alumni meetings of the two schools in cities across the country and on networks including *ABC-TV* in 1977, *ESPN2* in 1994 and

HDNet in 2003 and 2006 through 2011. The 2004 and 2005 games were telecast nationally on *DirecTV*.

FSU (Football): *Chief Osceola's Flaming Spear*

There is *no more dramatic before-the-game tradition in college football than Chief Osceola's at* **Florida State** *home games. Since 1978*, before every opening kickoff at *Doak Campbell Stadium* in Tallahassee, a student wearing war paint, dressed in authentic Seminole Indian attire and astride his horse

Renegade, rides to midfield while carrying a flaming spear. There, he flings and *plants the spear* as more than 80,000 'Noles fans go nuts. While this may strike some as politically incorrect, *it has the full cooperation and blessing of the Seminole Tribe of Florida*. But first, a little history: **FSU's** *Osceola* is named for the legendary Seminole Indian chief of the 1800's, born in Georgia near the banks of the Tallapoosa River. In 1962, a Florida State sophomore named Bill Durham, a member of the homecoming committee that fall, envisioned a student dressed as *Osceola* charging onto the gridiron aboard an appaloosa named *Renegade*

and *planting a flaming spear at midfield*. Durham got no support for his vision until the autumn of 1977, after Bobby Bowden had become the 'Noles head coach. Durham approached the *Seminole Tribe of Florida*, explained his idea and sought their approval for a student to portray, and honor, the great chief. The *Seminoles* approved. And so, *before the 1978 home opener* against **Oklahoma State**, the legend of *Osceola* and *Renegade* debuted with the tribe's blessing. Since then, adorned in authentic regalia designed by the women of the *Seminole Tribe, Osceola* and *Renegade* have turned each opening kickoff into a traditional spectacle while paying homage to the original *Osceola* and the *Seminole Tribe*. Both rider and *Renegade* know how to make an entrance.

FSU (Football): *Sod Cemetery*

FSU has a *Sod Cemetery*, with *grave markers signifying big wins*. For almost six decades, *sod games* and the *Florida State University Sod Cemetery* have been a rich part of the Seminoles' college football history, commemorating many of their greatest victories. In 1962, as the Seminoles completed their Thursday practice in preparation of facing **Georgia** at *Sanford Stadium*, Dean Coyle Moore — a long-time professor and member of **FSU's** athletic board — issued a challenge: *"Bring back some sod from between the hedges at Georgia."* On Saturday, October 20, the Seminoles scored an 18-0 victory over the favored Bulldogs. Team captain Gene McDowell pulled a small piece of grass from the field, which was presented to Moore at the next football practice. Moore and **FSU** coach Bill Peterson had the sod buried on the practice field as a symbol of victory. A monument was placed to commemorate the triumph and *the tradition of the sod game was born*. Since then, before leaving for all road games in which **Florida State** is the underdog, all road games at the **University of Florida** and all *ACC championship and bowl games*, Seminole *captains gather their teammates to explain the significance of the tradition. Victorious captains return with a piece of the opponent's turf to be buried in the Sod Cemetery* outside the gates of the practice field. Away from home and against the odds, **Florida State** *sod games* represent the most difficult battles on the football field. The *Sod Cemetery* stands as a tribute to those triumphs, to be enjoyed by the Seminole faithful.

Harvard / Yale (Football): *The Game*

In many respects, *the Game* between **Harvard** and **Yale** is *the original template by which all other college sports rivalries are based*. The *first matchup* between the two schools *occurred in 1875*, in what historians consider to be *the second college football game ever played*. There have been a total of ten years since when the rivalry was not played, and four of those were due to World Wars I and II. As early as 1898, fans of both sides were referring to it as *the Game*. This rivalry also started the stadium construction boom. **Harvard** *Stadium*, built in 1903, is the oldest permanent concrete structure in the country, while the **Yale** *Bowl* (1914) became the model for numerous college football stadiums that followed. **Harvard / Yale** has declined in national relevance from its heyday in the early 20th century, but *the Game* is still capable of making noise on occasion. In fact, the most famous meeting between these two schools happened in 1968, when both teams entered *the Game* with perfect 8-0 records and the meeting ended in a tie thanks to a miraculous 16-point **Harvard** comeback in the final 42 seconds of play. *"Harvard Beats Yale, 29-29"* headlined *the Harvard Crimson* student newspaper the next day in what would become one of *the most famous sports headlines of all-time*.

Hope College: *The Pull*

What *began* back *in 1898* as a *tug-of-war* between high school sophomores and incoming freshmen has become an annual, autumnal tradition at **Hope College**

in Holland, Michigan. One that pulls at the heartstrings as well as the hamstrings, and almost every other muscle in the human body. *The Pull*. Tug-of-war, taken to the max. "To the realm of art," Michael Finkel wrote in a 1996 *Sports Illustrated* article. "Or lowers it to the theater of the absurd." Picture this: Since 1898, across the cold Black River, 150 feet wide at this particular point, **Hope** freshmen are on one shore, sophs on the other. A rope spans the Black River. But to call this line a rope hardly does it justice. Just as, Finkel wrote, *"Referring to The Pull as a tug-of-war is like calling Buckingham Palace a nice house."* This particular rope, the Moby Dick of ropes, is made of three-strand Manila hemp – the best use of hemp since Woodstock? It is two inches thick, 600-foot-long and weighs-in at 648 pounds. On one side are 18 freshmen *Pullers* and 18 sophomore *Pullers* on the far bank. *Pullers* pull, yet far more than their own weight. Tryouts for *The Pull* are open to any **Hope** freshmen or sophomore. An advisory: Practice can be – no, make that is – brutal. Pull wannabes may have to pull on trees, trucks, or on hefty *Pull* alumni. Eventually, 18 *Pullers* are selected for each side, with two alternates per team. The chosen ones will obey the *Constitution of the **Hope** College Freshmen-Sophomore Pull*, a code of conduct of sorts with *a preamble, five articles and 27 bylaws*. *Pullers* are educated in the fine art of pulling by several types of coaches – regular coaches, and an anchor coach as examples. There is also a *Moraler* for each

Puller. *Moralers* are *The Pull's* equivalent of individual cheerleaders. And upperclassmen coach each team. So it's actually the even-years (freshmen & juniors, as an example) against the odd-years (sophs and seniors). The entire college is involved! When a *Puller* chooses his own personal *Moraler*, oftentimes *a tux, a rose, and a bended knee are involved.* "Will you please be my *Moraler*?" How can anyone refuse? And then there is the *Pull-pit.* It's a foxhole about the size of a 2' cube. This is where each *Puller* will do most of his work, and agonizing. In the early years of *The Pull*, teams were prone for the first 15 minutes or so, then stood up simultaneously and pulled from an upright position 'til the bitter – or glorious – end. Nowadays, Pullers dig their own pits – 2 feet deep, 2 feet wide –, spacing them about 18 inches apart, one behind the other. Each pit is reinforced with plywood at the foot, or the end closer to the Black River. As Zach *Lunatic* Johnson explained to Finkel in 1996, "We dig our own graves." The *Puller* lies on his side in the hole, bracing his feet against the plywood, two hands on the rope between his legs. *The Pull* also has its version of a flak jacket: large vests worn by each Puller, cushioned with rolls of toilet paper, or perhaps shag carpet remnants. This is all synchronized, too. Like wrestlers, *Pullers* have moves that must be coordinated: *Heaves. Strains. Counter-rocks. Lock-downs.* All orchestrated by the *head Pull coach*, "Playing the part of the coxswain," as Finkel wrote. Done while standing on a table in front of the first pit and signaling moves. The *Moralers*, in turn, call the signals to the Pullers, since they are often too focused to pay attention to the *head Pull coach*. With the rope already sprayed with fluorescent orange paint in front of each team's first pit, a whistle is blown. *The Pull* begins. And the crowd that often approaches several thousand, goes crazy! *Moralers* are also each *pullers* individual cheering section, often whispering words of encouragement into their *Puller's* ear for 3 hours, or more. The *Pullers* and *Moralers* have long become as one. It's more that urban legend that *many Pullers and Moralers eventually get married due to the true intimacy of the combined effort for The Pull.* Also believe this: not every Puller's a guy. In 1995, Keri Law – *the Sally Ride of the Pull* – became the first woman chosen as a *Puller.* Law, class of 1999, would have competed in that 1995 event but she injured her knee in practice. But she did compete as a Puller in the 1996 Pull. *You go, Keri.*

Some fun *Pull* Facts:

- o *2017 was the 120th Pull;*
- o *The four years when The Pull wasn't held: 1918, 1943 & 1944 (War Years), and 1957 (a flu epidemic on the Hope campus prompted its cancellation);*
- o *The Longest Pull: 1977 – 3 hours, 51 minutes. It was called a draw, one of four ties in Pull history (along with 1916, 1926 and 1952). It also prompted a rule change in 1978: The Pull was limited to a maximum of 3 hours. At the end of 3 hours, judges may declare a winner by measuring the rope again;*
- o *The Shortest Pull: 1956 – 2 minutes, 40 seconds;*
- o *The Shortest Pull after new rules were implemented in 1978: 67 minutes; and,*
- o *Shortest Winning Margin: In 1995, the sophomore class of 1998 won by 2 feet, 10 inches.*

Pull-on, **Hope**.

Indiana (Basketball): *Greatest Timeout in College Basketball*

It's called the *William Tell Overture Timeout* during **Indiana University** home basketball games. It's enough to make the late Clayton Moore, the *Lone Ranger* of TV legend, smile. During the under-8:00 minutes media timeout in the second half of each Hoosier home game, the **IU** Pep Band and cheerleading squad performs the *William Tell Overture* and transforms *Alumni Hall* into one hellacious home-court advantage. While the band blares the overture, cheerleaders race around the court carrying a myriad of eighteen **IU** flags. The *under-8:00 tradition*, which began more than 30 years ago, has often been called *the greatest college timeout in the college basketball.*

Iowa (Football): *Pink Locker Room*

For decades, *everything in the visitor's locker room at Kinnick Stadium has been painted completely pink.* From the walls and lockers all the

way to the urinals, everything is coated pink. Former **Iowa** head coach Hayden Fry started the tradition years ago. After majoring in psychology at **Baylor**, Fry believed that the color pink dampens aggressive and excited behavior, therefore giving his teams a mental edge. As part of a massive renovation of *Kinnick Stadium* in 2004, things got even pinker and that upset some **Iowa** law professors and students, who in 2005 protested the locker room on the grounds that it reinforced stereotypes of women and homosexuals as weak. The protests caused a stir for a while, but *public opinion seemed strongly in favor of the tradition.* As *Washington Post* columnist Sally Jenkins wrote that year, "I'm sure I should be more upset about the pink decor in the visitor's dressing room at **Iowa**. But as it happens, my violent knee-jerk reaction is that it's merely funny. If the armies of feminism want to change my thinking on that, they're going to have to slap electrodes to my pretty little forehead and zap me until I stop giggling."

Kentucky (Basketball): *Ashley Judd – Super fan*

Ashley Judd's *Essay on UK Basketball*, from her website, in 2004: "For 6 months beginning last September, I played the role of "Maggie the Cat" at the Music Box Theatre on Broadway, and I was always highly entertained during my curtain calls when I heard shouts from the audience of, *'Go Big Blue!, Go Cats,'* and the like (they were more frequent than you might think!). I even saw homemade signs, raised by theatre goers who wanted to joyfully express our mutually held passion for college basketball of a certain ilk as well as see Tennessee Williams' great play. But, while I treasured my opportunity on that stage, interpreting one of the greatest roles of all time, I deeply lamented that it prevented me from attending any and all games played by my beloved **University of Kentucky** Wildcats. That is why in February, when during about my 150th performance I severely injured my left foot, the first thought I had after, "OUCH!' was, "Lord, I can probably catch the rest of the games." And indeed, very shortly after I had surgery, I begged my ortho for permission to take a short flight ("But Dr. Ferrell, it's so close! And I'll keep it elevated the whole time!) to **South Carolina** (82-62, **UK**), where I blissfully watched my Wildcats absolutely dominate the Gamecocks on their *Senior Day* (sorry fellas, we do that to **Florida** a lot, too). People often ask me to try to explain why Kentuckians are so nutty about **UK** basketball, like I wear the *Fetish of Abidos* and should know these things. I can only speculate that it is because the Commonwealth is so diverse, from the mountains of the east, from where my family hails going back many generations, to the Bluegrass, where we have our proud tradition of raising the world's best Thoroughbreds, to the west, where the soil is so fertile and our crops are raised, and that basketball provides one single thing to unite us all (hmm, this sounds like the one true ring in *Lord of the Rings*!), of which we can all be proud, about which we can all dialogue (endlessly, I might add). And as a state that has had its hard times, basketball has given us something to distract us from hardships, from coal mines and strikes and poverty, and given us something positive about which to dream. And that dreaming is universal: a pilot once told my Nana that when he flies over the state, he can tell when **UK** is playing. The roads are empty. I was blessed to grow up in different parts of Kentucky, with both my heritage and the bulk of my time having been spent in the eastern part of the state, of which coach Rupp said, "I will lift up mine eyes to the mountains, from whence commeth my help." (That's about the steady stream of boys from the mountains who during 100 years of **UK** basketball have made this program what it is, people.) I took basketball for granted; it was always just there. The school I attended in the 12th grade, Paul G. Blazer, which was earlier called Ashland High School, won the state championship many times, and the *National* in 1928 (*check for possible other nationals titles!*); the wonderful Larry Conley, with whom my dad played junior high ball, came out of there to famously become the heart and soul of *Rupp's Runts*. I loved hearing my Aunt Margaret talk about Papaw Judd taking her and other kids, some of whom died before I came along, to *Memorial Coliseum* in Lexington to see games, driving on old route 60 as the highway hadn't been built yet. And I know that while I was in school elsewhere, my family watched the games on TV with the volume turned down to listen instead to Caywood Ledford's radio broadcast, and I dream of them doing so. When we moved to Tennessee in 1979, I used to wait endlessly on Saturday mornings for the SEC games to come on, and I'd sigh when I saw *Rupp Arena*, wistfully reckoning I knew half the people in the gym. That's a lot of people for a 13 year old to know, but I was homesick. **Kentucky** basketball helps keep 3 generations of my family actively in touch. My great aunts and uncles in Lexington join me for what games I am able to attend, and they send me charming letters accompanying local press clippings about my team, with reminders that our rooms at their houses are still ready and waiting for any spontaneous trips my husband and I might be able to make. My Uncle Mark, whom I adore and revere, and I talk shop; my Aunt Middy told me recently she occasionally gets out their tape of the *'98 Comeback Cats* defeating **Duke**, just to watch it again for renewed pleasure. My dad and I talk about **Kentucky** basketball both practically and poetically, and when he works *CBS* games he calls me so we can bitterly complain (again) about *ACC Billy*. This time we spend together on the premise of **Kentucky** basketball leads to my not only treasuring my relative's company but to an ongoing education about my family's history and fond recollections of those who have gone before us. One unexpected aspect of my fandom that I love is my total equality with all **Kentucky** fans. I am not an actress, I am not a movie star, and I am Judd only insofar as people express pride in their native daughters. I can go to games alone, and have done so many, many times, even on the road. In 2002 I hopped on a plane to **Florida**, took a cab to the gym, and just walked-in, afterwards returning to the humid night air chuffed with my team's 70-68 win and feeling as free as I do when I walk the woods of our farm. At least at that game, however, Donna Smith was expecting me; she wasn't when my brother-in-law's car went out in the first 30 minutes of the *12 Hours of Sebring* race and my husband and I suddenly found ourselves flying home much earlier than expected. I organized the plane to drop him off in Nashville and carry me on to St. Louis to see my Cats. There, I again I took a cab, and just walked the halls of the arena, exchanging hellos and hoots with the faithful, then surprising my friends at the team ticket table. They were able to cough up a ticket for me and I had conniptions of glee along with rest of the *Big Blue Nation* as we watched Tayshaun Prince score 41 points, just like Jack Goose Givens had against **Duke** 20 years earlier in that same gym to bring **UK** its *5th of 7 national titles*. Fans want to celebrate **Kentucky**, talk about match ups, go over specific players and how they are playing (Cliff's defense is awesome! Chuck and Erik pass like they are telepathically connected! How much do you love Ravi's hustle? That Thomas is going to contribute big time next year! I got to meet Joe Crawford and Rajan Rondo!), not chat me up about what movies I have coming or where Salma is. You have no idea what an epic relief that is to me. And, knowing **Kentucky** fans the way I do, I must add: I am not the number one fan. *Number One fans* are many, we are legion. I am just a little more visible than most (except for our *Elvis fan* at the SEC tourney each year!). *I have had the pleasure of getting to know many teams and players*. I get to go backstage, if you will, and enjoy the young men, their basketball IQ, their friendships and bonds, see residuals of game plans and X's and O's on the board, and the quality all-around life education coach Smith and his exceptional staff are giving them. Not to hurt anyone's feelings, but Tony Delk is still my favorite; that boy could flat out play, and while he was awesome to watch doing the obvious things which lead him to be *MVP* of the *'96 Final Four*, he won me over with his defense and the way he could get any sucker in foul trouble. Tony and I went to *Carnegie Deli* in NYC after **UK** won it all and the team party had petered out, and we ate a hilarious amount of food and drank milkshakes, waiting for the papers to come out. Now, who else has a memory like that? *The 2002-03 squad came to our* *house* (fan nirvana, anyone?) after they beat **IUPUI** (***get score, can't find my yearbook***) in Nashville and my friend Cathy, Aunt Dot, and I cooked for them. We were all mutually awestruck, so they ended up eating a whole heck of a lot less than the boosters who came over the next night and were far less numerous! Coach loved our countryside setting, and he kept trying to get the town boys to believe he wanted them to take a walk in the woods with a kerosene lantern. One guy was nearly hysterical at the thought (I'm not naming names!). I made a JuCo joke that Antwain Barbour and I still chuckle over. *The fellas signed a wall that goes down to the basement with fond sentiments in addition to their names and numbers.* That wall, which is

also graced by distinctions granted to me by the people of Kentucky (*Kentucky Colonel, National Arts Award*, etc.) is almost as dear to me as my grandmother's pearls. If I didn't want our future families to be able to see it, I'd have it cremated with me when I go. I really have far too many wonderful memories to even begin sharing, so I'll leave you with my most recent. It's also my most emotional. I went to *Rupp* for *Senior Day*, cast, sinusitis, bronchitis and all (84-62, **UK**). Each home game, *during the first time out in the second half, our cheerleaders (12 time National Champions) slide around the floor spelling "**Kentucky**" and a special person from the crowd is asked to come out to make the "Y," something I have done both alone and with my family.* (Some actually say the way I fired up the crowd with my *hyperactive Y* in 2002 when we were down to **Tennessee** helped us come back to win! Mr. Wildcat was looking at me, mouth gaping and amusement on his face, even some of the players in the huddle couldn't help but stare. But it ended up right, 64-61, **UK**). Anyhow, that day, cheerleader Jason Keough hoisted me onto his brave shoulder to carry me and my **UK** blue cast out to half court, and before the PA had even had a chance to introduce me, I saw that the entire gym (that's 23,000 + people! Have you ever seen a picture of that place?) was giving me a standing ovation. It was the most extraordinary feeling, something you can readily see in my face in the photograph of me with my arms opened wide and eyes closed, soaking up and reciprocating the love and esteem my kindred were giving me. They knew I hadn't been to *Rupp* all season. They know how much it all means to me, how much it meant to my Papaw Judd and Uncle Brian and all those others about whom I have told you. Back at the *Music Box Theatre*, at that very moment my play was closing without me, but I was having the best curtain call of my entire life right there in *Rupp Arena*, feeling adored by the people who mean so very much to me: The people of Kentucky."

Miami (Football): *Smoke Show*

Perhaps nothing sums up the mystique of the **Miami** dynasty in the 1980s and 1990s better than ... *the Smoke. Players run through the tunnel onto the field as white smoke engulfs them, the sound of a hurricane blaring through the speakers.* There is no more intimidating sight than seeing the Canes literally emerging from thin air, like ninjas ready for a fight. But did you know the tradition was started in the 1950s as a way to increase fan interest? **UM** transportation director Bob Nalette decided fire extinguishers would be used to create the smoke. Today, the smoke and the sound of a hurricane are all that is really needed to get everybody in **Miami** juiced-up for a game.

Michigan (Football): *Touch the Banner*

It's an iconic entrance at an iconic stadium to the tune of an iconic fight song. If you haven't seen **Michigan** *touch the banner* at **Michigan** *Stadium*, you haven't been paying attention. Before every game, Wolverines players charge out of the tunnel and *leap to touch the Go Blue: M Club Supports You banner* as the band plays *The Victors*. The tradition *began in 1962* as coach Bump Elliott, looking for a way to inspire his 1-5 team, had boosters hold a banner in the tunnel for players to touch on their way to the field. The banner moved to midfield the next year. Players cherish the banner tradition and abide by two rules: *Don't miss and don't trip.*

Middlebury College: *Picking-Up Butch*

At one college, the *Big Man on Campus* can be found in a wheelchair, fair weather or not. *No finer tradition exists* in the land than in Vermont. At **Middlebury College** where, for more than a half century, freshmen football and basketball players have been *Picking-Up Butch*. That's what they call a *tradition which began in a blizzard in 1961*. Butch Varno was 13 then, born with cerebral palsy and wheelchair-bound on one snowy Saturday during a **Middlebury** Division III football game. Butch's grandmother, a housekeeper at the college dorms, had wheeled him to the stadium about a mile away from their home. During the game, the snow fell and kept falling, and on the way home the elderly lady had trouble pushing Butch. Roger Ralph, then a **Middlebury** student and football player, happened to drive by. He stopped, got out of his car, lifted Butch out of his wheelchair, and took the boy and his grandmother home. With that, *a tradition was born*. Before each opening kickoff, **Middlebury** freshmen basketball players drive to the nursing home where Butch now lives. During hoops season, football players do the honors. Freshmen lift Butch from his wheelchair and into a  college-provided specialty vehicle. They sit beside him during games, helping him to his feet to stand for *The Star Spangled Banner*. They converse with, and especially listen, to Butch. They hold his hands so that he doesn't get tense late in a nail-biter of a ballgame. They hand-feed Butch hot dogs, and take him to the bathroom, before taking him back to the nursing home. "He always likes a hot dog and a Coke," Clark Read, then a 19-year-old power forward, told sportswriter Rick Reilly back in 2003. "It's kind of weird at first, sticking a hot dog in his mouth. The trick is to throw out the last bite so he doesn't get your fingers." "After 30 minutes with Butch, I felt as comfortable with him as anyone I knew," John Donnelly, a senior guard in 2004, told Reilly. "It was nothing like I expected," Donnelly said of his first football adventure with Butch. "He was talking your head off the whole time: 'Hey, buddy, hey buddy...'" "He's always got something to say," Donnelly continued. "What's amazing is how he never gets down. He's always positive. I've never heard a single negative thing out of his mouth. And he's always smiling, loves to see you, no matter who you are." "It kind of puts into perspective how lucky we are to be at this school, playing sports, to be part of this community. He would love to be out there playing basketball, football." "That's the hardest part about having CP: the inconvenience," Butch said. "It took so much away from me. It just totally wiped out my damn career." In a perfect world, in another life, Butch would have liked to be a lawyer. Why? "To help out poor people," he said, "handicapped people." Instead, in this life, as Jack Wilkinson wrote in 2004, *"He's become* **Middlebury's** *inspiration to its sons and daughters of privilege*. In turn, many of them have helped Butch with his daily physical therapy, some also helping him learn to read and study and finally earn his GED. "Without them," he told Wilkinson, "I'd probably be in an institution." Without people like Sarah Smith. "My bread and butter," Butch said one winter's day in 2004. "My motivator ... emotional leader ... best friend ... my big sister." Then a senior and pole vaulter on the track team while majoring in environmental policy, Smith was Butch's primary tutor and therapist and most ardent advocate. She organized a team of students to assist Butch. "Totally amazing," Smith said of her four years working with Butch. For his birthday in November, 2003, Smith and some girlfriends bought Butch a more comfortable seat cushion for his wheelchair. *"Heave the Heap"* was the slogan for Smith's fundraising campaign that ultimately bought Butch a new wheelchair. Smith's most pivotal role was in preparing Butch for the GED high school equivalency diploma exam, then enabling him to take it and pass it. "Without her, I'd be totally wiped out, confused," he said. "She had guts from day one." Eighteen months. That's how long it took Butch to study for the GED. Smith, after finally convincing him to take the exam, tutored him in several subjects. Jeff Brown, then the **Middlebury** men's basketball coach, supplied Middlebury box scores so Butch could sharpen his mathematics skills. State *educators balked at allowing Butch*, for whom writing is very difficult, *to take the test orally. Smith fought. The educators finally consented*. Three days, it took Butch to take the tests. Science was the toughest. *But Butch Varno got – no, earned – his GED*. "The damn struggle was over," Butch recalled. "I just cried. Sarah took me somewhere where I could cry. Don't mention I cried. Men really don't cry." **Middlebury** threw him a graduation party. Someone found a cap and gown for him to wear. Butch flashed his **Middlebury College** ring, the one with his name engraved and also football and basketball logos. He smiled a lot. At least until that May, and every May. May means graduation. "Every year, Butch is an emotional wreck," Jeff Brown told Wilkinson in 2004. "His number one senior graduates, and someone else has to step into that role." The role of the seemingly irreplaceable Smith. "Sarah, that I love," Butch told Wilkinson, his eyes welling with tears. "She helped me through a lot of B.S." "People said I couldn't do things: 'He can't read. He can't write,'" he said, weeping. "She helped me show them I could." "These kids care what happens to me," Butch told Rick Reilly. "They don't have to, but they do. I don't know where I'd be without them. Probably in an institution." But, as Reilly wrote, "That's not the question. The question is, *where would they be without Butch?*" "It makes you think," Ryan Armstrong, then a **Middlebury** freshman wide receiver, told Reilly in 2003. "We're all young athletes. Going to a game or playing in a game, we take it for granted. But then *you go pick up Butch and, I don't know, it makes you feel blessed.*" And an amazing part of this wonderful tradition is that it's now into its 2nd generation, with sons of students that once picked up Butch, now doing the honors. How wonderful is that? And Butch Varno continues to make young athletes feel blessed. All 5-foot-3, 170 pounds of him, who showed them all. A 65+ year-old man who was dealt a bad hand and persevered, and triumphed. He's the better for that. So are the men and women of **Middlebury**. For them, for more than a half century, *Picking-Up Butch* has been a mutually uplifting relationship. *It's the finest tradition in all of college sports.*

Midnight Madness

Lefty started it. **Kentucky** transformed it. Now it can be found almost anywhere: The Madness. No, not *March Madness*. *Midnight Madness*. It has become almost a *secular hoops holiday, the premier preseason tradition in college basketball* and, yes, all of college sports. Especially at **Kentucky**. For that, we can thank the ol' Lefthander: Charles G. Lefty Driesell. *In 1970,* when Driesell was head coach at **Maryland**, he *wanted to get a head start on the season's first practice.* As Lefty later told *ESPN's* Darren Rovell in 2000, "The NCAA told us we could start practice on October 15. Well, I said, that means we can start practicing one minute past midnight on the 14th. So let's get a jump on everybody." As Rovell wrote: "There were no half-court student shots for tuition, or slam dunk contests or hip-hop music to introduce the

Terps to thousands of screaming fans." None of those things that are now staples of *Midnight Madness*. Instead, Lefty took his team to *Byrd Stadium*, the football stadium, for a one-mile *midnight run*. "So we ran our mile on the football field and used the lights from our cars so no one could cut the corners," said Driesell, who actually started his *Madness* at 12:03 a.m. But that's OK. That's Lefty. "It first started out as a gimmick to show that we could start practice before everyone else did," he told Rovell. "Now, everyone does it. "The next year, we must have had 1,000 people watching us run the mile. And the following year, one of my players, Mo Howard, *suggested that we have an inter-squad scrimmage*. Well, I thought that was a pretty good idea, and we had about 8,000 people watching us that year in *Cole Field House*." Howard, however, got hurt in the scrimmage and missed the first few weeks of the season. And, there were other potential pitfalls, including the **Maryland** faculty. "The only bad thing," Lefty told Rovell, "was that if October 15 was on a Wednesday, and you had the practice at midnight on Tuesday, all the teachers complained that the guys couldn't study. So that's *why the NCAA changed it [the starting date of practice] to the first Saturday in October*." After leaving **Maryland**, Driesell coached at **James Madison** and at **Georgia State**. At **GSU**, Lefty and his athletic director, Greg Manning, decided to schedule the first Panthers practice of 2000 on a Saturday morning. *Morning Madness*? Not exactly. "I think it's great that a lot of teams started doing [*Midnight Madness*]," Driesell told Rovell that year. "It gets people talking about basketball." Besides, Lefty said, "College kids stay up all night anyway." So why did he bypass *Friday Midnight Madness* for a morning start? "I don't like staying up to 12 o'clock," Lefty said to Rovell. "I'm 68 now. I'm usually fast asleep by 12. I'll enjoy the sleep and we'll have a better practice on Saturday anyway." A much better season, too. The following March, Lefty led **Georgia State** to just its second NCAA tournament. The Panthers upset **Wisconsin** 50-49 in the first round. Alas, in the second round, **Georgia State** lost to a superior **Maryland** team, 79-60. Lefty didn't lose any sleep over it. More *Midnight Madness* moments: In 1982, **Kentucky** officially promoted a pre-season celebration of *Midnight Madness* ... and *has since turned it into an annual spectacle*. A few years ago, a marriage proposal at one *Midnight Madness* event went viral on the internet. In 1985, *Late Night in the Phog* debuted at **Kansas** in *Phog Allen Fieldhouse*. The Jayhawks practiced, yes, but there were giveaways for fans, classic **KU** videos on the overhead scoreboard screens, some players shooting half-court shots, others throwing down thunderous dunks to roars. Most *Midnight Madness'* schools will include a 3-point shooting contest with a dunk-a-thon and long-range heaves. The *Madness* is now often a coed event, for both men's and women's teams, especially at colleges like **UConn** and **Baylor**, whose 6-foot-8 Brittany Greiner – the *National Player of the Year* in 2012 when **Baylor** went 40-0 and won the *National Title* – can dunk with the big boys. *Midnight Madness*, by any name, is also used as a recruiting tool. *Scout.com* estimated that in 2007, 160 of the top high school basketball recruits in the country attended *Midnight Madness* somewhere. That number has since increased exponentially. And now, in the 21st

century, *Midnight Madness* has become even more lavish and extravagant, with celebrities included. One year, **Michigan State** coach Tom Izzo rode onto the court at the *Breslin Center* astride a Harley-Davidson. Izzo was dressed like a hippy, as in *Easy Rider*. Then he posed with *Sparty*, the Spartans' in-costume mascot. That **Michigan State** team won the 2000 *National Championship*. The following season for *Midnight Madness*, the Spartans – wearing boxing gloves and green satin robes – were introduced as they stepped through the ropes of a boxing ring. Izzo? He arrived in a  white stretch limousine, dressed in a black tuxedo. Another year, Billy Donovan, the two-time NCAA-winning **Florida** coach, rose up out of a coffin in the *O-Dome* during *Midnight Madness*. In 2012, Izzo made another grand entrance at the *Breslin Center* attired in an *Iron Man* costume while his wife and children were dressed as other *Marvel Avengers*. The *IZZone* student section went bananas. In 1994, on the **University of Cincinnati** campus, a student named Cory Clouse brought down the house. Having already won the slam dunk and 3-point shooting contests, Clouse launched a half-court shot in *the Shoe*, as the on-campus *Shoemaker Center* is still known. Clouse cleanly nailed the 47-footer to earn a free year of college tuition, and more. *Dick Vitale jumped into his arms*. And more importantly, in the summer of 1995, Cory Clouse won an *ESPY* for his *Midnight Madness* moment. At **Indiana**, it's *Hoosier Hysteria*. *Tubby's Tipoff*, they called it at **Minnesota**. In Madison, it's *The Night of the Grateful Red* at **Wisconsin**. At **Missouri's** *Midnight Madness* in 2012, Keion Bell dunked over six people lined up in size-order from the foul line to the basket. Wagner's Josh Thompson dunked over his parents, standing back-to-back, even if Dad got conked in the head. Brittney Griner nearly threw down *a 360-degree dunk*. But nobody – and we mean nobody – does *Midnight Madness* like they do it in the Bluegrass. At **Kentucky**. In October of 1982, coach Joe B. Hall, recalling Lefty's stroke of *Midnight genius*, invited **Kentucky** fans to attend *Midnight Special*, the first practice of that season. More than 8,500 fans showed up in old 12,000-seat *Memorial Coliseum*. It shortly became *Midnight Madness*. And, by any name, it's in a class all its own. In 1986, a fire marshal ordered the doors of *Memorial* closed two hours before the *Madness* was scheduled to start. More than 12,500 *Big Blue zealots* were already inside, with hundreds more stuck outside. In 1990, according to the **UK** website, Wildcats fans reveled in a *Big Blue New Year*. In 1991, *fans lined up 36 hours in advance for Back in the Spotlight*. For the first time in the Rick Pitino era, **UK** was off probation and again eligible for the postseason. The doors were closed 45 minutes after they opened, the earliest closing ever. All four Kentucky recruits who attended *Big Blue Madness* that year – Rodrick Rhodes, Jared Prickett, Tony Delk and Walter McCarty – verbally committed to **UK** the next week. In 1996, Kentucky would win the NCAA title. In 1992, *Big Boo Madness* appeared on Halloween Night. *Fans began arriving five days early for the event, then 17.* And finally there was Wally Clark, *who got in line to claim his spot 38 days before more Madness ensued*. Jump ahead to 2000: Some tickets – all are free – were available on the internet for the first time. All 700 were gone in the first 13 minutes. The remaining 8,000 were long gone in 10 minutes to those who'd waited in line. In 2002, to celebrate the 100th season of **Kentucky** basketball, popular long-time equipment manager Bill Keightley jumped out of an enormous birthday cake to the delight of the **UK** faithful. In 2005, *Big Blue Madness* was held in *Rupp Arena* for the first time, due to construction of the new basketball practice facility at *Memorial Coliseum*. *More than 23,000 tickets were snapped-up in less than 48 hours*. As the school also noted, **UK** fans *broke the national attendance record for a practice*. *Midnight Madness*, or *Big Blue Madness*, is annually televised by *ESPN* on several of its networks. Telecasts can last several hours, featuring footage from several colleges around the country. Just because you can't actually be there doesn't mean you can't watch *Midnight Madness*. At *Big Blue Madness 2012*, **Kentucky** raised its eighth *National Championship* banner from its title game win over **Kansas**. It also celebrated its seven previous titles, raising those banners, too. There were videos, skits, dancing. When coach John Calipari told the crowd, "I came here to win *National Championships* for you," the noise was deafening. The court at *Rupp Arena* was covered by an enormous white cloth, and used as a movie screen to show animations and highlights projected from high above. *Nearly 600 tents had been pitched outside Memorial Coliseum for the distribution of free Big Blue Madness tickets* – four to a person – on September 22. They were gone in a half hour. Good luck with trying to scalp some, not that some folks didn't try. And as for those four heralded freshmen? Kentucky fans got their first look at Nerlens Noel, Willie Cauley-Stein, Archie Goodwin and Alex Poythress together in action. They, too, all four of 'em, attended *Big Blue Madness* the previous year.

Mississippi State: *Cowbells*

The *most unique and certainly the most resounding symbol* of **Mississippi State University** *tradition is the cowbell*. Despite decades of attempts by opponents and authorities to banish it from scenes of competition, diehard **State** fans still celebrate Bulldog victories loudly and proudly with the distinctive sound of ringing cowbells. The precise origin of the cowbell as a fixture of **Mississippi State** traditions remains unclear. The best records have cowbells gradually introduced to the **MSU** sports scene *in the late 1930s and early 1940s*, coinciding with **Mississippi State's** football success prior to World War II. The most popular legend is that during a home football game

between **State** and arch-rival **Ole Miss**, a jersey cow wandered onto the playing field. **Mississippi State** soundly whipped the Rebels that Saturday, and **State College** students immediately *adopted the cow as a good luck charm*. Students are said to have continued bringing a cow to football games for a while, until the practice was eventually discontinued in favor of bringing just the cow's bell. Whatever the origin, it is certain that *by the 1950s cowbells were common at* **Mississippi State** *games, and by the 1960s were established as the special symbol of* **Mississippi State**. In the 1960s two **MSU** professors obliged some students by welding handles on the bells to they could be rung with much more convenience and authority. By 1963 the demand for these long-handled cowbells could not be filled by home workshops alone, so the *Student Government Association* bought bells in bulk and the *Industrial Education Club* agreed to weld on the handles. In 1964 the **MSU** Bookstore began marketing these cowbells with a portion of the profits returning to student organizations. *In 1974, the SEC adopted a rule against artificial noisemakers that made it illegal to ring a cowbell during games*. Despite creative efforts by **MSU** fans to circumvent the ruling and continue the tradition, *the ban was in effect until 2010*. That spring, the twelve schools of the SEC agreed to a compromise on artificial noisemakers, *acknowledging the role cowbells play in the history of* **Mississippi State University** *by amending the conference by-law*. In the fall of 2010, on a one-year trial with specified restrictions, *cowbells were permitted in Davis Wade Stadium for the first time in 36 years*. And due to **MSU** fans' notable adherence to the rules outlined by the league, cowbells have been allowed at **MSU** home football games since with similar restrictions in place. But it isn't just at home games. Fans always bring their bells to bowl games, and other games where they wish to make-a-statement.

Notre Dame (Football): *Painting the Gold Helmets*

On Monday evenings, prior to each game, *the team's student managers paint all football helmets gold*, using paint containing real 23.9 karat gold dust. The gold particles that are used on the helmet were collected from the re-gilding on the **Notre Dame** dome in 2007.

Notre Dame (Football): *Play Like a Champion Today*

As every **Notre Dame** player leaves the locker room for a home game, they slap a sign that says *"PLAY LIKE A CHAMPION TODAY."* That sign has been printed over 25,000 times onto coffee mugs, T-shirts, and many other novelty items. And you would think **Notre Dame** is happy for the rights to this sign. But, in reality, *all the money from reproducing the sign goes to the painter who made it* – Laurie Wenger. The story, of course, begins with Lou Holtz, who was the new football coach at **Notre Dame** in 1986. Lou is said to have been leafing thru old football photos and saw a sign in **Oklahoma's** locker room from the late 1940's – early 1950's that said *"Play like a Champion Today."* So Lou decided he must have a similar sign. He dispatched one of his assistant coaches to **Notre Dame's** sign shop. It took about three days to finish, and Holtz loved it and had it hung on the wall of a narrow

staircase leading to the field. "I told my players, 'Every time you hit this sign, I want you to remember all the great people that played here before you, all the sacrifices that your teammates have made for you, all the people, your coaches, your parents, who are responsible for you being here.'" Holtz believed in the sign so much that *he had Laurie make another one and took it with him to road games*. When one former player asked for a copy of the sign, the sign maker decided maybe a trademark might be appropriate. *Good call*. And even though she was employed by the school at the time, since the sign did not mention the school's name, *all was good with her personal trademark*.

Oklahoma (Football): *Boomer & Sooner*

The mascot present at all football games is the *Sooner Schooner*, a *Conestoga wagon*, pulled by two crème white ponies, *Boomer* & *Sooner*. In time for the 2005 football season, two new costumed mascots, based on the ponies who pull the *Schooner* were created, named appropriately, *Boomer* and *Sooner*. *The costumed mascots are identical to each other except for their eye color*. One has blue eyes, while the other has green eyes. Before, the *Boomer* & *Sooner* costume mascots, **OU** was also represented by *Top Dawg*. *Top Dawg* did some appearances at football games, but was *primarily used at wrestling and basketball events*. The *Sooner Schooner* leads the football team's entrance to the field.

Oklahoma / Oklahoma State (Various Sports): *Bedlam Series*

Bedlam. It's been the word of choice to describe the **Oklahoma / Oklahoma State** rivalry since the very *first football game between the two schools in 1904*. That game, played in cold and windy conditions, saw a punt carry over the Cowboys' return man and roll down a hill into an icy creek. Both teams dove in to recover the ball, and the *Sooners* eventually came up with it and scored a touchdown as a result. Why **Oklahoma** fought so hard for that ball in a game in which they won 75-0 is a mystery, but the tradition of craziness between these two rivals was born. It eventually came to incorporate a total of *17 other sports*, with the wrestling matches between the two national powerhouses being a marquee event. The *Bedlam Series* was officially formalized in 1999, with the winner of each head-to-head competition receiving points. In sports where there is no head-to-head matchup, the Big 12 final standings are used instead. No one sport can dominate the rivalry, which is a good thing, considering that **Oklahoma** has a nearly 5-to-1 lead in the all-time series on the gridiron.

Oklahoma / Texas (Football): *Red River Rivalry / 3 Trophies*

First played in 1900, the showdown between the *Longhorns* and *Sooners* – known far and wide as the *Red River Rivalry* – has become *one of college football's best and most bitter rivalries*. Though the **Oklahoma / Texas** series officially began in 1900, the game truly arrived *in 1929 – the year it was first played in the neutral-site city of Dallas*. The city is located approximately halfway between Norman, Oklahoma (home of the *Sooners*) and Austin, Texas (home of the *Longhorns*). *The storied old Cotton Bowl has played host to the game since 1937.* On game day – which is always scheduled in early October, *during the Texas State Fair* – the stadium is split in half, with **Texas** fans on one side of the 50-yard-line and *Sooners* fans on the other. The scene is similar to the one that plays out each year in Jacksonville, Florida, where **Florida** battles **Georgia** in another classic neutral-site rivalry. The good news is that the *Red River Rivalry* will likely remain in Dallas for a few years to come. The schools complained about the state of the *Cotton Bowl*, and publicly contemplated *making the rivalry into a traditional home-and-home affair*. But Dallas responded. An agreement increased the payout to each school for each game to $850,000 and also committed Dallas to a massive renovation of the *Cotton Bowl*. The *Red River Rivalry* gets its name from – what else? – the Red River, which separates the states of Texas and Oklahoma. For decades, the game was called the *Red River Shootout*, but starting in 2005, the name was officially changed to the *SBC Red River Rivalry*. The next year, it was changed once more, to the *AT&T Red River Rivalry*. No matter what it's called, however, this much is certain: the game is always a knock-down, drag-out affair *between two schools that truly don't like each other*. The series has been made especially bitter because of the fact that, dating all the way back to **Oklahoma's** Bud Wilkinson glory days in the 1950s, much of the *Sooners'* top talent has been recruited out of Texas. As former **Oklahoma** coach Barry Switzer once told *USA Today*: "No game carries with it the atmosphere, the excitement, the energy level that the **Oklahoma / Texas** game does. When you hit the floor of the *Cotton Bowl*, there's electricity. And if you don't feel it, you ought to have your saliva checked." The winner of the *Red River Rivalry* takes home, not just one but, *three different trophies*. The oldest is the *Golden Hat*, a bronzed ten-gallon hat, which is *given to the athletic department of the winning school*. The *Red River Rivalry Trophy*, first created in 2003, is *given to the student government of the winning school*. And the *Governors' Trophy is exchanged by the governors of each state*.

Ole Miss (Football): *Tailgating at the Grove*

Tailgating is an integral part of the college football experience. But while fans of every team *tailgate*, **Ole Miss** fans *do it with style and more than a little class. The Grove* is a shaded 10-acre patch of grass in Oxford, Mississippi, that on game days is filled with red and white and blue tents. More than a few candelabras can be seen, and food eaten by Southern belles and men in coats and ties, is often served on the best china. Don't forget a stop at the *Hot Toddy Potty* (seriously) after you've sipped your share of your favorite beverage.

Oregon: *Duck Mascot*

It began in 1947, when Oregon's first athletic director, Leo Harris, had a flash of athletic director genius. This was long before Phil Knight turned an athletic shoe company into a corporate colossus. More than a half century before the Nike founder outfitted his alma mater's football team in those wonderful uniforms the Ducks now don. Back in 1947, the **Oregon** *Ducks were just the Ducks*, if not just any Ducks. *Disney Ducks. Specifically, Donald Ducks*. Or as author Ray Franks wrote in his 1982 book *What's in a Nickname? – Exploring the Jungle of College Athletic Mascots*, *"Donald Duck and the Oregon Duck … one and the same!"* According to Franks, *"Until the 1920s*, the **University of Oregon** *had no athletic mascot*. But during that decade, the local media began referring to the **UO** teams as the *Webfooters*, eventually shortened to *Webfoots*. The name became official in 1926 when a student body election was held to designate a mascot. *Webfoots* won another election, this one in 1932, to again be named the mascot of the **UO** teams." Shortly after that, Franks found, "the name *Ducks began being substituted for Webfoots*, usually in newspaper headlines." In 1947, Leo Harris *reached a handshake agreement with Walt Disney: Donald Duck's likeness could serve as the* **Oregon** *mascot, as long as it was done, and used, in good taste.* The deal, unique at the time, stood for 20 years. *Walt Disney Productions* provided several versions of Donald for **Oregon's** use, which continued until the cartoon genius Disney died in 1966. *Upon his death, both parties realized no formal contract had ever been signed granting the* **University of Oregon** *the rights to Donald Duck's image.* As evidence, Harris could only offer a photograph taken two decades earlier showing the late Disney wearing an **Oregon** letterman's jacket with the **Oregon** *Duck* clearly visible on the front of the jacket. Not to worry. In 1973, Disney representatives agreed to negotiate the first written contract for **Oregon's** *athletic department to continue using Donald's image*. This was Donald Duck, a beloved worldwide, web-footed cartoon icon who was universally adored. Alas, even when Disney gave **Oregon** the OK to use Donald's cartoon image, there were problems. Jerry Frei, the *Ducks'* head football coach for five seasons from 1967-71, wanted Donald to sport teeth in his orange grill, to better portray his team's *Fighting Ducks* image. What was Frei thinking? Far worse was the moniker new **Oregon** men's basketball coach Dick Harter concocted upon

arriving in Eugene in 1971. Harter, a hard-nosed, hard-headed, defensive-minded authoritarian refused to even acknowledge the *Ducks* nickname, much less allow the image of Donald Duck to be used in connection with men's basketball. *The Kamikaze Kids*. That's what Harter called his players, insisting that any publicity materials from the university athletic media relations department refer to his team as just that. *The Kamikaze Kids*. Somewhere, Walt Disney was not smiling.

Oregon / Oregon State (Football): *Civil War*

In *the oldest college football rivalry in the Pacific Northwest*, **Oregon** and **Oregon State** have been engaged in a *Civil War* since they *first met in 1894*. This rivalry has seen both the lowest-of-lows and highest-of-highs: the 1983 game, commonly referred to as the *Toilet Bowl*, featured 16 turnovers and 4 missed field goals and was the last college football game to end in a 0-0 tie. On the other side of the coin, the 2009 game – a 37-33 **Oregon** victory – was *the first in series history in which the winner was guaranteed a spot in the Rose Bowl*. The winner of this game receives the *Platypus Trophy*, which is an animal that depicts *the features of both a duck and a beaver* (the two schools' mascots). For three years, from 1959 to 1961, *the trophy* was awarded to the winning school, before being lost for the next 44 years. It was rediscovered in 2005 and remains the game's unofficial trophy, and is awarded to the *alumni association* of the winning school.

Penn (Football): *Toast Toss*

"Here's a toast to dear old Penn"

Literally.

The *Toast Toss* happens *between the third and fourth quarters of every home football game at Penn*. For several decades, the tradition between the third and fourth quarter was for students to sing a song entitled *Drink a Highball*. They held their glasses high while singing, and when they reached the final line, *"...here's a toast to dear old Penn!"* they drank their highballs. Needless to say, the university tried to crack down on this practice and eventually banned alcohol from the stadium. The idea for the *Toast Toss* came from *The Rocky Horror Picture Show*. As you might know, that movie is very interactive, and includes a part where the audience throws toast at the screen. Members of the **Penn** Band saw the movie and got the idea to throw toast as they sang the final line of *Drink a Highball*. *It has been a tradition ever since*.

Rivalry Games

Once, while coaching the *New York Jets*, an exasperated Herm Edwards famously yelled at the press, "You play ... to win ... *THE* GAME!" Not just any game, but *The Game*. *The rivalry game:* that annual *Hatfield-McCoy* affair with your archrival. So what do you win? How about a $30,000 Waterford crystal football? That'd be nice, but that went to the *BCS National Champion*. Crystal's fine, but it's no *Floyd of Rosedale*. *T*hat sounds like a caller to a sports talk radio program – *"Floyd of Rosedale*, you're on the air." But it is actually the trophy given to the winner of the **Iowa / Minnesota** football game. *It's a trophy of a pig*. A pig named *Floyd*. In 1935, the governors of Minnesota and Iowa placed a wager on the *Gophers-Hawkeyes game*. The previous year, the *Gophers* had battered **Iowa's** Ozzie Simmons. So tensions were running higher than the price of pork futures. Especially after Iowa Governor Clyde Herring warned, "If the officials stand for any rough tactics

like **Minnesota** used last year, I'm sure the crowd won't." Clyde's gubernatorial counterpart, Floyd Olson (no relation to *Floyd of Rosedale*) responded, "Minnesota folks are excited over your statement about Iowa crowds lynching the **Minnesota** football team. I have assured them you are law abiding gentlemen and are only trying to get our goat … *I will bet you a Minnesota prize hog against an Iowa prize hog that Minnesota wins*." True to his word, Governor Herring walked into Olson's office after **Minnesota's** 13-6 triumph. He brought along *Floyd of Rosedale, a prize-winning hog*. And so began the handoff. *The ceremonial passing-of-the-pig*. Eventually, time passed, as did *Floyd*. In his memory, the winner of the **Iowa / Minnesota** game now claims a 15 and ½ -inch high, 21-inch long bronze statue of a prized porker: *Floyd of Rosedale*. The *Historically Black Colleges and Universities* often play their equivalent of bowl games during the season. They're called various *"Classics,"* and they are, especially when a rivalry is involved. You want cups? There is everything from the assorted *Governors'*

Cups, including **Georgia / GA Tech**, to the *Apple Cup*, which big-time rivals **Washington** and **Washington State** have fought over since 1900. And there is the delightfully-named *Apothecary Cup*. It pits the **Albany College of Pharmacy** and the **St. Louis College of Pharmacy**. The *Canal Cup*? That goes to the winner of the *Battle of the Bridge*, an all-sport competition between **Niagara University** and **Canisius College.** Those teams cross the *Grand Island Bridge* in upstate New York to play each other. The *most patriotic and meaningful trophy of all* is the *Commander-in-Chief Trophy*, awarded to the winner of the **Army**, **Navy** and **Air Force** football rivalries. If there's no outright winner, then the *Commander in Chief Trophy* stays put, until one of the *Service Academies* beats the other two in the same season. The *1899 Territorial Cup*? That goes to the winner of the annual **Arizona / Arizona State** football game. In 2001, the *1899 Territorial Cup* received NCAA Division I designation as *the oldest*

rivalry trophy in the United States. On November 30, 1899, Thanksgiving Day in Tempe, the then-**Arizona Territorial Normal School** beat **Arizona** 11-2 before *a reported crowd of 300*. Over the years, as with many rivalry trophies, the prized, silver-plated antique was misplaced. So for the *Big Game*, as **Arizona** and **Arizona State** called their rivalry, other awards needed to suffice. A *Governor's Trophy*, a *Victory Sculpture* by artist Ben Goo and a bronze *Saguaro Trophy*, were all used before, thankfully, the *1899 Territorial Cup* was finally discovered in the basement of a church that was being demolished. Since then, to ensure its safety, the (quite valuable)

Territorial Cup is moved from one school to another only under escort and with the supervision of gloved archivists. My family and I were very fortunate to see it awarded in 2013, for the victory in 2012. According to the NCAA, the previously oldest trophy was the **Michigan / Minnesota** *Little Brown Jug*, also awarded in 1899. The great thing about ancient, traditional rivalries is that each year, everything old is renewed again. What about a *Cortaca Jug*? The *Biggest Little Game in the Nation*. That's what *Sports Illustrated* anointed the November football rivalry between **Ithaca College** and **Cortland**, two campuses in New York about 20 miles apart. As for the *Cortaca Jug*: CORT-land vs. ith-ACA. Get it? The *Cortaca Jug* is the travelling trophy between these Division III teams who've developed one of the classic DIII rivalries. The **Ithaca** *Bombers* and *Red Dragons* of **Cortland** draw big crowds, often doubling the 5,000 capacity of **Ithaca's** *Butterfield Stadium*. There's often much at stake. In 1988, in the second-to-last week of the regular season, **Ithaca** and **Cortland** were ranked first and second nationally in DIII. **Cortland** prevailed; but three weeks later the *Bombers* beat the *Red Dragons* in the NCAA playoffs en route to winning the *Division III National Championship*. Nothing else, however, trumps taking home the *Cortaca Jug*. In the market for household furnishings? It's almost as if college sports' rivalries are an enormous, flea market. Need a *Beanpot*, perhaps? That's what the winner receives in Boston's yearly hockey classic between **Boston College, Boston University, Harvard and Northeastern**. How about a skillet? No ordinary frying pan. The *Iron Skillet* first awarded to the winner of the **SMU / TCU** game, back in their Southwest Conference halcyon days. A *beer barrel,* you say? Maybe not in these politically correct times? It goes to the winner of the **Tennessee** versus **Kentucky** football game. And while it is clearly a beer barrel, the sign on the side says *"ice water,"* in deference to the *Temperance Groups*, way-back-when. Yet you can still hope for a keg. The *Keg of Nails*, courtesy of either **Cincinnati** or **Louisville**. Anyone for a *War Canoe*? Or an authentic *Totem Pole* with two names? **Middle Tennessee** calls it *Harvey*. To **Tennessee Tech** students, it's *Sin-a-Ninny*. This pigskin tradition began in the 1960s before the *totem pole* disappeared for several years. How's this for a *Bucket List*? The *Bayou Bucket*, which goes to the winner of the **Houston / Rice** football game. The *Old Brass Spittoon* belongs to the winner of the **Indiana** versus **Michigan** football game. It's not to be confused with the *Brass Spittoon* awarded to the **New Mexico State / UTEP** football winner. The *Old Oaken Bucket*, which neither **Indiana** nor **Purdue** would ever spit into, dates perhaps to *Civil War* times. The actual bucket itself, not the game. The *Paint Bucket*, no primer necessary. And a personal favorite of mine: The *Slab of Bacon Trophy*, which **Minnesota** and **Wisconsin** long fought over in football until 1948. The two schools first played in 1890, when

Minnesota beat **Wisconsin** 63-0. More than a half century later, the *Slab of Bacon Trophy* was lost following a post-game melee in which students and spectators ran wildly around the field. **Wisconsin** officials say that the *Slab of Bacon* disappeared in 1945, yet the scores of every **Minnesota / Wisconsin** game from 1930-70 were written on the back of the *slab*. Regardless, it was replaced in 1948 by *Paul Bunyan's Axe*. On the six-foot long handle is emblazoned the results of each *Badgers-Gophers* game. That's great, but it's not a *Slab of Bacon*. And what goes better with bacon than eggs? The annual *Egg Bowl* between **Ole Miss** and **Mississippi State**. What about an *axe*? The *Axe* goes to the winner of *The Big Game* – the annual **Cal / Stanford** football epic. When it comes to **Cal / Stanford**, think big, really big. When it's the **Cal / Stanford** rivalry, everything – not just football's *Big Game* – is B-I-G. It's not **Cal / Stanford** volleyball, it's the *Big Spike*. Water polo? That's the *Big Splash*. Ice hockey? Easy: the *Big Freeze*. And **Cal / Stanford** Crew? That was the *Big Row*. But in 2011, it was renamed the *Jill Row,* in honor of Jill Costello, the **Cal** coxswain who lost her year-long battle with lung cancer. Ironically, Jill was a non-smoker. Some treasures are nothing to shake-a-*stick* at. The *Old Hickory Stick*, for example, goes to the **Northwest Missouri State / Truman State** football winner. Other gridiron riches sound almost *Olympian*. Think Gold, Silver, Bronze. There is the *Golden Hat*: the **Oklahoma / Texas** winner gets a ten-gallon cowboy hat on a wooden block. The *Silver Spade*: **New Mexico State / UTEP**. The *Bronze*

Derby: **Newberry / Presbyterian**. Boots? We have boots. The *Golden Boot*: **Arkansas / LSU**. The *Beehive Boot*: **BYU / Utah / Utah State**. The *Bronze Boot*: **Colorado State / Wyoming**. Instead of a *spittoon*, anyone care for a *Peace Pipe*? Or the *Shillelagh*, a Gaelic war club that's gone to the winner of the **Notre Dame / Southern Cal** football game since 1952. It's made of oak or thorn saplings from Ireland. The *Shillelagh* is adorned with *ruby red Trojan heads* with *the score and year* of **USC** wins, and *emerald-studded shamrocks* for *Fighting Irish victories*. In Los Angeles, the cherished *Victory Bell* goes to the winner in the *crosstown rivalry* between **UCLA** and **USC**. The winning school gets possession of the 295-pound *Victory Bell*, if only briefly. One of the *least-seen trophies in the land*, the *Victory Bell* sits in a vault for all but two days of the year. It's displayed in the stadium during the first three quarters of the **UCLA / USC** game, and on the following Monday, on the winning team's campus. Then it goes back into hiding. There's also *weaponry* to be won, from a *Musket* to a once-upon-a-time *Kit Carson Rifle* (no longer awarded), to a *Cannon* with a few screws loose. The **University of Nevada** and **UNLV** play for the *Fremont Cannon*. At 545 pounds, *it's the heaviest* and among the most expensive trophies in college football, and a replica of a howitzer cannon used by explorer John C. Fremont on an 1843 expedition in the *Sierra Nevada's*. The *Sweet Sioux Tomahawk* was once awarded to the winner of the annual **Illinois / Northwestern** football game. In these 21st century times, the *tomahawk* has been replaced with the *Land of Lincoln Trophy*. It's a bronze replica of *Honest Abe's stovepipe hat*. Speaking of hats, in 1993, **Lycoming College** and **Susquehanna University** turned their game into a *Stagg party*. The annual *Stagg Hat Game*. The trophy: *the late Amos Alonzo Stagg's actual fedora* he wore as the grand old man of college football coaching. Stagg won 314 games in a legendary career that began at the **University of Chicago** and ended at **Susquehanna**. His hat was bronzed and later given to the university as a gift. It sat displayed in a trophy case for several years before the *Stagg Hat Game* began in 1993. But, sadly, the game is no longer played due to conference alignment. And then there's the non-paralleled **Lafayette / Lehigh** game — *the most played and longest uninterrupted rivalry in college football*. They've tackled each other 150+ times since 1884 with one interruption, in 1896. I witnessed the 148th rendition, when they announced the 150th game would be played in *Yankee Stadium*. And the crowd went wild! These two Pennsylvania campuses are just 17 miles apart (a resemblance to **Duke** and **UNC's** distance apart). *The Rivalry*, as it's simply known, is so ancient that *it predates football trophies*. How cool is that? The winning team *gets the game ball, painted with the final score and date*. **Lafayette / Lehigh** has been the subject of several books and a *PBS* television documentary narrated by the late, great sportscaster Harry Kalas. Since 1938, **North Dakota** and **North Dakota State** have slugged it out on the gridiron in hopes of winning the *Nickel Trophy*. It weighs 75 pounds and is a large *replica of a nickel*. And, of course, it has been the object of many raids, thefts, recoveries, and returns over the years. But don't try to pilfer the *Chief Caddo Trophy.* It's the *largest football trophy in the country*,

and goes to the winner of the **Northwestern State / Stephen F. Austin** football game. The *Chief's* a big dude, standing 7'6", and weighing more than 320 pounds. He's over

50 years old, having been carved from a 2,000-pound black gum log after the 1961 rivalry game. The statue is named in honor of the *Caddos*, a Native American tribe indigenous to the area. Legend has it that a *Caddo* chief and his two sons were responsible for settling Nacogdoches, Texas, and Natchitoches, Louisiana, each school's respective cities. **Michigan / Minnesota** have the rich history of *the Little Brown Jug*. But of the many hundreds of *rivalry trophies* not mentioned here, please don't forget the ultimate parting gift – when either **Iowa** or **Minnesota** brings home the bacon – *Floyd of Rosedale*.

Rose Bowl

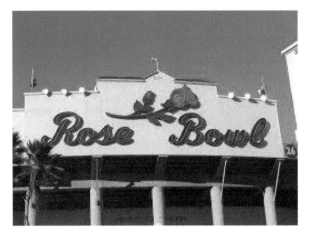

Nicknamed the *Granddaddy of Them All*, the *Rose Bowl* is *the oldest postseason game in college football*. The game, long known for its scenic setting, frequently ends just as the sun goes down over the *Arroyo Seco* on *New Year's Day*. It is also preceded by the *Tournament of Roses Parade*, which draws upwards of 700,000 spectators every year. Contrary to popular belief, the *Rose Bowl* was not always a grudge match between the Pac 12 (or its predecessor, the PCC) and the Big 10. The first *Rose Bowl*, a 49-0 **Michigan** victory over **Stanford**, that was called midway through the third quarter, was considered such a failure that *the game was not played again for 15 years*. Once football was reinstated, the *Tournament of Roses Committee* was not exactly eager to invite Big Ten opponents. The next thirty *Rose Bowls* included only two current members of the conference, one of which (**Penn State** in 1923) was an independent at the time. It was not until *1947 that the Rose Bowl became an annual matchup between the two conferences*, with the two champions guaranteed to meet in Pasadena every year until the advent of the *BCS* in 1998. For many years, the *Rose Bowl* was the largest football stadium in the country, holding a maximum capacity of 104,091 at its peak. While it has since been down-sized, it is still the largest stadium that hosts a bowl game and remains one of the most coveted tickets of the college football postseason. The *Rose Bowl* also *introduced television to the sport*, as the 1952 game between **Illinois** and **Stanford** was among the first to be seen by a national audience.

Southern Cal (Football): *Conquest & Traveler*

Whenever **USC** scores, the band plays *Conquest*, and since 1961, *Traveler –* their beautiful white horse *– gallops around the Coliseum.* The current horse is Traveler VII. Traveler's rider is dressed as an idealized Trojan warrior, and is often mistaken for Tommy Trojan -- the Trojan portrayed in USC's

famous Trojan Shrine statue; however, the rider is unnamed and simply designated as a Trojan warrior with Traveler recognized as the official mascot. For the original Trojan rider, USC used its connections to the film industry to procure the costume worn by Charlton Heston in *Ben Hur.* That costume proved to be too heavy for extended use, so a leather uniform was made for the 1962 season, and the same costume has been used since. And, interesting to me is the fact that each of Traveler's riders is a USC alumni, not a current student, as is the case with riders of most other horse mascots.

Streaking

Yes, *streaking* (running naked) still exists on many campuses, sometimes to even raise money for charity. Most are yearly events, although others happen more often. Below are a few examples:

Bucknell	*Lacrosse Streaking*
UC – Davis	*Naked Mile*
UC – Santa Cruz	*First Rain*
UC – Berkeley	*Moffitt Library*
Caltech, San Luis Obispo	*Streak Hathaway*
Centre College	*Running the Flame*
Concordia University	*Naked Man Snow Angel Run*
Denison University	*Naked Ultimate Frisbee*

Fredonia State	*Naked Library Run*
Chicago	*Regenstein Library*
Dartmouth College	*Blue Light Challenge*
Hamilton College / Colgate / Princeton / Williams	
Streak Competitively Against Other Schools	
Lawrence University	*Senior Streak*
Lewis & Clark College	*Naked Mile*
North Carolina	*The Undergraduate Library*
Michigan	*Naked Mile*
Notre Dame	*LaFortune Student Center*
Penn State	*Mifflin Road*
Princeton	*Various Running-a-Streak*
Rice	*Baker 13*
Swarthmore College	*Dash for Cash*
Tufts	*Naked Quad Run*
Union College	*Naked Nott Ride*
Vermont	*Naked Bike Ride*
Virginia	*Rotunda to Statue of Homer*
Wheaton College	*Kingdom Run*
William & Mary	*Naked Triathlon*
Yale	*Naked Punt Returns*

Taylor University (Basketball): *Silent Night*

A favorite in-game tradition of mine is *Silent Night*, as only the crowd at tiny **Taylor University** in Upland, Indiana, can perform it. On a weekend in December, just before final exams and for more than 25 years now, **Taylor** students play the *pajama game*. They *wear pajamas to the gym and, at least initially, no one speaks or cheers*. Not when the teams warm up, not when the starting lineups are introduced, not even when play begins. Not until **Taylor** *scores their 10th point*. Then the gym erupts. Fans stand and roar. Students race up the sideline and across the baseline. It's a sonic boost to the *Trojans'* ego, and the small gymnasium at the NAIA evangelical Christian school in Upland, Indiana, might as well be *Alumni Hall*. "It sounds like an episode of Oprah, and she's giving something away," Tony Reali of *ESPN's Pardon the Interruption* once said on an episode of *PTI*. And *with about two minutes left to play*, and irrespective of the score, while the teams continue to play, the **Taylor** *crowd links arms and sings a heartfelt rendition of Silent Night – all three verses*. After the game,

students gather at the campus student center, where they enjoy Christmas music, baking and eating Christmas cookies, addressing Christmas cards to our troops, making gingerbread houses, and singing the inevitable Christmas songs with a karaoke machine. The climax of the night is when the university president and his wife *read the students the Christmas Story*. A one-time assistant coach conceived the *Silent Night Game* in the late 1980s. A decade later, it was a full-house, full-blown Christmas tradition and wonder. In its 2010 Christmas issue, *Sports Illustrated* paid tribute to the hoopla of *Silent Night, when all isn't calm but all is bright and right in* **Taylor's** *little corner of the world*.

TCU (Football): *The Frog Horn*

TCU's mascot, the *Horned Frog*, spits blood from its eye as a defense mechanism, and is certainly *among the most unique school mascots*. But why not reverse *"Horned Frog"* into *"Frog Horn"*? The *Horned Frogs* blow a 120-decibel train horn at key times during football (and some soccer and baseball) games. This tradition *began in 1958*, when two students hoisted a home-made contraption onto a railing at the stadium, and waited for the Frogs to score. When they did, the enterprising young men would wrench open a valve and everything would come to a standstill as the stadium filled

with the roar of a borrowed train whistle that the boys had cobbled onto the end of an air canister. But turning it off wasn't so easy, and the thing blasted for 15 minutes before the air finally ran out. The game was stopped and officials ungraciously escorted the boys from the stadium. But the Frogs beat Texas, 22-8 that day. Fast-forward to 1994 when football coach Pat Sullivan asked an alumni group why they had no football traditions to get the crowd involved? Someone remembered the 1958 prank, and enlisted a few other friends to help him recreate the sound. A university trustee was CEO of *Burlington Northern Railroad*, and gladly agreed to help. Four hours later preliminary drawings for a new contraption were faxed for approval. A small group of men at *Burlington's* Springfield, Missouri maintenance shop had less than four weeks to complete the horn, but the challenge energized them. Never at the railroad had they ever built anything like this. Rumor has it that the maintenance men put about 14 coats of paint on it. During subsequent planning meetings, the trailer with a horn – since *patented by the railroad* – expanded to include marquee lights for **TCU** logos, green flashing eyes and purple theatrical smoke that poured from two chrome horns on top. Those extras, of course, meant additional equipment under the cowling, so it overheated during a test drive. Vents were added to the body, which was all hand machined in the Springfield shop. A local artist was hired to paint the face after agreeing to give the beast a ferocious look. A bell from an old steam locomotive was also added. The shiny new *Frog Horn*, weighing in at 3,000 pounds, was loaded onto a C-47 and flown to Fort Worth. The horn was rung for the first time before the 1994 home opener against **Kansas**. No one at **TCU** (including the administration) had been told about the *Frog Horn*, so its debut was a surprise. Since 2002, Jason Lesikar (class of 2002) has lovingly cared for **TCU's** famous *Frog Horn*, keeping it in running condition and managing it at games. Jason gets help from a spirit organization, since it takes one person to watch the game and cue a second handler to ring the bell or blow the horn at the right time (a very important task since blasts at the wrong time can violate NCAA rules), and one person to keep others at an appropriate distance. Jason recently invited me to the *secret / secure facility* on his ranch west of town where he handles all the maintenance and repair — mostly out of his own pocket. It's a fairly needy piece of machinery — now almost 25 years old, after all, and parts are not only expensive, they are sometimes hard to locate. In recent years Jason crafted new fenders and replaced the fog machines and more light bulbs than he can count. Occasionally he has to crawl inside during a game to keep it blasting and flashing. "It's a big asset, but it's also a big responsibility," Jason says. "Getting to work on it has been a huge honor." One thing no one has fixed is a *dent near the front* that an opponent (reportedly a **Texas Tech** player) put there with his helmet in a moment of extreme frustration at the Frogs' success on the field. "It's part of its history," Jason says, "so we've left it there."

Tearing Down Goalposts

Many traditions revolve around *tearing down goalposts* after significant victories. Sometimes the goalposts end up in a local lake (as in the case for **Northwestern**, and Lake Michigan), or sometimes they are *paraded through*

town and reside at a local student bar. **Northwestern** even has blog related to this on *www.laketheposts.com*. But with safety a paramount concern, very few goalposts currently meet their demise after a victory. And if overwhelming security isn't deterrent enough, many goalposts can now be *remotely lowered to the ground* after time expires. Those goalposts cost almost twice as much as non-lowering ones ($13,000 per set versus $7,000). Each goalpost is baked at 400 degrees for 15 minutes and it takes thirty people about thirty-five hours to make one set. And, of course, the color must be a powder coating of *DuPont aero yellow*. In 1981, in the midst of a 34-game football losing streak – then the longest in FBS history – **Northwestern** fans celebrated a 61-14 home loss to **Michigan State** by *tearing-down the goal posts* and marching through the streets of Evanston, Illinois, shouting, "We're the worst!" Then they tossed the goal post into Lake Michigan. A new tradition, and word, were born: *"Laking"*. And at **Missouri**, students often celebrate huge wins by hauling the goal posts 17 blocks from *Faurot Field* to *Harpo's Tavern*.

Tennessee (Football): *Running Through the Block-T*

At the climax of the **Tennessee** band's pregame show, the musicians form in a wide open *"T" formation for the players to run* through as they exit the tunnel. The tradition

began in 1964 when then-head coach Doug Dickey introduced the *"T"* on the player's helmets. The pregame routine followed shortly after and has become a permanent home game staple for the band, and for the team. The *"T"* has occasionally been formed for road games, most notably at *Liberty*

Bowl Memorial Stadium in Memphis, at **Vanderbilt** *Stadium* in Nashville, and at various other major bowl games.

Texas: *Bevo*

While *Bevo* began as a tradition in 1916, the **Texas** *Longhorn*, has actually been a fixture on the **UT** sidelines since 1966. The *Longhorn* mascot epitomizes the pride and tradition of **Texas** football, and it's one of the best known stories on the **UT** campus: During a late night visit to Austin, a group of Texas A&M Aggie pranksters *branded* the University's first longhorn mascot *"13-0," the score of a football game won by* **Texas A&M**. In order to save face, **UT** students altered the brand to read *"Bevo"* by changing the *"13"* to a *"B,"* the *"−"* to an *"E,"* and inserting a *"V"* between the *"dash"* and the *"0."* For years, Aggies have proudly touted the stunt as the reason the steer acquired his name. But was the brand really changed? And is that why he's called *Bevo*? **A&M** says yes, while **Texas** says no.

Texas A&M (Football): *Midnight Yell Practice*

Before each home football game, as many as 50,000 fans attend – at midnight – an event called *"Midnight Yell Practice."* The event was *first held* in 1931, and really isn't a *practice*, since everyone in attendance already knows the famous

yells (not cheers). **A&M** is famous for their tradition of *the 12th Man,* and even licenses this term to the *Seattle Seahawks,* of the NFL, for $5,000 per year. The *Yell Practices* are also held (not at midnight) at various venues for away games. As an example, when **A&M** played at **South Carolina** for the first time, the *Yell Practice* was held on the steps of the *South Carolina State House.* Five *yell leaders* – three seniors and two juniors – are elected to one-year terms by the student body. *Sports Illustrated* named *Midnight Yell Practice* as one of the *100 Things You Gotta Do Before You Graduate.* I attended *Midnight Yell Practice* a few years ago with my great friend, Ken Weingart, before **A&M** hosted their very first SEC game. It was an amazing experience.

Texas A&M (Football): *Student Bonfire*

The tragedy of *the 1999 bonfire collapse* that killed twelve Aggies caused the cancelling of the university sponsored event *held yearly, since the early 1900's,* on the Wednesday before the **Texas** game. But in 2002 a group of **A&M** students *restarted the bonfire tradition,* as an unsanctioned university event, held off-campus. *The university sponsored event had 8,000 students involved with the construction,* while the current event has approximately 2,000. Ruling over all construction activities are the *Redpots,* a name derived from the cardinal color of the team's helmets. The *Redpot* job is nearly full-time, but is quite the resume item. The project begins in mid-September, and *includes thousands of trees, each felled by-hand.* The resulting tower is approximately 45' tall, but in deference to the 1999 accident, all logs must touch the ground. After three weeks of construction, *more than 15,000*

Aggies gather in person, with another 50,000 watching online. In 2013, *CollegeSpun* wrote an article about a *Groom's Cake* they had recently seen. The *Groom's Cake* is an excellent representation of the **A&M** *Bonfire*, and it even has a *Longhorn* roasting at the very top.

Texas A&M: *Reveille*

To the freshmen in the **A&M** corps of cadets, she's *"Miss Reveille, ma'am,"* and *her rank is higher than any other student's in the corps of cadets.* She is *NEVER crated, NEVER un-groomed,* and *NEVER left alone. Reveille attends classes with her*  *handler,* and based on tradition, *if she barks in class, class is immediately dismissed.* Former-Reveilles are *laid-to-rest outside the stadium, where a scoreboard is mounted on the stadium's wall, so that the revered-mascots can keep up with the game.* Also before each home game, *flowers are placed on the Reveille graves. In 1989 twenty thousand mourners attended Reveille IV's funeral – a burial with full military honors.*

Venues – Iconic Places to Watch a Game

There are places we'll remember all our lives, though some have changed. Some forever, not for better, while some have gone and some thank God, remain. All these places had their moments, and nearly all will again … and again … and again. They're *the great venues in college sports*. Venues that *have witnessed wonderful traditions*. The stadiums, arenas, and playing fields are the scenes of so many keepsakes. They're places in the heart, and in our collective memory banks. Where to begin? Why, almost anywhere … In Knoxville, in *Neyland Stadium* on a football Saturday. Once the *Volunteer*

Navy's docked on the *Tennessee River* and satisfied their tailgate appetites, **UT** fans walk on *Peyton Manning Pass* to watch their Vols play. Remember when a freshman tailback named Herschel (no last name needed) introduced himself to Bill Bates and the rest of the country one night in Knoxville? In Athens, games are played *between the hedges*. Rest-in-peace, all you *Uga's entombed in Sanford's canine mausoleum*. As *Sports Illustrated* noted in

1997, in declaring *Uga V* the *Number 1 Mascot* in the land, and an *SI* cover boy: "If you can't appreciate the swaggering gait and Churchillian physiognomy of Uga V, the Bulldogs' bulldog, you must be a cat lover." It's not just the games people play, but where they play them. As an example, in downtown Lexington, Kentucky where *Rupp Arena* — for its sheer size (capacity 23,500) and the rabidity of **Kentucky** basketball fans — is *Big Blue Heaven*. **Florida State** baseball at *Dick Howser Stadium* has become one of college baseball's best and toughest venues. Named for the late Kansas City Royals manager and **FSU** coach, and the

Seminoles' first baseball All-American, the stadium is now home to *Mike Martin Field*. Martin coached nearly four decades in Tallahassee, where baseball's long been a happening. In Baton Rouge, of course, stands one of two *Death Valleys* (**Clemson** has the other). It's *Tiger Stadium*, and nothing compares to a Saturday night game in *Death Valley*. Joe Cahn, the self-proclaimed *Commissioner of Tailgating*

wrote a book about that fine art and says, "The best place to tailgate is wherever you are that weekend." *LSU can be up*, *LSU can be down*, but *LSU's best weapon remains … sunset.* ESPN.com once proclaimed *Death Valley* "The scariest place to play in America." And then there's Billy Cannon's *Halloween Night* run in 1959. That's when Cannon, who would win the

Heisman Trophy, saved the unbeaten and top-ranked Tigers. With **LSU** trailing *Number 3* **Ole Miss** 3-0 in the fourth quarter, Cannon returned a punt 89 yards for a touchdown and a 7-3 triumph. And Death Valley erupted like Vesuvius. The seismograph on **LSU's** campus registered the event as a small earthquake. In Charlottesville, only select students live in the rooms on *the Lawn* at *Mr. Jefferson's University*. But at **Virginia** football and basketball games and other sporting events, or just at the drop of a hat, everyone can – and does – sing *The Good Old Song of Wahoowa*. The *biggest stadium in the country*? *The Big House*, as **Michigan** *Stadium* – capacity 109,901 – is

known and beloved by the Wolverine faithful. **Penn State, Tennessee, Ohio State, Alabama** and **Texas** also exceed 100,000 in capacity. There's nothing parochial about *Notre Dame Stadium.* It's one of the quintessential college stadiums and campuses in the country. It's Rockne, Leahy, Ara and Holtz. It's home to *seven Heisman Trophy winners, none of whom has had his number retired*. It's *Touchdown Jesus*. It's where *Rudy* finally got into a game, and where the movie *Rudy* was filmed. It also inspired a wonderful T-shirt that I once saw: *"Rudy Was Offsides."* In the Pacific Northwest, *Autzen Stadium* at **Oregon** became an electric atmosphere during the Ducks' offensive blitzkriegs under head coach Chip Kelly. And the speed just keeps coming. In **Washington**, a $250 million remodeling of *Husky Stadium* debuted in the 2013 opener against **Boise State**. The view from the shore of *Lake Washington* and *Portage Bay* has long been idyllic. Tailgating – or *Sailgating*, as many Huskies fans have done for decades, is enjoyed at one of the most picturesque settings in the nation. Back in Eugene, **Oregon's** Hayward Field reigns as *track and field's most cherished venue*. It's the home of numerous NCAA, USTAF *National Championships*, and frequent *United States Olympic Trials*. *Franklin Field* at the **University of Pennsylvania** is renowned for the *Penn Relays*, the annual weekend-long track and field carnival held in the hallowed old stadium in Philadelphia. It's where, legend has it, a sportswriter once looked at all the meet officials with their stopwatches and cracked, "These are the souls that time men's tries." At the *Drake Relays* in Des Moines, Iowans know and love their track and field. Back to the West Coast, and down to Los Angeles, the home of **UCLA**. Or rather, to Pasadena, where the Bruins play their home games in the *Rose Bowl*. Whenever the sun is setting over the stadium's rim, it's one of the signature sights in college sports. In Madison, at *Camp Randall Stadium*, between the third and fourth quarters, Badgers fans do the *Jump Around*. It's done to the ballistic sound of a *House of Pain* tune. When nearly 80,000 fans jump up and down, the stands actually shake. At **Texas A&M** in College Station, when Aggie fans link arms and sway back and forth during games, the *Kyle Field* press box moves, too. Honest. **Penn State's** *whiteout* of 100,000 plus fans turn *Beaver Stadium* just that: *white*. For those who prefer driving and tailgating, New York offers one of the absolute best venues: **West Point**. *The United States Military Academy*. Especially the tailgating at historic *Buffalo Soldier Field* and the atmosphere inside *Michie Stadium*. Every home football game at **Army** begins with a special delivery: four members of the famed *Black Knights Parachute Team* leap out of a helicopter one at a time, all attempting to land on the Black Knights logo on the 50-yard line in *Michie*. *One hand-delivers the game ball*. In Durham, North Carolina, *Cameron Indoor Stadium* has its own *crazies*. The *Cameron Crazies*, those privileged

Dukies who help give coach Mike Krzyzewski and his Blue Devils *one of the great home-court advantages*.

They camp outside in any weather / temperature, in

their tent city *Krzyzewskiville*, waiting to get tickets and prime locations once inside *Cameron*. Yes, they can be very amusing, even clever at times. In Chapel Hill, first in *Carmichael Auditorium* and now in the cavernous *Dean Dome*, **North Carolina** basketball remains royalty under ol' Roy. Since returning to **UNC**, Roy Williams has won three *National Championships* with the Heels (2005, 2009, and 2017). Spontaneous celebrations still occasionally break out on Franklin Street after big wins. In lacrosse, there's no place like *Homewood: Homewood Field*, the home of **Johns Hopkins** lacrosse in Baltimore. The *United States Lacrosse Museum* and *National Hall of Fame* is housed there, too. The Blue Jays have won 44 *National Championships*, including nine Division I titles since the first NCAA tournament in 1971. Whether at *Homewood* or away, in whatever football stadium

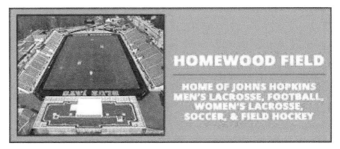

the men's *Final Four* is now held, lacrosse is the fastest-growing sport in the nation. It's a three-day, family affair, and a Memorial Day weekend happening with NCAA Division I, II and III titles at stake. The sport's burgeoning popularity has long been a staple at **Syracuse**, which plays its home games in the *Carrier Dome*. The Orange holds the most NCAA titles in the DI era with ten. **Syracuse** also has a numbers' tradition. It *awards jersey # 22 to its best all-around player*. The player with the most talent, most flair, and most creativity. Back in the day, it would've been the football star who once wore # 44 in both football and lacrosse: Jim Brown, whose *football 44 is now retired*. For the best in women's lacrosse, which is also booming, just go to Evanston, Illinois. To **Northwestern**, who won the 2012 title for its seventh NCAA championship in eight years. Jay Bilas, who played on Mike

Krzyzewski's first *Final Four* team and is now a broadcaster, said of **Butler's** *Hinkle Fieldhouse*: "It's the *Fenway Park of College Basketball*." If you're a true hoops fan, you must go to *Hinkle* (capacity 10,000), where the baskets are still 10 feet high and the magic lives on. What about *the Carnegie Hall of college basketball*? That's how **Indiana's** *Assembly Hall* is known. It's where the Hoosiers take the floor in *their classic red-and-white, candy-striped warm-up pants* to the fight song played by the **IU** *Pep Band*. It's the home of the *best timeout in college basketball*, as the under 8:00-minute timeout in the second half is known. The band plays the *William Tell Overture* while the cheerleaders and flag-bearers wave flags all over the court. *The Cathedral of College Basketball*. That's how *the Palestra* is widely known, loved and revered. It's the ancestral home of the *Big-5*: **Penn**, **St. Joseph's**, **Villanova**, **Temple**, and **LaSalle**. The Palestra's capacity is 8,722 with all wooden bleachers. It's a holy place that long housed the *Holy War*, as **St. Joe's / Villanova** is known, and other showdowns between the *Big-5*. Four of them sometimes played doubleheaders. Now add **Drexel**, a short walk from *the Palestra*, and it's an occasional *six-team City Series*. *The Palestra* has a *plaque on the wall just inside the main entrance that says:* "To win the game Is Great ... to play the game is Greater ... but to love the game is the Greatest of all." In women's basketball, UConn has the *Gampel Pavilion* on their campus in

Storrs – where many *National Champions* have practiced and played. Just like Pat Summitt did with the **Tennessee** Lady Vols. And as a result, in the cavernous *Thompson-Boling Arena*, the court was renamed *The Summit*. No embellishment needed. Not for a woman who changed an entire sport. I was in attendance at one of the last games coach Summitt coached, and feel

very fortunate for having seen her. It's no coincidence that the *Women's Basketball Hall of Fame* opened in Knoxville in 1999, with Summitt leading the inaugural class of inductees. Farewell, *Big East*. At least the *Big East* tournament we knew and loved in *Madison Square Garden*, in those Saturday night finals that seemed more like heavyweight title fights. And what about the original *Orange Bowl* when the 'Canes entered the field from a tunnel and *through a cloud of smoke* –and then smoked the opposition. When the **Cal / Stanford** game is played in Berkeley, lucky students view the game for free from *Tightwad Hill*. There's *the Pit* in Albuquerque, with its mile-high altitude. It's the home of the **New Mexico** Lobos and the site of the *1983 NCAA Final*, when Jim Valvano's **NC State** Wolfpack shocked Houston's Phi Slamma Jamma 54-52 on Lorenzo Charles' last second dunk of an air ball. It's also where a head coach from a prominent conference once told his team, "Don't worry about the altitude. We're playing the game indoors." *Pauley Pavilion* no longer strikes fear into opponents' hearts. At least not like it did when John Wooden worked his basketball wizardry and his **UCLA** Bruins were the *greatest dynasty in college sports history*. Between 1964 and 1975, Wooden's teams won 10 NCAA championships in 12 years, seven consecutive from 1967 to 1973. UCLA won a record 38 straight NCAA tournament games, and his Bruins compiled an NCAA-record 88-game winning streak from 1971-74 before falling at Notre Dame 71-70. He was, and shall ever remain, *the Wizard of Westwood*. Wooden, an Indiana native and **Purdue** All-American from 1932-34, was the first person to be inducted into the *Naismith Memorial Basketball Hall of Fame* as *both a player and a coach*. As each of Bill Walton's four sons became basketball players, Walton would write some of Wooden's maxims on their lunch bags each day. **UCLA** now plays with a statue of Wooden outside the north entrance, and where the corridor on the east side of *Pauley* is named *Wooden Way*. They play on the *Nell & John Wooden Court*, as it was named in 2003 for Wooden and his

beloved Nellie, his wife of 53 years who died in 1985. Wooden mourned her daily until his death on June 4, 2010, at the age of 99. *Now, in the new-and-improved Pauley, Wooden's gold-upholstered seat – Seat 6, Row B, right behind the Bruins' bench – stands out among the blue seats.* On Saturday, February 2, 2013, **Oklahoma State** went to Lawrence, Kansas. To *Allen Fieldhouse*, where the Cowboys hadn't won since 1990: where second-ranked **Kansas**, on an 18-game winning streak, had won its last 33 home games on *James Naismith Court*. Where Bill Self's Jayhawks were an astonishing 102-1 in their previous 103 games in *the Phog*, as *Allen Fieldhouse* is known and beloved by **KU** fans, while feared and dreaded by opponents. Somehow, **Oklahoma State** won 85-80. You can look it up. The numbers don't lie. They do, however, reinforce this truth: *Allen Fieldhouse* is not only the best venue in college basketball, but the most daunting and toughest, too. They invented the game, let's start from there. Dr. James Naismith, who invented the game of basketball in 1891 at the YMCA in Springfield, Massachusetts, came to **Kansas** in 1898 to teach and coach. And Naismith's successor at **Kansas**? The Phog. Dr. Forrest *"Phog"* Allen, considered the *father of basketball coaching*. Two assistants who apprenticed under him: Dean Smith and Adolph Rupp. Allen is the man behind the Phog. That's what all Kansas fans call *Allen Fieldhouse*. The enormous sign is up there, high above the stands behind the north basket, and serves as a warning to opponents, one and all: *Pay Heed All Who Enter, Beware of The Phog.* It's how one of those classic pre-game videos on the four-sided scoreboard above center court begins – only to be followed by words appearing on the screen, one after the other: *"The Nation's ... Biggest ... Home Court Advantage ..."* Larry Brown's 1988 Jayhawks, led by Danny Manning, entered the NCAA Tournament as a 6th seed. "If **Kansas** wins," Dick Vitale said, "I'll kiss the Jayhawk on the floor of *Allen Fieldhouse*." *Danny & the Miracles* upset Oklahoma 83-79 in the *Championship* game. Eventually,

Vitale kissed the floor in the Phog. **Kansas** fans are prideful. They love their Jayhawks. They pack *the Phog* and root like crazy. When an opposing player fouls out, they stand and lift their arms overhead and sway them back and forth. *Waving-the-Wheat*, it's called. You

know, like a field of Kansas wheat swaying in a prairie breeze. Of course, they chant *Rock Chalk, Jayhawk, KU!* **Kansas** fans are proud and loud. Never more so than on February 25, 2012, in the final *Border War* game with **Missouri** before the Tigers' move to the Southeastern Conference. When Thomas Robinson blocked a last second shot in regulation and sent the game into overtime, the crowd set an *Allen Fieldhouse* noise record of *127 decibels*. That's loud. That's *the Phog.* "It's Fenway," **Kansas** basketball operations director Barry Hinson told Vahe Gregorian of the *St. Louis Post-Dispatch.* "Wrigley. Old Yankee Stadium. It's the Coliseum. I mean, it is. And it's set down in a small town in Midwest America. On *Naismith Drive.*"

Virginia Tech (Football): *Lunch Pail*

Virginia Tech's *lunch pail* symbolizes the Hokies' tireless, blue-collar approach to the game, but also inspires current players *to uphold that tradition*. It all began in 1995, when then co-defensive coordinators Rod Sharpless and Bud Foster brought the pail back from New Jersey and decided to *use it as a motivational tool* for that season's defense. Sharpless' mother-in-law found the now-famous original *lunch pail* in Mercerville, New Jersey, where it had belonged to a coal miner. Throughout the season, *the pail holds the players' defensive goals, weekly goals, and keys to success for the week*

as well as a mission statement that was signed by each player before the season began. And, of course, *little bits of opponents' turf from road wins also have become part of the tradition.*

Wake Forest (Basketball): *Kernkraft 400*

You have heard the song, but almost certainly don't know the title. It's the song that is *often played before a kickoff* at a football game – the one where all the students spontaneously jump up-and-down. Ahhh. Now you know what I mean. The song, as an anthem for college sports, started at **Wake Forest**, and for that, you can thank Splank. That's the name Florian Senfter, a German artist from Munich, performs under. He's the guy who wrote, recorded and popularized *Kernkraft 400* by *Zombie Nation*. It's the techno-pop, non-stop ditty that college basketball crowds – and many football fanatics, too – have been hopping up-and-down-to for more than a decade during timeouts when the home team's rollin' and the house is a'rockin'.

According to Tom O'Toole of *USA Today, Kernkraft 400* first surfaced at a **Marquette University** basketball home games in 2002. Later that season,

Todd Scheel, whose Milwaukee company, *FX in Motion*, introduced *Kernkraft 400* at Marquette games, brought it south to **Wake Forest** for a big TV game against **Duke** on February 13, 2003. It was the day before *Valentine's Day*. When **Wake**, led by Chris Paul, won in double-overtime, **Wake Forest** fans fell in love with the song. And *America saw the Wake students' reaction to it*. A tradition was born. Soon, college basketball, indeed much of college sports, followed suit. "I think one of the reasons it was successful for **Wake Forest**," Dan Hauser, then the marketing director at **Wake**, told O'Toole, "is that we played it for a conference game, we won and it was a team with Chris Paul." And a mania was born. In 2006, according to a story in *The Daily Collegian*, the student newspaper at **Penn State**, the university began judiciously using the song at football games in *Beaver Stadium*, capacity 100,000 plus. With the student section jumping up-and-down to *Kernkraft 400*, there were concerns about possible structural damage to the stadium itself. All this thanks to Splank –who is well aware of his song's popularity at American sports events, and its impact on the games people play. He's heard his song played during the *Olympic Games*, and knows a Belgian soccer team that plays it after each goal is scored. But there is one musical-mulligan Splank wished he had taken. The title: *Kernkraft 400.* The title translates to *"Atomic Energy 400."* Had Splank known his song would become such a sporting phenomenon, particularly on college campuses, he indicates, "I would have chosen a friendlier name." But regardless of the title that no one knows, this is one *rockin' college sports tradition* that rocks-on to this day.

Walks

They walk *the Walk*. So many teams do it now. It's become *one of the most treasured traditions – and most copied – in college football*. It's the pre-game *Walk*. Whether from the athletic dormitory, through a parking lot near the *Tate Center* at the **University of Georgia**, down *Yellow Jacket Alley* on the *Flats* at **GA Tech** to *Bobby Dodd Stadium*, or straight from the football complex to the stadium and into the locker room. They walk *the Walk*. They do so as hundreds – usually thousands – of fans line the route, clear a path, clear their throats and cheer their heroes. "It's the most copied tradition in all of college football," former **Auburn** athletic director David Housel once said of his school's traditional *Tiger Walk*, which had its genesis in the early 1960's. Yet some *Walks* go way, way back-back-back in time. "You're just thinking about how many people have been walking down here," Sam Schwartzstein, the fifth-year senior starting center and a tri-captain on **Stanford's** 2012 Pac 12 and *Rose Bowl* champions told a school videographer on the day he took his final *Walk*. "It's been going on since the 1920's." "I greatly value *the Walk*, a tradition I came to know and embrace as a young **Stanford** fan while my dad coached here," said Jim Harbaugh, whose father, Jack, was a Cardinal's assistant coach in the early 1980s. Jim was **Stanford's** head coach from before becoming head coach of the San Francisco 49ers, and now, of course is coaching at **Michigan.** In the 1950's, **Stanford** players would dress in the old *Encina Gym*, and walk *the Walk* from there to *Stanford Stadium.* Now, they begin at the *Arrillaga Family Sports Center*, pass by

countless tailgate parties, thousands of fans, and see everyone from the infamous *Stanford Band* to the band's mascot — the hilarious *Tree*. It's **Stanford's** way for

players to meet fans, kiss Mom and get their game faces on. On their final *Walk*, **Stanford** seniors wear *"My Last Walk"* T-shirts with the date printed on them. The *Stanford* Band does-their-thing behind the team on *the Walk*, and **Stanford's** fans go nuts. There's nothing pedestrian about *the Walk*, wherever it takes place. Especially in *the Grove*, a 10-acre patch of land on the **Ole Miss** campus and considered by most to be *the most beautiful, bucolic and best spot for tailgating in the country. Sports Illustrated* once anointed **Ole Miss** the *Number 1 tailgating school in the nation,* while, not to be outdone, *The Sporting News anointed the Grove as the Holy Grail of tailgating sites.* Their signature cheer – *"Hotty Toddy!"* – could break out at any moment. *"Are you ready?" "Hell Yes! Damn Right! Hotty Toddy, Gosh Almighty! Who the Hell are we? Hey! Flim Flam Bim Bam, Ole Miss by Damn!"* In *the Grove*, as most everywhere on campus, the *speed limit is 18 miles per hour*. In honor of Archie Manning, who wore *number 18* while becoming the greatest quarterback and most beloved football player in **Ole Miss** history. But on *Manning Way*, the road around *Vaught-Hemingway Stadium*, the posted *speed*

limit is 10 miles per hour, not 18 miles per hour, in honor of Eli's uniform *number 10*. Before kickoff, when it's time *to Walk*, **Ole Miss** players march into *the Grove* and then beneath an arch that bears these words: *"Walk of Champions. Win or Lose, Champions."* The *Mother of All Walks*, however, took place in 1989, at the *Loveliest Village on the Plain* – at **Auburn University**, on that long-awaited day when **Alabama** finally deigned to come to **Auburn**. The ***Auburn /Alabama*** rivalry, considered by many to be the most bitter and fierce rivalry in the college game, is unlike any other. It was interrupted early in the 20th century over a dispute between the two schools. So the Tigers and Crimson Tide did not play from 1907-1948. When the *Iron Bowl* rivalry was finally renewed, it was played at *Legion Field*, the allegedly neutral stadium in Birmingham. But the game in Birmingham always seemed to have an air of **Alabama** arrogance. In 1958, after Paul Bear Bryant left **Texas A&M** and returned to his alma mater, the Tide ruled the rivalry. Bryant, one of the greatest coaches in college football history, belittled **Auburn**, dismissing it as *"that little cow college across the state."* Bryant refused to play at **Auburn**, and never did. He died in 1982, barely a month after coaching his last game. But during the 1980's, once Pat Dye became the **Auburn** coach and built an SEC power, coach Dye and **Auburn** officials began pressuring the SEC and politicians to force **Alabama** to play **Auburn** on a home-and-home basis. That day finally arrived on Saturday, December 2, 1989. *The day the Tide came to Auburn.* Ivan Maisel, an

Alabama native and long-time *ESPN* senior writer, on-air commentator and college football historian, was there that epic day. "Only once have I genuinely feared for my safety," Maisel later wrote. "That was at *Tiger Walk* in 1989." **Alabama** was 10-0 and ranked 2nd in the nation. **Auburn**, 8-2, was ranked 11th. Over 20,000 fans lined both sides of Donahue Drive as the **Auburn** players walked *the Walk* from their football dorm down the hill to the south end of *Jordan-Hare Stadium*. Maisel later wrote: "The **Auburn** fans roared, their eyes glazed with a mixture of fervor, pride, passion and perhaps a touch of the *Jack Daniels*. We [he and another sportswriter] were five or six deep and couldn't get any closer to the street. We were also hemmed in,

and didn't have the zeal-fueled adrenaline to ward off the elbows and other parts of the bouncing, heaving, deafening masses. I no longer had any interest in taking notes, which was just as well, because the noise and the lack of space made it impossible. My own adrenaline kicked in, and I worked my way into an open space." Later that day, after **Auburn** upset the Tide 30-20 before a delirious, then-record crowd of 85,319 in *Jordan-Hare*, Dye would say, "I'm sure that [scene] must have resembled what went on the night the wall came down in Berlin. I mean, it was like they [**Auburn** fans] had been freed and let out of bondage, just having this game at **Auburn**." "You'll never see that commotion again," David Housel said. "The Children of Israel entered the Promised Land for the first time only once." Yes, beating undefeated, Number 2 **Alabama** was extremely satisfying. *"But the victory on the field, while important, paled beside the victory off the* *field,"* Maisel wrote. *"Because when **Alabama** arrived on campus, **Auburn** had arrived, too."*

Washington State (Football): *College GameDay Flag*

Tom Pounds proves that just one person, even with no connection to TV sports, can change what America sees on TV each week. Not that he began with any grandiose plan in mind. Having graduated from **Washington State** in 1981, he was struck by a suggestion in 2003 on the school's *cougfan.com* sports site from a **WSU** alum living in Austin. That alum had seen somebody

unfurl the **WSU** flag at an *ESPN College GameDay* show at **Ohio State** and wondered: Why not ask someone to wave the **WSU** school flag in the background during the upcoming *GameDay* show in Austin for the **Kansas State / Texas** football game? Makes perfect sense. All Pounds had to do was stay up past midnight, with his mom, to make a flag, begin driving at dawn to drive 800 miles to Austin and end up getting sworn at by unwelcoming fans at the

GameDay set who failed to grasp the idea's inherent nobility. Plus, the alum in Austin couldn't make it. Pounds says he never met him, "I hope to someday," and doesn't even know the identity of the man who first waved the flag at **Ohio State**. The story could have stopped there. But then Pounds heard from a seminary student in Minneapolis: not an alum, but a **WSU** fan that had seen the flag and offered to drive it to a *GameDay* in Madison, Wisconsin. From there, the relay has gone on. Pounds, has assembled an online network of around 120 flag-bearing contacts that have offered to help keep this wonderful tradition going. The streak is uninterrupted and is often mentioned by the announcers on GameDay. Pounds has personally waved the flag several times. The flag relay inspired a non-profit corporation (*Ol' Crimson Booster Club*) that has raises funds to cover the flag-wavers' expenses. One flag that was used is displayed at the alumni center at **WSU**. Pounds says the flag-waving has provoked fisticuffs in Gainesville, **Florida** and Eugene, **Oregon**, but most often draws respect from the crowds. I'm not certain when the second flag (identical, except with **Washington State's** opposite team color) was added, but if you look closely each Saturday morning in the fall, you may be able to spot each of the flags. I had the opportunity to personally wave-the-flag in 2012, as well as speak with a couple of the **WSU** alums doing the waving. It was a wonderfully unique experience.

West Virginia University: *Burning Couches*

WVU student's *burn couches*. They burn them because the basketball team won. They burn them because the football team won. They burn them because the football team lost. They burn them because Bin Laden was killed. They burn them because it snowed. WVU student's *burn couches*. It's what they do. The practice, immortalized in song and in generations of carbon patches on the roads of Morgantown, may be nearing an end. Until recently, couch-burning had been a misdemeanor, with only a $1,000 fine to back it up. Now, *it is a felony arson charge*, which carries the possibility of up to three years in prison. There is even a rhyming *educational and awareness campaign.* Students will *Learn Not to Burn* from stickers, magnets and flyers around campus, and presumably also be able to earn 3-6 credit hours in the freshman core curriculum.

Williams College (Football): The Williams' Walk

Williams College is an academic powerhouse, and competes for National Championships in most every sport. The prestigious private school in Williamstown, Massachusetts, in the scenic heart of the Berkshires, is home to what *Sports Illustrated* called in 1992, *The Best Post-Game Tradition in America*. The history of *The Williams Walk* – following a homecoming victory over either arch rival **Amherst**, or **Wesleyan** – *dates back to 1971*, Bob Odell's first season as the Ephs' head coach. Odell neither initiated *The Walk*, nor encouraged it. *It just happened, as many great college sports' traditions do*. That November 13th, **Williams** broke a three-game losing streak to **Amherst** with a 31-14 win at *Weston Field*. The field looks more like a high school gridiron, and tickets are not necessary. It is low-key but high-quality football. In 1971, in the traditional finale of **Williams'** eight-game schedule, the Ephs – who'd been outscored 115-49 by **Amherst** in the three previous meetings – finally and *literally turned the corner*. "We were just so darn happy to have beaten **Amherst**, it did not surprise me to see our team *go out the main gate and head up towards Spring Street*," Odell said. "I just thought, well, isn't that nice, the boys look like they are having a little fun." Odell walked over to his car, hopped in and drove back to *Cole Field House*. *But a tradition had been born*. Many an Eph, still in uniform, has marched up Spring Street toward town after a big homecoming win over **Amherst** or **Wesleyan**. But that November day was the first time the team made *The Walk* en masse – as one. Sixteen years later, *St. Pierre's Barber Shop* became the destination of choice. David Williams, an Eph star and Williamstown resident, told Roger St. Pierre that if the Ephs won and ended a four-year *Walk* drought, the boys would be dropping in to celebrate. This came after St. Pierre had told **Williams'** tales of earlier *Walks*, and wondered if the custom could be revived. "It was such a great tradition that he wished the players still did it," said Mike McLaughlin, class of 1989 and a senior on that team. "The week before *homecoming*, Dave told Roger that when we won, we'd be making *the Walk*. Roger and his long-time assistant Vern said they'd be ready for us." "There were only about 10 of us and we were all underclassmen," McLaughlin continued, "but we made *the Walk*. When we got to the barbershop, Roger and Vern were *ready inside with beer and some hearty congratulations*." There were *victory cigars*, too. Well-aged stogies, for a triumph well-earned. "The crowds walking up Spring Street all took notice, and they seemed to get a kick out of it," McLaughlin said. Even Montgomery's twin brother, Gordon, who played for **Amherst**, stopped by – showered and dressed in a sport coat and tie by then – happy for his brother if not for the day's outcome. "You can't really get 75 to 100 football players into *St. Pierre's*," David Montgomery said." But you can if *you win the homecoming game*." Dick Farley, the Ephs' new head coach that season, coached until 2003 and is now in the *College Football Hall of Fame.* He was 16-0-1 in homecoming games, the lone blemish a 0-0 tie with **Amherst** on a quagmire on *Weston Field* in 1995. "It's something the kids started and they got excited about it," Farley said of *the Walk*. "They don't want to be the team that doesn't walk, I know that much. But I've never seen it and I've no idea what goes on inside [the barbershop], except I've seen a few of the haircuts days later." At times, a photographer has been admitted to the barbershop shenanigans. A videographer, too, and the occasional celebrity. But mainly it's *Roger and the Ephs, celebrating with cigars*. Sodas and water are the beverages of choice now as the barbershop rocks to the rhythm of

Est. 1908
"Only 3 hours from Fenway Park"

18 Spring Street
Williamstown, MA 01267   413-458-5861

the **Williams** fight song and the cheers of victory. Eph parents and fans gather outside the shop to cheer and await the victors. In 2007, *ESPN's GameDay* was on hand for the 122nd game versus **Amherst**. *GameDay* host Chris Fowler popped into *St. Pierre's* briefly to congratulate the Ephs and thank them for allowing *ESPN* access to their homecoming and *the Walk* after a 20-0 victory over **Amherst**. Now the Williamstown Police Department closes Spring Street to traffic and hundreds of fans gather along the street and storefronts, some even watching from second-floor apartments. Many more gather outside *St. Pierre's* to see who, and what, will emerge from the barbershop. Some Ephs have their hair, uh, styled, others shaved or shorn. Hey, the hair grows back and *the Walk* remains in memory. "Beating **Amherst** is always a wonderful thing because they're such worthy opponents," said ex-Eph Ernie Smith. "At the time, there was nothing better. My days at **Williams** and that day in particular will always remain as a highlight in my life." *"There is no other tradition in college football today that means more to the student-athletes than the Walk,"* said former **Williams** coach Mike Whalen, who won his first five homecoming games. "Our players understand that in order to take *the Walk* up Spring Street, they must prepare as hard as they possibly can during the week before the game. If they're successful and earn the victory, then they're rewarded with *the Walk* with their teammates, supported by our fans, student body and families. On November 14, 2009, the morning of homecoming, a group of **Williams'** football alums gathered to honor one of their own. Dave Shawan was the guy *who led the Ephs up Spring Street on their initial Walk in 1971*. Thirty-eight years later, that reunion of football alumni also included Shawan's sister, Diane. Shawan died in 2008, succumbing after a long illness. He was

memorialized that morning in *St. Pierre's Barber Shop*. There, *a plaque was unveiled commemorating the birth of the Walk on November 13, 1971* – the day Dave Shawan first led **Williams** up Spring Street. Ever since, no one in college football walks *the Walk* like the Ephs.

Wisconsin (Football): *Jump Around*

On October 10, *1998*, a **Wisconsin** *football tradition was born* when a *House of Pain* song blasted through the stadium speakers and 80,000 people shook the place by *jumping up-and-down* to the song. After an uproar over an administration attempt to nix the song, the chancellor reversed the decision and it continues still, between the 3rd and 4th quarters of each home football game. The entire stadium shakes as students and fans jump around. The *Rose Bowl* has traditionally not allowed schools to engage in many of their own traditions, but in 2012, they made an exception for *Jump Around*. They also allowed **Oregon's** similar tradition of *Shout*. In the event that the *Rose Bowl* had not relented, **Wisconsin** fans were being urged to download the song onto their phones / MP3 players, and play it in unison, as they all jumped around. Also as a contingency, the **Wisconsin** *Band* learned the piece. This is often called the *rowdiest three minutes in college football.* When I personally witnessed *Jump Around* a few years ago, I was amazed that even the players all participate. And the coaches seem not to mind.

Yells, Cheers, and Chants

They say "Rock Chalk!" You say *"Rockar!"* They say *"Rammer Jammer!"* You say *"Stockar!"* The chanters are mighty **Kansas** – *"Rock Chalk, Jayhawk, KU!"* And mighty Alabama's *"Rammer Jammer Yellowhammer!"* They are two of the behemoths in big-time collegiate sports. But what about that "Rockar" and *"Stockar"*? It's from tiny **Bethany College** in Lindsborg, Kansas, a comparative *Little House on the Prairie* athletically. An NAIA school but, like the Jayhawks and Crimson Tide, one that takes its sports seriously. They are the Swedes – as Bethany's teams are known. And their traditional yells, cheers and chants are as cherished as **KU's** and **Alabama's**. One cheer in particular: *"ROCKAR! STOCKAR! THOR OCH HANS BOCKAR! KOR IGENOM! KOR IGENOM! TJU! TJU! TJU! BETHANIA!"* ROCKAR! STOCKAR! That legendary cheer, *yelled in Swedish* and based on Swedish mythology, began at the turn of the 20th century. Back in the Bennie Owen era at **Bethany**, when the *Terrible Swedes*, as they were then known, were feared and respected by all. In December *1902*, a group of students, dissatisfied with the old school yells, *used their Swedish mythology studies to create a new one*. An instant classic, if you will. Several members of the class of 1904 memorized the words and, before a crucial football game, performed the first public rendition of Rockar! Stockar! It was a figurative home run. *A tradition like no other*. And you thought **Georgia's** *How 'Bout Them Dawgs*? was cool. Actually, it is. So is the **Alabama** fan base, whenever the Tide rushes into the end zone and another

How 'bout Them Dawgs

Rammer Jammer Yellowhammer chant begins. It's a hybrid of *The Rammer Jammer*, a student newspaper back in the roaring '20s, and the *Yellowhammer*, the state bird of Alabama. Originally, the cheer was performed by the 'Bama crowd before football games. Hence, the lyric "We're gonna beat the hell outta you!" The you being **Florida** or **LSU** or, ideally, **Auburn**. Now, it's chanted towards the end of a game, when victory's certain and all's well in *Bear Bryant's hound's tooth hat world*. Let the screaming commence, with one lyrical change: *"Hey **Auburn**! Hey **Auburn**! Hey **Auburn**! We JUST BEAT the hell out of you! Rammer Jammer, Yellowhammer, gave 'em hell, Alabama!"* At **Arizona** basketball games,

during the first four minutes of each half or until the first media timeout of each period, the band and student sections ratchets-up some chants. Each dribble by an opposing player begets a *"Boing!"* Every pass, a *"Pass!"* Every shot, a hopeful *"Brick!"* You get the idea. In 1960, **Baylor's** yell leaders introduced *a new hand signal*. The *Bear Claw* is made by slightly curving all five fingers inward to form a claw. It's accompanied by a *Sic 'em, Bears!* yell. Initially, the reaction to the *Bear Claw* and the *Sic 'em shout* was mixed, by students and faculty alike. It became, believe it or not, a topic of heated debate on campus. The *Claw* and *Shout* were employed sporadically until 1972, when Grant Teaff became **Baylor's** new football coach and embraced both shticks. They became sporting staples, symbolizing **Baylor's** athletic pride. The *Bear Claw* is held aloft during the singing of *That Good Old Baylor Line*. UC – Irvine's mascot? An anteater. Not an actual anteater, but *Peter the Anteater: a* student in anteater's clothing. There is no one *Peter the Anteater*. Several students don the mascot costume for games and performances throughout the school year. Salary: $10 an hour. Nice work if you can get it and you can probably get it if you try out. The coolest part? *Zot.* What? The *Zot, Zot, Zot chant* at athletic events, very popular among **UCI** students. The *Zot* is the sound made by the tongue of an anteater in the comic strip B.C. as it flicks out to catch an ant. *Air Ball! Air Ball!* – a cheer said to have originated at **Duke**. At **Cornell**, the operative hockey word isn't *Eh*? but *Boring!* That's what Big Red fans *taunt when the visiting team is introduced*. They also *shake newspapers, then crumple and throw them on the ice*. Those Ivy guys and gals are also fond of shouting *Safety School!* during games. It's another way of belittling opponents' universities. Whatever the sport may be at **Furman University**, Paladins' fans invoke what's known as the *Implication Cheer*. It's brilliant in its simplicity: *FU all the time! How 'Bout Them Dawgs?* How'd that come about? Grammar, be damned. **Georgia** fans in the mid-to-late 1970s began invoking the phrase regularly, especially during the 1978 season when the Bulldogs and their opportunistic *Junkyard Dogs* defense pulled off several unlikely, come-from-behind victories. It isn't a question so much as a declaration. Even the little guys yell their lungs out. Even tiny **Goldey-Beacom College** in Wilmington, Delaware. In the early days, before it became **Goldey-Beacom** in 1951, **Goldey College** specialized in business, bookkeeping and, yes, penmanship. Logically, it would follow that they actually composed and published this as the official ***Goldey College** Yell* for all sporting events: *Debit, credit, petty cash; half length, double length, curve and dash; coalescents, F-V hook, Journal, ledger, entry book!* Good luck making a last second one-and-one free throw when Lightning fans yell that. No less a sportsman than Teddy Roosevelt proclaimed *Rock Chalk, Jayhawk, KU!* as the best cheer he'd ever heard. Our rough-riding 26th president (1901-1909) was not alone in that regard. The legendary **Kansas** chant was

created in 1886 by some science club students at **KU**. The original words began: *Rah, Rah, Jayhawk...KU!* repeatedly. The first two times slowly, then increasing in  speed. But the *Rah Rah's* were replaced with *Rock Chalk*, a reference to the chalk rock – or limestone – found at nearby *Mount Oread* in Lawrence, Kansas, but also common around the state. It was later certified as the university's official rally call. At **Louisiana-Lafayette**, Ragin' Cajun fans do the funky *Hot Boudin chant*. You can, too: *Hot Boudin, Cold Cush Cush, Come on Cajuns Push! Push! Push!* And then you can wash it down with another Abita. More than 20 years after his death, they still chant: *This is Hank's House! This is Hank's House!* At **Loyola Marymount University** basketball games in Los Angeles, the crowds – so much smaller now than when Hank Gaithers played and scored, soared and rebounded – keep Hank Gaithers' memory alive. He was a 6-foot-7, ferocious rebounder and scorer who in 1989 became the second player in NCAA Division I history to lead the nation in both scoring and rebounding. But Gaithers also suffered from an irregular heartbeat. On March 4, 1990, he collapsed and died of a heart attack during a game against **Portland University**. Somehow, **Loyola** – led by Bo Kimble, Gathers' closest friend – reached the *Elite Eight* in the NCAA Tournament before losing to eventual *National Champion* **Nevada-Las Vegas**. *Bo even shot a late game*

free throw left handed to honor his friend, Hank. **Wisconsin** hockey fans invented the *Sieve! chant* for when opposing goalies allow goals. **Michigan** crowds took that a taunting step further: *You're not a goalie, you're a sieve! You're not a sieve, you're a funnel! You're not a funnel, you're a vacuum! You're not a vacuum, you're a black hole! You're not a black hole, you just suck!* At **Minnesota**, the operative phrase is *Ski-U-Mah!* It's pronounced SKY-YOU-MAH. But then, you knew that. In *1884*, two **Minnesota** rugby players, John W. Adams and Win Sargent, tried to come up with a team yell. They took the word *Ski*, a Sioux battle cry meaning victory, and combined it with *U-Mah* –

representing the University of Minnesota. You say Starkville, I say *Cowbells*. The most, uh, resounding symbol of tradition at **Mississippi State** is the *cowbell*. Cowbells decorate

offices and homes of **MSU** alumni. Many are passed down through generations of Bulldog fans, like heirlooms or *Faberge Eggs*. **Penn State**: *WE ARE … PENN STATE*. Still. And at **Texas**, the world renowned *Hook 'em, Horns*

sign, created by head cheerleader Harley Clark in 1955, was voted *the nation's top hand signal* by *Sports Illustrated*.

Traditions Personally Witnessed by the Author

I would love to visit YOUR favorite Tradition. Please invite me at
stan.beck@collegesportstraditions.com

- *$2.00 Bills (Football),* **Clemson**
- *The 12th Man (Football),* **Texas A&M**
- *1899 Territorial Cup Presentation (Football),* **Arizona / Arizona State**
- *2001 Space Odyssey (Football),* **South Carolina**
- *7th Inning Stretch (Baseball),* **Manhattan College**
- *A Capella National Anthem (Basketball),* **Harding University**
- *Aggie War Hymn (Football),* **Texas A&M**
- *"Air Ball" (Basketball),* **Duke**
- *Allstate Goalpost Nets (Football),* **various teams**
- *Alma Mater (Various Sports),* **Notre Dame**
- *Announcing the Score of Slippery Rock Games (Football),* **Michigan**
- *Baptist (Southern) Tunes, (Various Sports),* **Wake Forest**
- *Bats in the Stadium (Football),* **Texas A&M**
- *Battle for the Leather Helmet (Football),* **Clemson / Boston College**
- *Battle of the Blues (Basketball),* **Duke / North Carolina**
- *Beer Sold at College Games (Football),* **various teams**
- *Bench Celebrations (Basketball),* **various teams**
- *Best Damn Band in the Land (Football),* **Ohio State**
- *Between the Hedges (Football),* **Georgia**
- *Bevo (Football),* **Texas**
- *Big Bertha (Football),* **Texas**
- *Big Red's Birthday Party (Mascots),* **Western Kentucky**
- *Bill Snyder's Windbreakers (Football),* **Kansas State**
- *Blimpworthy Events (Football),* **various teams**
- *Blowing a Conch Shell (Swimming),* **Rollins College**
- *Boomer Sooner (Football),* **Oklahoma**
- *Bowden Bowl (Football),* **Clemson / FSU**
- *Buck-I-Guy (Football),* **Ohio State**
- *Budweiser Jingle (Football & Basketball),* **GA Tech**
- *Calling of the Hogs (Football),* **Arkansas**

- *Cameron Crazies (Basketball),* **Duke**
- *Candy-Striped Warm-Up Pants (Basketball),* **Indiana**
- *Carrying Coach off the Court after a National Championship (Basketball),* **UConn**
- *Checkerboard Baselines (Basketball),* **Tennessee**
- *Chicken Fried Tailgate Song (Football),* **various teams**
- *Chief Osceola & Renegade (Football),* **FSU**
- *Clapping Until Team Scores (Basketball),* **Tennessee**
- *Cockaboose (Football),* **South Carolina**
- *College Football Playoff (Football),* **various teams**
- *College GameDay (Football),* **Texas A&M, Army / Navy**
- *College GameDay Flag (Football),* **Washington State University**
- *Colored-Lights on the UT Tower (Various Sports),* **Texas**
- *Commander in Chief Trophy Presentation (Football),* **Army / Navy**
- *Cowbells (Football),* **Mississippi State**
- *Cutting a Hockey Net (Ice Hockey),* **Boston College**
- *Cutting Down Basketball Nets (Basketball),* **NC State**
- *Dawg Walk (Football),* **Georgia**
- *Demon Deacon's Motorcycle Entrance (Football),* **Wake Forest**
- *Dogpile (Baseball),* **various teams**
- *Donald Duck is Oregon Mascot (Football),* **Oregon**
- *Dotting-the-"I" (Football),* **Ohio State**
- *Drake Relays (Track & Field),* **Drake University**
- *Duel in the Desert (Basketball),* **Arizona / Arizona State**
- *Earning Your Golf Bag (Golf),* **GA Tech**
- *Fans Commuting to a Game on their Boats (Football),* **Clemson, Tennessee**
- *Fans Gathering on the Field After a Football Game (Football),* **Clemson**
- *Fightin' Texas Aggie Band (Football),* **Texas A&M**
- *First-Friday Parade (Football),* **Clemson**
- *Fish Toss (Ice Hockey),* **New Hampshire**
- *Five Dollies (Football),* **Stanford**
- *Flowers Placed on Reveilles' Graves (Football),* **Texas A&M**
- *Flyovers (Football),* **various teams**
- *Flyover During National Anthem (Football),* **Army / Navy**

- *FOY-ODY Sportsmanship Trophy Awarded (Football),* **Alabama / Auburn**
- *Free Throw Defense (Basketball),* **various teams**
- *Frog Horn (Football),* **TCU**
- *Frozen Four (Ice Hockey),* **various teams**
- *GA Tech Fight Song (Basketball / Football),* **GA Tech**
- *Gamecock Walk (Football),* **South Carolina**
- *Games Attended at Iconic Venues*
    - *Alexander Memorial Coliseum (Basketball),* **GA Tech**
    - *Alumni Stadium (Football),* **Middlebury College**
    - *Amalie Arena (Hockey; Basketball),* **Men's Frozen Four, Women's Final Four, ACC Men's Basketball Tournament**
    - *Assembly Hall (Basketball),* **Indiana**
    - *AT&T Stadium,* **College Football Playoff Championship**
    - *Atlanta-Fulton County Stadium,* **various teams**
    - *Autzen Stadium (Football),* **Oregon**
    - *Barclays Center (Basketball),* **ACC Men's Basketball Tournament**
    - *BB&T Field (Football),* **Wake Forest**
    - *Ben Hill Griffin Stadium (Football),* **Florida**
    - *Birmingham Crossplex (Track),* **DII National Championship**
    - *Black River (The Pull),* **Hope College**
    - *Bobby Dodd Stadium at Historic Grant Field (Football),* **GA Tech**
    - **Boston College** *Alumni Stadium (Football)*
    - *Bridgestone Arena (Basketball),* **Women's Final Four**
    - *Bryant-Denny Stadium (Football),* **Alabama**
    - *Cameron Indoor Stadium (Basketball),* **Duke**
    - *Camp Randall (Football),* **Wisconsin**
    - *Capital Centre (Basketball),* **ACC Men's Basketball Tournament**
    - *Capital City Club (Golf),* **NCAA DI Men's National Championship**
    - *Carnesecca Arena (Basketball),* **St. John's**
    - *Charlotte Coliseum (Basketball),* **ACC Men's Basketball Tournament**
    - *Clemson Memorial Stadium,* **Clemson**

- Cotton Bowl, **Texas / Oklahoma**
- Dan McGill Tennis Complex (Tennis), **NCAA DI Men's and Women's National Championships**
- Darrell K Royal – Texas Memorial Stadium (Football), **Texas**
- Death Valley, (Football), **Clemson**
- Death Valley, (Football), **LSU**
- Doak Campbell Stadium (Football), **FSU**
- Drake Stadium (Track & Field), **Drake University**
- Edmund P. Joyce Center (Basketball), **Notre Dame**
- Fisher Stadium (Football), **Lafayette**
- Fitton Field (Football), **College of the Holy Cross**
- Folsom Field, (Football), **Colorado**
- Frank Howard Field (Football), **Clemson**
- Gator Bowl (Football), **various teams**
- Georgia Dome, **various teams**
- Georgia Tech Recreation Center (Swimming), **NCAA DI Swimming & Diving National Championships**
- Greensboro Coliseum (Basketball), **ACC Tournament**
- Harvard Stadium (Football), **Harvard**
- Historic Barron Stadium (Football), **NAIA National Championship**
- Howey-in-the-Hills (Golf), **DIII National Championship**
- Infinite Energy Arena (Gymnastics), **NCAA DI National Championship**
- Iron Bowl (Football), **Alabama / Auburn**
- Jordan-Hare Stadium (Football), **Auburn**
- KFC Yum! Center (Volleyball), **DI National Championship**
- Kyle Field (Football), **Texas A&M**
- Lawrence Joel Veterans Memorial Coliseum (Basketball), **Wake Forest**
- Legion Field (Football), **Alabama / Auburn**
- Louisiana Superdome (Football), **various teams**
- M&T Bank Stadium (Football), **Army / Navy**
- Madison Square Garden (Basketball), **various teams**
- MetLife Stadium (Football), **Army / Navy**
- Michie Stadium (Football), **Army**
- Municipal Stadium (Football), **NAIA Championship**

- o Neyland Stadium (Football), **Tennessee**
- o Notre Dame Stadium (Football), **Notre Dame**
- o Odle Arena (Basketball), **Taylor University**
- o Original Orange Bowl (Football), **Miami**
- o Original Sugar Bowl (Football), **Tulane**
- o Raymond James Stadium (Football), **College Football Playoff National Championship**
- o Rhodes-Reaves Field House (Basketball), **Harding**
- o Rome Tennis Center (Tennis), **ACC Championship**
- o Rose Bowl (Football), **UCLA / Penn State**
- o Rupp Arena (Basketball), **Kentucky**
- o Sanford Stadium (Football), **Georgia**
- o South Commons Softball Complex (Softball), **NAIA College World Series**
- o Spectrum Center (Basketball), **ACC Basketball Tournament**
- o Stegeman Coliseum (Basketball), **UGA**
- o Sun Bowl, **UCLA / Virginia Tech**
- o Sun Devil Stadium (Football , **Arizona State**
- o TD Ameritrade Park (Baseball), **College World Series**
- o The Big House (Football), **Michigan**
- o The Horseshoe (Football), **Ohio State**
- o The Omni (Basketball), **Men's Final Four**
- o The Palestra (Basketball), **Ivy League Tournament**
- o The Swamp (Football), **Florida**
- o Thompson-Boling Arena (Basketball), **Tennessee**
- o Tiger Stadium (Football), **LSU**
- o Toyota Stadium (Football), **FCS Championship**
- o University of Phoenix Stadium (Football), **Fiesta Bowl; College Football Playoff National Championship**
- o USA Softball Hall of Fame Stadium (Softball), **College World Series**
- o Vaught-Hemingway Stadium (Football), **Ole Miss**
- o Williams-Brice Stadium (Football), **South Carolina**
- Garnet & Gold Guys (Football), **FSU**
- Gator Chomp (Football), **Florida**
- Golden Hat Trophy Presentation (Football), **Oklahoma / Texas**
- Governor's Cup (Football), **Georgia / GA Tech**

- *Governors' Trophy (Football),* **Oklahoma / Texas**
- *Greatest Timeout in College Basketball (Basketball),* **Indiana**
- *Hang on Sloopy (Football),* **Ohio State**
- *Head of the Charles (Crew),* **various teams**
- *Helen of Troy Hairdryers (Football),* **Sun Bowl**
- *Helmet Stickers (Football),* **FSU**
- *"Hey, John" (Ice Hockey),* **New Hampshire**
- *High-Five (Various Sports),* **Louisville**
- *Hook 'em Horns Hand Sign (Football),* **Texas**
- *Hokey Pokey (Football),* **Virginia Tech**
- *Home Games Away From Home (Football),* **Georgia**
- *How 'Bout Them Dawgs? (Football),* **Georgia**
- *Howard's Rock (Football),* **Clemson**
- *Howdy (Football),* **Texas A&M**
- *Ice-skating Cheerleaders (Ice Hockey),* **Minnesota**
- *IZZone (Basketball),* **Michigan State**
- *Johnny Football (Football),* **Texas A&M**
- *Jump Around (Football),* **Wisconsin**
- *Keeper of the Frog Horn (Football),* **TCU**
- *Kernkraft 400 (Basketball),* **Wake Forest**
- *Kiss-Your-Date (Football),* **Texas A&M**
- *Krzyzewskiville (Basketball),* **Duke**
- *Le Regiment de Sambre et Meuse (Football),* **Ohio State**
- *Leaping to Touch Banner (Football),* **Michigan**
- *Lei Worn by Navy Coach for Army / Navy Game (Football),* **Army / Navy**
- *Leland Stanford Junior University Marching Band (Football),* **Stanford**
- *Little Red Flag (Football),* **Harvard / Yale**
- *Little Three (Football),* **Williams / Wesleyan**
- *Live Eagle Mascot (Football),* **Auburn**
- *Local Hotel Duplicates Traditions (Football),* **Notre Dame**
- *Lunch Pail (Football),* **Virginia Tech**
- *MacArthur Bowl Presentation (Football),* **Clemson**
- *March-On (Football),* **Army / Navy**
- *Martha, the Mop-Lady (Basketball),* **Indiana**
- *Mascot Pushups (Football),* **various teams**

- *Midnight Yell Practice (Football),* **Texas A&M**
- *Mike the Tiger at LSU Home Games (Football),* **LSU**
- *Miss Reveille, Ma'am (Football),* **Texas A&M**
- *Moralers (Tug-of-War),* **Hope College**
- *Most Exciting 25 Seconds in College Football (Football),* **Clemson**
- *Most Played Southern Rivalry (Football),* **Auburn / Georgia**
- *Most Played Rivalry (Football),* **Lehigh / Lafayette**
- *Mutual Respect Rivalry (Football),* **Army / Navy**
- *My Old Kentucky Home (Football / Basketball),* **Kentucky**
- *Nation's Top Hand Signal (Football),* **Texas**
- *Notre Dame Fight Song (Football / Basketball),* **Notre Dame**
- *Nova, the War Eagle (Football),* **Auburn**
- *Number 1 Mascot (Football),* **Georgia**
- *Open the Gate (Football),* **Wake Forest**
- *Orange Balloon Release (Football),* **Clemson**
- *Palmetto Bowl (Football),* **Clemson / South Carolina**
- *Peyton Manning Pass (Football),* **Tennessee**
- *Picking-Up Butch (Football & Basketball),* **Middlebury College**
- *Pink-the-Rink (Ice Hockey),* **Fredonia State**
- *Pitt Script Helmets (Football),* **Pitt**
- *Planting a Flaming Spear at Midfield (Football),* **FSU**
- *Play Like a Champion Today (Football),* **Notre Dame**
- *Players Respecting the National Anthem (Basketball),* **Virginia Tech**
- *Players Running Through the Block-T (Football),* **Tennessee**
- *Presidential Walk From One Sideline to the Other at Halftime (Football),* **Army / Navy**
- *Prisoner Exchange (Football),* **Army / Navy)**
- *Pullers (Tug-of-War),* **Hope College**
- *Quick Cals (Football),* **Ohio State**
- *Radcliffe Crew (Crew),* **Radcliffe**
- *Raising Helmets During Alma Mater (Football),* **Notre Dame**
- *Ralphie's Pre-game Run (Football),* **Colorado**
- *Ramblin' Wreck (Football),* **GA Tech**
- *Rama Jama National Championship Burger (Football),* **Alabama**
- *Rammer Jammer Yellowhammer! (Football),* **Alabama**
- *Red River Rivalry (Football),* **Oklahoma / Texas**

- *Reunion of All Reunions (Football),* **Army / Navy**
- *Reveille Graves (Football),* **Texas A&M**
- *Ringing the Chapel Bell (Football),* **Georgia**
- *Rivalry Games Attended*
  - *Alabama / Auburn (football)*
  - *Arizona / Arizona State (basketball)*
  - *Army / Navy (football, boxing)*
  - *Auburn / Georgia (football)*
  - *Clemson / South Carolina (football)*
  - *Duke / North Carolina (basketball)*
  - *Georgia / GA Tech (football, basketball, baseball)*
  - *Lafayette / Lehigh (football)*
  - *Michigan / Ohio State (football)*
  - *Oklahoma / Texas (football)*
  - *Williams / Wesleyan (football)*
- *Roll Tide Roll Cheer (Football),* **Alabama**
- *Rolling-the-Quad (Various Sports),* **Wake Forest**
- *Rolling Toomer's Corner (Football),* **Auburn**
- *RUF/NEKS Shotguns (Football),* **Oklahoma**
- *Sandstorm (Football),* **South Carolina**
- *Sawing Varsity's Horns Off (Football),* **Texas A&M**
- *Script Ohio (Football),* **Ohio State**
- *Script Oh No (Football),* **Michigan**
- *Shout (Football),* **Oregon**
- *Silent Night (Basketball),* **Taylor University**
- *Simulating a Bowling Game (Baseball),* **Vanderbilt**
- *Sing-Second (Football),* **Army / Navy**
- *Skull Session (Football),* Ohio State
- *Smokey the Cannon (Football),* **Texas**
- *Smoking a Victory Cigar (Football),* **Williams College**
- *Sod Cemetery (Football),* **Clemson**
- *Sooner Schooner (Football),* **Oklahoma**
- *Speed Limit of 18mph (Football),* **Tennessee**
- *Spike Squad (Football),* **Georgia**
- *Spirit Spots (Football),* **Army / Navy**
- *Spirit Walk (Football),* **Texas A&M**

- *St. Pierre's Barber Shop (Football),* **Williams College**
- **Stanford** *Band (Football)*
- **Stanford** *Tree (Football)*
- *Storming-the-Court, after a #1 team has been defeated,* **Miami** *over* **Duke** *in 2013*
- *Super Fans (Basketball / Football),* **various teams**
- *Tailgating at the Grove (Football),* **Ole Miss**
- *Tailgating with the Volunteer Navy on the Tennessee River (Football),* **Tennessee**
- *Taps (Football),* **Texas**
- *Team Not-Named Harvard (Crew),* **Radcliffe**
- *Team Up North (Football),* **Ohio State**
- *Texas Fight Song (Football),* **Texas**
- *Textile Bowl (Football),* **Clemson / NC State**
- *The Eyes of Texas (Football),* **Texas**
- *The Game (Football),* **Harvard / Yale**
- *The Good Old Song of Wahoowa (Basketball / Football),* **Virginia**
- *The Hokey Pokey (Football),* **Virginia Tech**
- *The Irish Guard (Football),* **Notre Dame**
- *The Notre Dame Fight Song (Football / Basketball),* **Notre Dame**
- *The Pull (Tug-of-War),* **Hope College**
- *The Rivalry (Football),* **Lehigh / Lafayette**
- *The Swarm (Football),* **GA Tech**
- *The Victors Fight Song (Football),* **Michigan**
- *The Williams Walk (Football),* **Williams College**
- *Tie-Dyed Nation (Basketball),* **Wake Forest**
- *Tiger Pushups (Football),* **Clemson**
- *Tigerama (Football),* **Clemson**
- *Touchdown Jesus (Football),* **Notre Dame**
- *Touching the Banner (Football),* **Michigan**
- *T-shirt Gatling Gun (Basketball / Football),* **various teams**
- *Two-Bits (Football),* **Florida**
- *Ugas' Mausoleum (Football),* **Georgia**
- *Untraditional Uniforms (Football),* **Oregon**
- *Upside Down Hook 'em Horns Sign (Football),* **Oklahoma**
- *Walk of Fame at Denny Chimes (Football),* **Alabama**

- *War-Chant Arm Motion (Football & Basketball),* **FSU**
- *We Are … Penn State (Football),* **Penn State**
- *We Are the Boys of Old Florida (Football),* **Florida**
- *Welcome to the Jungle (Football),* **Wake Forest**
- *White Jerseys for Home Games (Football),* **LSU**
- *William Tell Overture Timeout (Basketball),* **Indiana**
- *Woo Pig, Sooie (Football),* **Arkansas**
- *World's 9th Best Infantry (Football),* **Alabama**
- *Wrestling Title Belt (Football),* **Alabama**
- *Yell Leaders (Football),* **Texas A&M**

Bibliography

Alabama / Auburn: Iron Bowl Remains: A Curious Iron Bowl Trend: Fans Leaving Cremated Remains on the Field, www.al.com/sports, John Talty, November 25, 2015

Alabama: Celebrating Bear Bryant's Birthday: Fans Tip Hat to Bryant on 100th, Dan Wolken, USA Today, September 12, 2013

Alabama: Countdown Clock: The 2016 Alabama Football Countdown Clock, www.bamahammer.com, Charles Evans, January 13, 2016

Alabama: Evergreen Cemetery: Evergreen Cemetery Across from Bryant-Denny Stadium, ESPN.com, Alex Scarborough, August 25, 2015

Alabama: Fan's Christmas Lights: Alabama Fan Syncs Christmas Light Display Up with Eli Gold's Cotton Bowl Highlights, www.tide1029.com, Ben George January 5, 2016

Alabama: Roll Tide: The Mysterious Origins of the Phrase "Roll Tide," www.rollbamaroll, C.J. Schexnayder, October 14, 2013

Alabama: Walk of Fame at Denny Chimes: The Walk of Fame at Denny Chimes, www.prideofthetide.com, retrieved April 11, 2017

Alabama: Wrestling Belt: Why Alabama Players Have a Wrestling Title Belt on the Sideline, SB Nation, Jason Kirk, January 9, 2017

Alabama First Round NFL Draftees: Riding the Tide, USA Today, Ellen J. Horrow and Karl Gelles, April 27, 2017

Allstate Goalpost Nets: It's Good! The Story Behind Allstate's Field Goal Nets, Sports Business Journal, Terry Lefton and Michael Smith, May 26-June 1, 2014

Alumni Games: Watch. 90-Year-Old Kansas Alumni Scores Second TD in Two Years, CBS Sports, Chip Patterson, April 11, 2016

Amherst: Mascot Selection Timeline, www.amherst.edu, March 27, 2017

Arizona State: Curtain of Distraction: Michael Phelps Anchors Curtain of Distraction in Sun Devils' Rout, ESPN.com, retrieved April 20, 2017

Arizona: Race Track Program: Trainers Schooled in Business Side at Arizona, USA Today, Dan Wolken, June 2, 2015

Arkansas: Linemen Fly First Class: Promising Time for Arkansas, from Ground (game) Level to 36,000 feet, USA Today, George Schroeder, September 23, 2014

Arkansas: Woo Pig Sooie: Woo Pig Suing? Arkansas Gets Sound Trademark for Call, Michael Smith, Sports Business Journal, July 28, 2014

Armed Forces Classic: www.espnevents.com, retrieved April 16, 2017

Army / Navy: Spirit Spots: The Good, the Bad and the Goats, the Military Times, Kevin Lilley, December 9, 2016

Army / Navy: Tradition and History Wrapped into 115th Army / Navy Game, Fox News, Sarah Blansett, December 13, 2014

Army / Navy: The Greatest Game Ever Played: Tim Reynolds, the Atlanta Journal-Constitution, February 12, 2016

Army: Pillow Fight: West Point Bans Cadet Pillow Fight after 30 Injured, Fox News, Associated Press, November 25, 2015

Army: The Marshall Plaque: Goodyear Print Advertisement, Winning Traditions Driven by Goodyear, 2015

Ashley Judd – Kentucky Super fan: ashleyjudd.com, retrieved April 27, 2017

Athletes Seeking Trademarks: Looking to Future, More NCAA Athletes Seek Own Trademarks, USA Today, August 27, 2015

Athletes' Programs to Complete Degrees: Programs Offer Alternative Path for Athletes to Finish Degrees, Sport Business Journal, Kristi Dosh, August 18, 2014

Auburn: Rolling Tradition Will Roll-On at Auburn, Laken Litman, USA Today, 2014

Auburn: Toomer's Corner: Oaks Back at Toomer's Corner, Atlanta Journal-Constitution, Associated Press, February 2, 2015

Auburn: Toomer's Corner: Tireless Fight Ends to Save Auburn's Oaks, Mike Lopresti, USA Today, April 24, 2013

Auburn: Toomer's Corner: Turning Tragedy into Great Beauty, Atlanta Journal-Constitution, Howard Pousner, May 30, 2014

Autism Speaks: Coaches Unite for Autism Speaks, Atlanta Journal-Constitution, Ken Sugiura, February 6, 2015

Baylor: Bezos River Commute: Where Boats Meet Bears: University Makes Most of Riverside Location, Sports Business Journal, Don Muret, September 8, 2014

Beer Sales at College Events: Tapping Into New Stream of Revenue, USA Today, Dan Wolken, June 23, 2014

Big 10 Trophy Games: Game Report: Iowa 10, Wisconsin 6, www.thegazette.com, Nate Meier, October 3, 2015

Boston College: Live Eagle Mascot: Meet Welles, Boston College Football's Live Eagle Mascot, Brian Favat, www.bcinterruption.com, November 2, 2013

Bowl Games Swag: Want a New Gift Suite Choice? Take a Seat. David Broughton, Sports Business Journal, December 9-15, 2013

Bowl Games Swag: Thanks for Playing, Sports Business Journal, David Broughton, March 10-16, 2014

Bowl Games Swag: Unique Bowl Gift a Heady Memento; Ken Sugiura, Atlanta Journal-Constitution, December 27, 2016

Boxtorow National Championship Poll: Grambling Crowned HBCU National Champions, www.boxtorow.com, Donal Ware, December 20, 2016

Bradley: Kaboom, the Gargoyle Mascot: Finally, a Mascot to Call Their Own, Champion Magazine, Spring 2014

Brown: One for Me Program: Exploring Opportunities One Class at a Time, Champion Magazine, Michelle Brutlag Hosick, winter 2013

Busted Brackets: March Madness Toast, Janice Hough, www.leftcoastsportsbabe.com, 2017

Butler University: Bulldog Mascot Walks with Each Graduating Class: Butler Mourns Death of Beloved Mascot, Nicole Auerbach and Daniel Uthman, USA Today, September 3, 2013

Butler: Mascot ACL Tear: Butler Mascot Blue III Has Torn ACL, the Indianapolis Star, Joe Tamborello, September 29, 2016

Caltech: Win a Ball Signed by Five Nobel Prize Winners: Revenge of the Nerd, Chris Ballard, Sports Illustrated, November 23, 2015

Caltech: Probation: Caltech is on NCAA Probation. No, Really, the Los Angeles Times, Bill Plaschke, July 15, 2012

Caltech / MIT Rivalry: Wikipedia.org/, retrieved April 1, 2017

Central College: Baseball Graduation: One Thousand Words, Champion Magazine, Dan Vander Beek, spring 2015

Chicken Fried Tailgate Song: Zac Brown Band's 'Chicken Fried' Most Popular Tailgating Song, the Atlanta Journal-Constitution, Melissa Ruggieri, October 2, 2015

Cincinnati: Cincinnati's Midday Madness, The Court They Played On, the Sporting News, Roger Kuznia, October 17, 2013

Clemson: Fan Tattoo: Clemson Fan Keeps Promise, Gets Dabo Swinney Tattoo, CBS Sports, Tom Fornelli   , December 14, 2015

Clemson: Omaha Challenge: Omaha Challenge a Hit with Players, Clemsontigers.com, Brian Hennessy, December 5, 2014

Coaches Beat Cancer: Coaches Donate Time for Cancer Fundraiser, Mark Snyder, Detroit Free Press April 13, 2015

Coaches' Superstitions: Champion Magazine, winter 2013

Coast-to-Coast Men's Basketball Event: Plans in Place for 4-Team Basketball Trip in 2018; Joe Rexrode, USA Today, February 2, 2014

Cockabooses: As Tailgate Host Rails, What Else to Do but Chug? NY Times, College Football Spotlight, Marc Tracy, September 28, 2014

Coker College: Senior Players Graduate by Walking Down the 3rd Base Line: An Electric Day for Coker Baseball, Greg Johnson, Champion, Spring 2013

College World Series: Dogpile: The Art of the Dogpile, ESPN.com, Mitch Sherman, June 25, 2014

Cutting the Nets: Leading Off, Sports Illustrated, April 21, 2014

Dartmouth: Tackling Robots: Dartmouth Football Introduces Robotic Tackling Dummies in Practice, USA Today, Avery Stone, August 27, 2015

Dartmouth: Some of the Best College Hockey Traditions, NCAA.com, Beth Maiman, January 12, 2017

Dear World: Coach K Sends Moving Letter to His Late Friend, Jim Valvano, USA Today, Nate Scott, December 5, 2016

Dear World: Duke Building Close-Knit Clan, USA Today, Nicole Auerbach, November 13, 2014

Die-Hard Fans: Die-Hard College Sports Fans Defy Expectations, Duke Today, Jackie Ogburn, March 16, 2015

DII Community Engagement: Community, Championships Come Together in Division II, Champion Magazine, Rachel Stark, summer 2014

Drake University: Beautiful Bulldog: Lucey Named Beautiful Bulldog, Luke Meredith, Associated Press, April 21, 2014

Final Four Floor: Building the NCAA's Final Four Floor, ESPN the Magazine, April 10, 2017

Flyovers: Preparing for Takeoff, Ryan McGee, ESPN the Magazine, February 2, 2015

Franklin College: Grizzly Grandparents: Friend off the Court, Champion Magazine, Hannah Meister, winter 2016

FSU: Renegade Makes a Road Trip: Seminoles' Steed Renegade Makes a Long Ride West, Sights & Sounds, 2014

FSU: The Garnet and Gold Guys: Insider Spotlight, ESPN the Magazine, September 29, 2014

FSU: Chief Osceola: Legendary Florida State Coach Bobby Bowden Plants the Spear at Midfield, USA Today, Nick Schwartz, October 27, 2013

GA Tech: Earning Your Golf Bag: Tech Glad NCAAs at Crabapple, Ken Sugiura, the Atlanta Journal-Constitution, May 27, 2013

Games Played Outside the USA: List of College Football Games Played Outside the United States; www.wikipedia.com, retrieved April 16, 2017

Georgetown: Kale: Hoyas to Have Kale Giveaway Night, www.espn.com, Darren Rovell, February 3, 2015

Georgia: Lone Trumpeter: The Singular Story behind Redcoat's Lone Trumpeter, Atlanta Journal-Constitution, Kristen Miller, retrieved April 9, 2017

Georgia: Spike Squad: UGA Basketball Coach Mark Fox Paints Body for Bama Game, William McFadden, www.dawgnation.com, October 3, 2015

Goalposts Do Not Grow on Trees, Steve Wulf, ESPN the Magazine, September 2, 1013

Goodyear Blimp: Spirit of Goodyear Retired, ESPN the Magazine, April 14, 2014

Goodyear Blimpworthy Events: Goodyear Website, September 1, 2016

Grand Valley State: First Pitch: A Purposeful Pitcher, Champion Magazine, David Pickle, spring 2013

Heisman Trophy: With Heisman Tucked Away, Spotlight Falls to Look-Alikes, NY Times, Richard Sandomir, December 13, 2015

High Five: History of the High Five, ESPN the Magazine, Jon Mooallem, August 8, 2011

Iowa: The Swarm: Goodyear Print Advertisement, Winning Traditions Driven by Goodyear, 2015

Kansas State: Bill Snyder's Windbreakers: No Bowl Jackets for Bill Snyder, www.espn.com, Associated Press, September 27, 2014

Kansas State: Mascot: Kansas State Student Suffers Seizure after Getting Tackled during Pregame Ritual, the Bleacher Report, Kyle Newport, November 3, 2013

Kansas State: Where No Band Has Gone Before, www.slate.com, Jake New, September 10, 2015

Kansas: Ugly Sweater Game: KU Basketball Fans Break Holiday-Sweater World Record, KU Sports.com, Rochelle Valverde, December 19, 2015

Lehigh / Lafayette: Not Your Average Foes, Champion Magazine, fall 2014

Louisiana / Lafayette: Blackjack Landry Statue: Blackjack Landry Statue Unveiled at Cajun Field, Daily Advertiser, Tim Buckley, September 29, 2012

Louisville: Men's Swimming & Diving Teams' Support: Watching the Cardinals Women's Volleyball Team, Igor Guryashkin, ESPN the Magazine, December 9, 2013

LSU: Mike the Tiger: LSU Ends Practice of Bringing Live Tiger into Stadium, Begins Search for Mike VII, CBS Sports, Chip Patterson, January 19, 2017

MacArthur Bowl: Hall of Fame Provides New Home for Trophy, Atlanta Journal-Constitution, Tim Tucker, April 25, 2015

Manager Games: These Scrimmages Count, the NY Times, Zach Schonbrun, February 21, 2016

Mansfield: Night Game: After 121-Year Blackout, Night Football Returns to Mansfield University, www.wbur.org, September 7, 2013

Marshall: Fountain Ceremony: www.marshall.edu, November 14, 1970 Remembered, retrieved April 2, 2017

Maryland: Lifetime Degree Guarantee: Maryland to Offer Lifetime Degree Guarantee, USA Today, Tess Quinlan, August 19, 2014

Mayor's Cup: This Cup Runneth Over, Champion Magazine, Jared Thompson, summer 2015

Michigan / Notre Dame: Breakup: Michigan and Notre Dame Have Different Versions of Their Breakup, NY Times, September 7, 2014

Michigan State: Dairy: Thriving Saturdays with the Help of Sundaes, and Flavors for Everyone, NY Times, Campus Corner, Marc Tracy, September 13, 2015

Michigan: Announcing the Score of All Slippery Rock Games: Slippery Rock's Tie to Michigan is in Name Only, Always Cheered, the New York Times, Marc Tracy November 8, 2015

Michigan: Jim Harbaugh Smashing a Buckeye on a Grave: Jim Harbaugh Smashed a Buckeye with a Hammer at Bo Schembechler's Grave, the Washington Post, Des Bieler, November 24, 2015

Michigan: Team Trips: Jet-set Jim: Harbaugh intends to take Michigan team abroad every year, ESPN.com, Dan Murphy, February 1, 2017

Mike Slive Tradition: Slive Savors Role in SEC's Golden Age, George Schroeder, USA Today, August 29, 2014

Mississippi State: Cowbells: Mississippi State Traditions, www.hailstate.com, retrieved April 8, 2017

Monmouth University: Bench Celebrations: USA Today December 2, 2015, Nicole Auerbach

Mount St. Joseph: Lauren Hill: An Unforgettable Sunday Afternoon for Lauren Hill, www.espn.com, Alyssa Roenigk, November 5, 2014

Mr. Irrelevant: NFL Draft's Irrelevants? Says Who? The New York Times, Ken Belson, April 30, 2017

National Champions Visiting the White House: Florida State Waits on Busy Obama, Corey Clark, Tallahassee Democrat, June 22, 2014

National Championship Rings: Manufacturing of the FSU Championship Rings, ESPN the Magazine, April 28, 2014

National Championship Rings: Loyalty's Rewards: Cubs Give 20 Fans Honor of Presenting Series Rings, USA Today, Nancy Armour, April 12, 2017

National Championship Visits to the White House: Obama Snubs NCAA Hockey Champions, the Free Beacon, Bill McMorris, April 22, 2015

National Championships: Lost Titles: Fringe Benefit of College Football Playoff? No More Mythical Titles, CBS Sports, Dennis Dodd, June 24, 2014

Naval Academy: Lei worn by Coach during Army / Navy Game: Heritage, Lucky Charm Tied Together, Gary Mihoces, USA Today, December 14, 2013

Naval Academy: March On: Insider Spotlight, ESPN the Magazine, November 10, 2014

NCAA Organization: And Then There Were Three, Champion Magazine, David Pickle, summer 2013

Nebraska: Big Red Express: Tim Miles, Bo Pelini Taking Big Red Express Train throughout Nebraska Today, www.thespun.com, Andrew Holleran, June 28, 2014

Nebraska: Help with Starting Careers: Nebraska Program Gives Athletes Help in Starting Careers, USA Today, Nicole Auerbach, May 30, 2016

North Dakota: Fighting Sioux Nickname: The Sioux Nickname Is Gone, but North Dakota Hockey Fans Haven't Moved On, the NY Times, Pat Borzi, March 1, 2016

Northeastern: Jock-the-Vote: Athletes at Northeastern Team-Up to Jock the Vote, Champion Magazine, fall 2014

Notre Dame: Bagpiper: Notre Dame's Unlikely Tradition: the Lacrosse Bagpiper, the Chicago Tribune, Philip Hersh, May 21, 2015

Notre Dame: Leprechaun: Job Demands a Fiery Spirit; a Fiery Beard is Optional, New York Times, College Football Spotlight, Marc Tracy, September 6, 2015

Notre Dame: Play like a Champion Today Sign: Paint like a Champion, Rick Reilly, www.espn.com, December 21, 2012

Notre Dame: Recruiting Letters: Notre Dame Returns to Recruiting with Gold, www.thescore.com, Kimberly John, January 9, 2015

Notre Dame: Trick-Shot Monday: Top-10 Trick Shot Monday Moments, Pat Sullivan, www.slapthesign.com, June 30, 2016

NYC Colleges Home Games: There's No Place like Home, Champion Magazine, summer 2016

Ohio State: Buck-I-Guy: Insider Spotlight, ESPN the Magazine, February 2, 2015

Ohio State: Fired Band Director Says Sexual Report Inaccurate, USA Today, Laken Litman, August 5, 2014

Ohio State: Gold Pants Pin: An Ohio State Football Tradition, SB Nation, Jeanna Thomas, June 3, 2013

Ohio State: Governor's Proclamation: Sign of the Apocalypse, Sports Illustrated, December 30, 2015

Ohio State: Mirror Lake Jump: OSU Students Unhappy with Mirror Lake Jump Changes, Antonio Venegas, www.collegespun.com, November 25, 2013

Ohio State: Script Ohio: A Band Shows Flair Even as It Sticks to the Script, the New York Times, Melissa Hoppert, November 29, 2015

Oklahoma: Mex the OK Mascot: Oklahoma Mascot Mex Buried in Memorial Stadium, ESPN.com, Jake Trotter, August 25, 2015

Ole Miss: Chucky Mullins Bust: Mullins' Lasting Mark on Ole Miss, Atlanta Journal-Constitution, David Brandt, September 7, 2014

Oregon: Four Sport Athlete: Brenner Breaks the Mold, USA Today, Jeffrey Martin, USA Today, May 29, 2013

Oregon: Phil Knight's Locker, ESPN.com, Chantel Jennings, August 25, 2015

Oregon: Speed School: So You Think You Can Run, College Football Playbook, ESPN the Magazine, John Brant, September 16, 2013

Oregon: Uniforms: Meet the Men Who Dress the Ducks, ESPN.com, Darren Rovell, January 11, 2015

Oregon: Untraditional Uniforms: Uniform Expression, Laken Litman and Paul Myerberg, USA Today, January 6, 2015

Palestra: Palestra Packed Full of History, USA Today, Nicole Auerbach, February 7, 2017

Palestra: The Palestra, College Hoops Cathedral, USA Today, Rem Rieder, January 22, 2016

Pittsburgh / Penn State: Rivalry: With Penn State Next, Pitt Glad to End Drought of Rivalry Games, USA Today, Nicole Auerbach, September 6, 2016

Pittsburgh: Heinz Red-Zone: Heinz Field's Gant Bottles to Spur Fans' Anticipation, Post-Gazette, Tom Barnes, October 20, 2001

Pittsburgh: The Pitt Script: Pitt's Helmets Return to Script of Glory Days and a Title Year, Dave Caldwell, The New York Times, November 15, 2015

Pranks: Acing the Pranks, Roy Rivenburg, LA Times, retrieved April 1, 2017

Pranks: Best Rivalry Pranks in College Football History, the Bleacher Report, Carl Stine, May 2, 2013

Pranks: College Pranks We Wish We Thought Of, www.mentalfloss.com, Ransom Riggs, retrieved April 1, 2017

Pranks: Eleven of the Greatest Class Pranks in History, www.mentalfloss.com, Julie Winterbottom, retrieved April 1, 2017

Pranks: Top Four Rivalry Pranks in the NCAA, www.theodysseyonline.com, MacKenzie Mitchell, retrieved April 1, 2017

Presidents and College Football: Presidents and College Football, the White House Historical Association, Joel Tresse, retrieved April 11, 2017

Robert Morris: Athletic Scholarships for Video Gaming: Sign of the Apocalypse, Sports Illustrated, September 15, 2014

Rutgers: Cannon: Demanding Liberty or Death, or Maybe a Touchdown, NY Times, Campus Corner, Marc Tracy, September 21, 2014

Saint Joseph: Hawk: Last Flap, ESPN the Magazine, Chris Jones, April 14, 2014

San Jose State: Coach Dancing: San Jose State Coach Shows off Dance Moves from His Old Job with MC Hammer, Fox News, April 12, 2017

Service Academies Adjusting Their Schedules: DOD Change Opens Door for Robinette, USA Today, Lindsay H. Jones, March 22, 2017

Service Academy Nominations: Pride and Patronage, USA Today, Gregory Korte and Fredreka Schouten, September 16, 2014

Simon Fraser: Border Crossing, Champion Magazine, Rachel Stark, winter 2017

Sonic's School Spirit: Sonic Puts School Spirit Where Mouth Is, Bruce Horovitz, USA Today, August 20, 2013

Southern Mississippi: SMTTT: Sting Easing for Southern Miss, George, Schroeder, USA Today, August 13, 2013

Stanford: Iowa Senate Bill Targets Stanford Band Controversy, www.desmoinesregister.com, William Petroski, February 3, 2016

Stanford: LSJUMB, http://lsjumb.stanford.edu/, retrieved April 12, 2017

Stanford Offensive Line: Stanford Offensive Line Ops for Major Challenges, USA Today, Dan Wolken, April 28, 2017

Storming-the-Field: SEC Schools to Face Fines up to $250K for Fans Rushing the Field / Court, www.al.com/sports, Natalie Williams, May 29, 2015

Suits and Sneakers Week: Coaches Versus Cancer, www.nabc.com, retrieved April 8, 2017

TCU: Frog Horn: Hhaaaaaah! The Frog Horn! TCU Magazine, Nancy Bartosek, fall 2010

Teams supporting Others After a Tragedy: Tragedy Brings Tigers, Tide Together, ESPN.com, Gene Wojciechowski, May 4, 2011

Tearing Down Goalposts: Editorial, David Callaway, USA Today, April 25, 2014

Tennessee: Skeletons Inside Neyland Stadium, Anthropology Research Carried Out Inside Neyland Stadium, ESPN.com, David Hale, August 25, 2015

Texas A&M: Kyle Field Bats: Kyle Field a Friend to Bats, ESPN.com, Sam Khan, August 25, 2015

Texas A&M: Monuments: A&M Unveils Statues Paying Homage to Aggie Traditions at Kyle Field, The Eagle, Sam Peshek, September 6, 2014

Texas A&M: Student Bonfire: This Texas A&M Fan's Groom's Cake Features an Aggie Bonfire Complete with a Roasting Longhorn, Tyler Moorehead, www.collegespun.com, December 21, 2013

Texas A&M: Student Bonfire: Zoom, Scott Eden, ESPN the Magazine, December 22, 2014

Texas A&M: Yell Leaders: At Texas A&M, Fans are Fluent in the Science of Yelling, NY Times, Campus Corner, Marc Tracy, September 7, 2014

Trophy Games: Ranking 60 College Football Rivalry trophies, SB Nation, Evin Demirel, November 26, 2014

UCLA: UCLA Has Gone from Cubs to Grizzlies to Bruins, Sports Illustrated, Evan Scott Schwartz, September 30, 2014

UConn: Carrying the Coach off the Court after a National Championship: Leader of the Pack, Geno Auriemma, Sports Illustrated, April 20, 2015.

UNLV: Khem Kong Puppet: ESPN the Magazine, Rachel Ullrich, January 29, 2014

UT Chattanooga: Moc Walk a Daily Practice Tradition, Times Free Press, Stephen Hargis, November 28th, 2014

Utah: Changes to Fight Song Lyrics: University of Utah Changes Fight Song Lyrics from Man to Fan, www/nbcnews.com, July 3, 2014

Various Traditions: The Old College Try, Champion Magazine, Megan Fernandez, Amy Wimmer Schwarb, Ali Smith, Kayci Woodley, spring 2016

Virginia Tech: National Anthem: This Coach Hosted Veterans to Teach His Players to Respect the National Anthem, the Federalist, Bre Payton, September 26, 2016

Virginia Tech: Virginia Tech's Cannon Deeply Rooted in History, Sports Illustrated, Evan Scott Schwartz, September 2, 2014

Virtual Reality: New Use of Virtual Reality Adds Another Dimension to Coaches' Recruiting Tactics, the NY Times, November 21, 2015

Wisconsin: Camp Randall: Camp Randall the Site of Former Confederate Prison, ESPN.com, Mitch Sherman, August 25, 2015

Zero Waste Initiative: Oil Isn't the Only Natural Resource in Texas, fall 2013

Zero Waste Initiatives: Lacing Up, Champion Magazine, fall 2013

Zero-Waste Initiatives: Greening of College Sports Has Potential for Community Change, Christine Costa, Sports Business Journal, August 19, 2013

Alabama / Auburn Iron Bowl – al.com

Alabama Bear Bryant Statue – pinterest.com

Alabama Countdown Clock to Spring Game – depositphotos.com

Alabama Evergreen Cemetery – al.com

Alabama Players Smoking Cigars – bamahammer.com

Alabama Rama Jama National Championship Burger -- lentwithoutbacon.com

Alabama Rammer Jammer Yellowhammer*!* – redbubble.com

Alabama Roll Tide – Hyundai

Alabama Soldier of Fortune Magazine – maxim.com

Alabama Walk of Fame at Denny Chimes – remax-alabama.com

Alabama Wrestling Belt – proambelts.com

Allstate Good Hands Nets – boldip.com

Amherst Mammoths – twitter.com

Amherst / Wesleyan / Williams Little Three – collegesquashassociation.com

Arizona / Arizona State Territorial Cup – Wikimedia Commons

Arizona Camp Tontozona – engage.asu.edu

Arizona Linda Ronstadt – jensenbrazilsblog.com

Arizona Racetrack Industry Program – harnesslink.com

Arizona State Michael Phelps – youtube.com

Armed Forces Classic – retireenews.com

Army Marshall Plaque – marshallfoundation.org

Army / Navy Game – sportstravel.com

Army / Navy Spirit Spots – military.com

Army Pillow Fight – holykaw.alltop.com

Army T-shirt Tank – cbssports.com

Auburn Last Roll – pinterest.com

Auburn Oak – lauraandreades.com

Auburn Tiger Walk – auburn.edu

Auburn Toomer's Corner – treehugger.com

Aztec Bowl – americanfootballinternational.com

Basketball Manager Games – chrome.google.com

Baylor Bezos River – reddit.com

Baylor Immortal 10 – Baylor University

Baylor Sic 'Em Jersey – ftw.usatoday.com

Beehive Boot – en.wikipedia.org

Beer at College Games – collegian.csufresno.edu

Big 10 Rivalry Games; Paul Bunyan's Ax – sbnation.com

Bowl Games Swag – sportsbusinessdaily.com

Boxtorow Poll – boxtorow.com

Bradley Kaboom Mascot – twitter.com

Busted Brackets – interbasket.net
Butler Hinkle Fieldhouse – 19nine.com
Cal / Stanford Big Game – ruleoftree.com
Caltech Basketball Signed by Nobel Prize Winners – upperdeckstore.com
Caltech Cannon – hacks.mit.edu
Caltech Hollywood Sign – content.time.com
Caltech / MIT Mugs – mitadmissions.org
Caltech Revenge of the Nerds – si.com
Caltech Scoreboard – brennen.caltech.edu
Calvin / Hope Rivalry – athletics.hope.edu
Case Western Baird Brothers Trophy – Case Western University
Cheerleader with Upside Down Sign – mouthfrog.com
Cincinnati Midday Madness – gobearcats.com
Clemson Dabo Swinney Tattoo – sbnation.com
Clemson Howard's Rock – Clemson University
College of Wooster Bagpipers – woosterathletics.com
Colorado Running of Ralphie – University of Colorado Athletics
Cutting Hockey Nets – twincities.com
Dartmouth Tennis Balls on Ice – ivyleaguedigitalnetwork.com
Dartmouth Tackling Dummies – consumeraffairs.com
Duke Coach K Dear World – duke.247sports.com
Duke Cameron Indoor – Duke University
Duke Krzyzewskiville – commons.wikimedia.org
Duke Mascot Head – usatoday.com
Fans Storming a Football Field after a Victory – GA Tech athletics
Final Four Court – chron.com
Flyovers – theaviationist.com
Franklin College Grizzly Grandparents – franklingrizzlies.com
FSU Sod Cemetery – colmel.wordpress.com
FSU Chief Osceola and Renegade – ©Mike Olivella
FSU Garnet and Gold Guys – FSU Athletics
Georgetown Hail to Kale – washingtonpost.com
Georgia How 'bout Them Dawgs – dawgwear.net
Georgia Lone Trumpeter – dawgnation.com
Georgia Players Off the High Dive – gamedayr.com
Georgia Spike Squad – courtesy of Spike Squad
Georgia Uga Burials – University of Georgia
Georgia Urn – urnsdirect2u.com
Georgia Tech Golf Bag – kohls.com
Goodyear Blimp – bigmonkeyshouse.blogspot.com
Harding National Anthem – youtube.com
Harvard Little Red Flag – harvardmagazine.com

Harvey Mudd Victoria's Secret Campaign – fsufashiongirl.blogspot.com
Heinz Red Zone – bdeusa.com
Heisman Trophy – axs.com
Hope College Pull – the odysseyonline.com
Indiana Little 500 – axs.tv
Indiana Martha the Mop Lady – pinterest.com
Indiana William Tell Overture Timeout – youtube.com
Iowa Floyd of Rosedale – Iowa Athletics Communications
Iowa Grapple on the Gridiron – kwwl.com
Iowa Pink Locker Room – imgur.com
Iowa State / Missouri Telephone Trophy – realclearsports.com
Jimmy Valvano – speakola.com
Johns Hopkins Homewood Field – hopkinssports.com
Johnson & Wales Lacrosse Cart – ncaa.org
Kansas Christmas Sweater – fanatics.com
Kansas Phog – pinterest.com
Kansas Rock Chalk Jayhawk! – keywordsuggests.com
Kansas State Bill Snyder's Windbreaker – freewinningpicks.com
Kansas State Willie the Wildcat – pinterest.com
Kentucky Ashley Judd – secfanatics.com
Kentucky My Old Kentucky Home – kentuckypress.wordpress.com
Kentucky Rupp Arena – en.wikipedia.org
Kerncraft 400 – youtube.com
Krispy Kreme Challenge – raceentry.com
Lafayette / Lehigh Rivalry – web.mta.info
Lawry's Beef Bowl – sportscardinfo.wordpress.com
Lost National Championships – wikipedia.com
Linfield College End Zone Couches – Linfield College
Louisville High Five – youtube.com
Louisville Swimmers – themountaineernation.com
LSU Death Valley – pinterest.com
LSU Mike the Tiger – theredshtick.com
LSU White Home Jerseys – saturdaydownsouth.com
LSU Win Bar – tigerdroppings.com
MacArthur Bowl Trophy – courtesy of the National Football Foundation
Manhattan College 7th Inning Stretch – fscdena.org
Mansfield College First Night Game – joycetice.com
Marshall Fountain Ceremony – littlebitsofhistory.blogspot.com
McDaniel Drive-in Tailgating – McDaniel College
Miami Smoke Show Entrance – welcome.miami.edu
Miami Urn – memorials.com
Michigan / Jim Harbaugh Grave Walk – detroitsportsrag.com

Michigan / Notre Dame Rivalry – newmexico.undclub.org
Michigan Hail to the Victors – Hyundai Motor America
Michigan Road Trip to Rome – americamagazine.org
Michigan Slippery Rock Scores – flickr.com
Michigan The Victors – levysheetmusic.mse.jhu.edu
Michigan State / Zeke the Wonderdog – sbnation.com
Michigan State Dairy – msudairyclub.weebly.com
Michigan Touching the Banner – nshsdenebola.com
Middlebury College Picking Up Butch – courtesy of Middlebury College
Military Academy Appointments – davidyoung.house.gov
Mississippi State Cowbells – alumni.msstate.edu
Mississippi State Left Field Lounge – pinterest.com
Missouri Rock-M – komu.com
Missouri Truman the Tiger – mizzou.com
Monmouth Bench Celebrations – thekicker.com
Monon Bell – wasbash.edu
Mount St Joseph / Lauren Hill – pinterest.com
Mr. Irrelevant – twitter.com
NABC Suits & Sneakers Week – coaches.acsevents.com
National Champions Visiting the White House – pinterest.com
National Championship Rings – balfour.com
National Consortium for Academics & Sports – sportsbusinessdaily.com
National Signing Day – easttexasmatters.com
Naval Academy Coach Wearing Lei – US Naval Academy
Naval Academy March On – usna.edu
Naval Academy Painting Tecumseh – US Naval Academy
Navy's Goat Prank – brocouncil.com
NCAA DII Sports Festivals – ncaa.org
Nebraska Big Red Express – up.com
New Hampshire Fish Toss – ©Cody Smith Photography
North Dakota Fighting Sioux – pinterest.com
Northeastern Jock-the-Vote – vimeo.com
Norwich University Claw Machine – pinterest.com
Notre Dame Bagpiper – Notre Dame Athletics
Notre Dame Bookstore Basketball – nd.edu
Notre Dame Gold Helmets – Notre Dame University
Notre Dame Leprechaun – wikipedia.com
Notre Dame Play Like a Champion Sign; – Notre Dame University
Notre Dame Pot of Gold Recruiting Letter – notredame.247sports.com
Notre Dame Touchdown Jesus – nationfanthem.com
Notre Dame Trick Shot Monday – uhnd.com
Obituaries – amazon.com

Occidental College Latin Cheer – youtube.com
Ohio State Baby Blankets – btn.com
Ohio State Buck-I-Guy – keyword-suggestions.com
Ohio State Gold Pants – pinterest.com
Ohio State Mirror Lake Jump – youtube.com
Ohio State Script Ohio – catsmeow.com
Oklahoma Mex, the Mascot – findagrave.com
Oklahoma / Oklahoma State Bedlam – youtube.com
Oklahoma Boomer Sooner – flicker.com and soonersports.com
Ole Miss Fins Up – the odsseyonline.com
Ole Miss Chucky Mullins Bust – collegefootball.ap.org
Oregon Gameday Mascot Head – seattletimes.com
Oregon / Oregon State Civil War – thecivilwarseries.com
Oregon's Liz Brenner – usatoday.com
Oregon's Student Section – Lars Topelmann Photography
Oregon Uniform Combinations – gamedayr.com
Oregon State Congratulating Their Rival – opb.org
Palestra Box Office – courtesy of Stan Beck
Penn Toast Toss – crimsoneducation.org
Penn State We Are – pennstateclothes.com
Pitt Script Helmet – pittsburghpanthers.com
Pitt versus Penn State Rivalry – pittsburghmagazine.com
President's March Madness Selections – bostinno.streetwise.com
Radcliffe Crew – gocrimson.com
Red River Rivalry Trophy – diehardsports.com
Rice's Coaches' Table – ftw.usatoday.com
RISD Mascots – sundaydepression.com
Rose Bowl – commons.wikimedia.org
Rutgers Cannon – nytimes.com
Rutgers First Game Statue – offtackleempire.com
Saint Joseph Hawk – huffingtonpost.com
Saint Joseph Joe Lunardi Bracketology Class – friarbasketball.com
San Jose State Alonzo Carter Dancing – mwcconnection.com
SMU Peruna – smu.edu
Sonic School Spirit – barstoolu.barstoolsports.com
South Carolina Cockaboose – South Carolina Athletics
Southern Illinois Cardboard Boat Regatta – youtube.com
Southern Miss SMTTT – za.pinterest.com
Stanford Tickets Phone Number – abnewswire.com
Stanford Band / Leland Stanford Junior University Marching Band– courtesy of Robby Beyers
Sieve Chant – sites.google.com
Stanford Walk – stanforddaily.com

Streaking – fitisafeministissue.com
Superfan – elevenwarriors.com
Superfan Ashley Judd – cincinnati.com
Swarthmore / Ursinus Prom Dress Rugby – Swarthmore.edu
Taylor University Silent Night – courtesy of Taylor University
TCU Frog Horn – Jason Lesikar
Tearing Down Goalposts – luna.ku.edu
Tearing Down the Goal Posts – ponyfans.com
Teddy Roosevelt – kpfa.org
Tennessee Block T – utsports.com
Tennessee Skeletons in Neyland Stadium – strangeremains.com
Texas Bevo – dfw.cbslocal.com
Texas Hook 'em Horns – nbcdfw.com
Texas UT Tower – khou.com
Texas A&I Javelina – pinterest.com
Texas A&M 12th Man; – topbet.eu
Texas A&M Bats in the Stadium – goodbullhunting.com
Texas A&M Bonfire – texags.com
Texas A&M Fish Camp – iss.tamu.edu
Texas A&M Kingsville Tortilla Tossing – pinterest.com
Texas Tech Masked Rider – en.wikipedia.org
Texas Tech Will Rodgers Statue – orgsync.com
Tom Osborne Leadership Award – twicopy.org
Toomer's for Tuscaloosa – makeit-loveit.com
Trinity College Squash – ebay.co.uk
Tufts Jumbo Mascot – division3tennis.com
UCLA Bruins Mascot – sportslogos.net
UCLA Wooden's Seat – uclawbb.com
UNLV Khem Kong Puppet – lasvegasweekly.com
USC Conquest & Traveler – sweetstoimpress.com
Utica College Teddy Bear Toss – Utica College / Jamie Callari
Vanderbilt's Anchor Down – pinterest.com
Virginia Tech Hokie Stone – journeydownthescale.info
Virginia Tech Lunch Pail – turkeyrunner.com
Virginia Tech Skipper the Cannon – si.com
Virtual Reality Recruiting – anandtech.com
Washington State Gameday Flag – pinterest
West Virginia Gameday Sign – brobible.com
Western Kentucky Big Red Mascot – pinterest.com
Williams College St Pierre's Barber Shop – ephsports.williams.edu
Williams Walk – Williams College / Kris Dufour
Wisconsin Camp Randall Stadium – emaze.com

Wisconsin Jump Around – badgeofhonor.com
Wisconsin Slab of Bacon – Univ. of Wisconsin Athletics Communications
Wisconsin Cane Tossing – livenews.madison.com
Zack Brown Band Chicken Fried – youtube.com